Financial and Monetary Policy Studies

Volume 44

Series editor
Ansgar Belke
Essen, Germany

More information about this series at http://www.springer.com/series/5982

Frank Rövekamp • Moritz Bälz •
Hanns Günther Hilpert
Editors

Cash in East Asia

Springer

Editors
Frank Rövekamp
East Asia Institute
Ludwigshafen University
of Applied Sciences
Ludwigshafen, Germany

Moritz Bälz
Faculty of Law / Interdisciplinary Centre for
East Asian Studies
Goethe University
Frankfurt, Germany

Hanns Günther Hilpert
Research Division Asia
German Institute for International
and Security Affairs (SWP)
Berlin, Germany

ISSN 0921-8580 ISSN 2197-1889 (electronic)
Financial and Monetary Policy Studies
ISBN 978-3-319-59845-1 ISBN 978-3-319-59846-8 (eBook)
DOI 10.1007/978-3-319-59846-8

Library of Congress Control Number: 2017949280

Printed on acid-free paper

This Springer imprint is published by Springer Nature
The registered company is Springer International Publishing AG
The registered company address is: Gewerbestrasse 11, 6330 Cham, Switzerland

Preface

"Cash in East Asia" was the title of an international conference staged at the East Asia Institute in Ludwigshafen in May 2016. Recent years have witnessed an intensified international debate on the benefits and costs of moving towards a "cashless society". Against this backdrop, the conference brought together leading experts from academia as well as monetary authorities to explore economic, legal and policy perspectives on cash and its future role in East Asia. The papers delivered at the conference form the basis for this book.

The conference was made possible through the generous support of the *Deutsche Bundesbank* and the *Haniel Foundation*, which is gratefully acknowledged. Likewise, we wish to thank Springer International Publishing for accepting this volume into its series entitled *Financial and Monetary Policy Studies*. Finally, we are indebted to Chris Engert for his excellent work in the language correction and copy-editing of the manuscript.

Ludwigshafen am Rhein, Germany — Frank Rövekamp
Frankfurt am Main, Germany — Moritz Bälz
Berlin, Germany — Hanns Günther Hilpert

Preface

Contents

List of Contributors

Moritz Bälz holds the Chair of Japanese Law and its Cultural Foundations at the Goethe University, Frankfurt am Main, where he also serves as executive director of the Interdisciplinary Centre for East Asian Studies (IZO). Prior to being appointed professor, he worked as an attorney with the international law firm Freshfields Bruckhaus Deringer in New York and Frankfurt (2003–2008) and was Joseph Story Research Fellow at Harvard Law School (2002–2003). He is co-editor of the *Journal of Japanese Law* (*J.Japan.L*) and has published widely on topics of Japanese business law.

Hwee Kwan Chow is Professor of Economics and Statistics (Practice), Singapore Management University. She has a Ph.D. from the London School of Economics and was Lead Economist at the Monetary Authority of Singapore and Vice President at the Overseas Union Bank. She teaches Econometrics courses, and her main research areas are Monetary Economics, International Finance and Economic Forecasting. Chow is Associate Editor of the *Singapore Economic Review*, and her publications have appeared in the *Journal of Macroeconomics*, the *Open Economies Review* and the *International Journal of Forecasting*. She has provided consultancy services to ADB, ADBI, AMRO and several central banks.

Rüdiger Frank is a German national living in Vienna, Austria. He is Professor of East Asian Economy and Society at the University of Vienna and Head of its Department of East Asian Studies. He holds an M.A. in Korean Studies, Economics and International Relations and a Ph.D. in Economics. He has been researching North Korea ever since he spent one semester as a language student at the Kim Il Sung University in Pyongyang in 1991/1992. Currently, he is Vice Chairman of the Global Agenda Council on Korea of the World Economic Forum. In 2013, he was listed as one of the top 50 most influential German economists by the *Frankfurter Allgemeine Zeitung*. His editorial and advisory board memberships include the *European Journal of East Asian Studies*, the *Korea Review of International Studies*, the *Vienna Journal of East Asian Studies*, the *Journal of Asian Politics and History*,

Asian Perspective, *The Review of Korean Studies* and the *Seoul Journal of Korean Studies*. He is also a book series editor for Brill's Studies on East Asian Security and International Relations and Korean Studies Library. He is the author or editor of 13 books and over 200 book chapters and articles.

Erwin Gladisch trained as a bank clerk at the Gelsenkirchen savings bank and then studied at the University of Essen. He graduated with an M.A. in Economics. In 1982, Mr. Gladisch joined the *Deutsche Bundesbank* and completed a traineeship at the Head Office. He has held various positions at the *Deutsche Bundesbank*, including the audit department, the capital market department (trader for government securities at the Frankfurt stock exchange) and the back-office operations for securities. Furthermore, Mr. Gladisch has worked in different working groups of the Eurosystem, for example, the "Security working group" and the "Issue working group". Since the year 2000, he has been working in the cash department. His main issue is the study of the cash cycle in Germany, the developments of cash in other countries, and theoretical studies about the behaviour of people in the cash market.

Patrick Hess serves as Senior Market Infrastructure Expert at the European Central Bank (ECB). His prior positions include Senior Economist at the ECB's China Desk and relationship manager and expert in the TARGET2-Securities and TARGET2 projects. From 1996 to 2003, he worked for the *Deutsche Bank* in its corporate and transaction banking businesses. Patrick Hess holds an M.A. in Sinology and Economics from Heidelberg University and also studied at Beijing Foreign Studies University, Rijksuniversiteit Leiden and VU Amsterdam. His research and teaching experience, inter alia at the Institute of Chinese Studies in Heidelberg, focuses on China's financial system and economic policies.

Hanns Günther Hilpert is Head of the Research Division Asia at the German Institute for International and Security Affairs ("*Stiftung Wissenschaft und Politik*", SWP), Berlin. Formerly, he worked for the German Institute for Japanese Studies (DIJ), Tokyo (1999–2002), and the Ifo Institute for Economic Research, Munich (1989–1999). He has written and published many books and articles on the Japanese economy and on Asian trade and economic integration. His current research focuses on various policy-oriented economic issues of East Asia.

Woosik Moon is currently a Professor of Economics at the Graduate School of International Studies (GSIS), Seoul National University (SNU). He was a member of the Monetary Policy Committee, at the Bank of Korea, from April 2012 to April 2016. Prior to joining the Bank of Korea, he served as an advisor or policy evaluator in different Korean Ministries, including the Ministry of Foreign Affairs, the Ministry of Finance and Budget, and the Ministry of Education. He also worked as a research fellow at the Korea Development Institute. He received his Ph.D. in economics from the University of Paris-I, and his area of expertise is monetary economics, international finance and monetary integration.

Frank Rövekamp works as Professor of Asian Studies and Director of the East Asia Institute at the Ludwigshafen University of Applied Sciences in Germany. He also serves as Honorary Research Fellow at the Hong Kong Institute of Asia Pacific Studies of the Chinese University in Hong Kong and at the WTO Center of Aoyama Gakuin University in Tokyo. Previously, he worked in industrial enterprises and held senior management positions in Germany, Japan and China. His research interest covers monetary economics and issues of the political and economic systems in Asia.

Friedrich Schneider has been Professor of Economics at Johannes Kepler University of Linz, Austria, since 1986. He obtained his Ph.D. in Economics from the University of Konstanz in 1977. From 1991 to 1996, he was Dean of Social Science and Economics at the Johannes Kepler University of Linz and Vice President for Foreign Affairs of the Johannes Kepler University of Linz from 1996 to 2007. He was President of the Austrian Economic Association from 1997 to 1999, and, from 2005 to 2008, he was President of the German Economic Association. He has also been a consultant to numerous organisations including the EU Commission in Brussels, the International Monetary Fund and the World Bank. He has published extensively in leading economics journals including *The American Economic Review*, *The Quarterly Journal of Economics*, *The Economic Journal*, *Public Choice*, *Kyklos* and the *Journal of Economic Literature*. He has also published numerous books including *The Shadow Economy* (together with Colin C. Williams, The Institute of Economic Affairs, 2013) and *Readings in Public Choice and Constitutional Political Economy* (together with Charles K. Rowley, Springer Publishing Company, 2008). He was the editor of the *Journal of Public Choice* from 1991 to 2004 and *Perspektiven der Wirtschaftspolitik* from 2000 to 2004.

Masaaki Shirakawa was previously Governor of the Bank of Japan. He was appointed Governor in April 2008 and left the Bank in March 2013. He has also been Vice Chairman of the Board of Directors of the BIS since January 2011. Currently, he is professor at the Aoyama-Gakuin University and also a member of the Group of Thirty. Masaaki Shirakawa joined the Bank of Japan in 1972. At the Bank, he held key positions, including Executive Director in charge of monetary policy. Born in 1949, he studied economics at the University of Tokyo (B.A.) and at the University of Chicago (M.A.). He was also professor at the Kyoto University School of Government from July 2006 to March 2008.

Helmut Siekmann is Professor of Money, Currency and Central Bank Law at the Goethe University, Frankfurt am Main. He also serves as director of the Institute for Monetary and Financial Stability (IMFS). His research is focused on all aspects of government finance and the institutional framework of the European System of Central Banks. He has worked extensively on the EU provisions to secure stable government finances, the mechanisms to stabilise financial institutions and the supervision and control of financial markets. Professor Siekmann received his *doctor juris* and his postdoctoral degree ("Habilitation") from the University of Cologne. He also obtained a master's degree in economics ("*Diplom-Volkswirt*") from the University of Bonn. He was Professor of Law at the Ruhr-University Bochum from 1993 to 2006. He has been visiting professor at Saint Louis University School of Law (1996, 1999, 2001), Université d'Orléans (2003, 2004, 2005, 2006), Université Paris-Dauphine (2005, 2007), Université de Luxembourg (2009) and Donau-Universität Krems (2013). Professor Siekmann has contributed to numerous legislative projects at national and supranational level. He has also worked as counsel to constitutional bodies and represented them in constitutional courts. In 2010, the university Paris-Dauphine awarded him the degree "*docteur honoris causa*".

Franz Waldenberger is Director of the German Institute for Japanese Studies (DIJ) in Tokyo. He is presently on leave from Munich University where he holds the professorship for Japanese Economy at the Munich School of Management. His research focuses on the Japanese Economy, Corporate Governance and International Management. He has published numerous articles and books on the Japanese economy and is member of the editorial board of Japanese- and Asian-related social science and economics journals. He held positions as visiting professor at Osaka City University, Hitotsubashi University, Tsukuba University and the University of Tokyo and was Shimomura Fellow at the Research Institute of Capital Formation of the Development Bank of Japan. He is member of the German Japan Forum and a Member of the Board of the Japanese-German Business Association (DJW).

List of Abbreviations

AD	Anno Domini
AGD	Accountant-General's Department
AP	Associated Press
ASEAN	Association of Southeast Asian Nations
ATM	Automated Teller Machine
BBC	Basket-band-crawl
BEPS	Bulk Electronic Payment System
BIS	Bank for International Settlements
BoJ	Bank of Japan
BoK	Bank of Korea
CCP	Chinese Communist Party
CDFCPS	China Domestic Foreign Currency Payment System
CIS	Cheque Image System
COMECON	Council for Mutual Economic Assistance
CPF	Central Provident Fund
CPI	Consumer Price Index
CPSS	Committee on Payment and Settlement Systems
DVD	Digital Versatile Disc
EC	European Community/Communities
ECB	European Central Bank
ECJ/CJEU	European Court of Justice/Court of Justice of the European Union
EEC	European Economic Community
ESCB	European System of Central Banks
EU	European Union
FAO	Food and Agriculture Organization of the United Nations
FAOSTAT	FAO Statistics
Fed	Federal Reserve
FILP	Fiscal Investment and Loan Programme

Fintech	Financial Technology
FRBM	Fully Reserve-backed Money
FY	Financial Year
GDP	Gross Domestic Product
HVPS	High-Value Payment System
IBPS	Internet Banking Payment System
IC	Integrated Circuit
IMF	International Monetary Fund
IMPS	Intermediate Payment System
IS	Islamic State
IT	Information Technology
JGB	Japanese Government Bonds
KPW	Korean People's Won (North Korea)
KRW	Korean Won (South Korea)
KYC	Know-Your-Customers
MAS	Monetary Authority of Singapore
MERICS	Mercator Institute for China Studies
MIMIC	Multiple Indicator Multiple Causes
NEER	Nominal Effective Exchange Rate
NIRP	Negative interest rate policy
NYSE	New York Stock Exchange
OECD	Organisation for Economic Co-operation and Development
P-to-P	Person-to-person
PBoC	People's Bank of China
P2P	Peer-to-Peer
PIs	Payment Institutions
PoS	Point-of-Sale
PSD	Payment Services Directive
PSD2	Revised Payment Services Directive
QE	Quantitative Easing
QQE	Quantitative and Qualitative Easing
QR	Quick Response
REER	Real Effective Exchange Rate
S$NEER	Singapore Dollar Nominal Effective Exchange Rate
SEM	Structural Equation Model
SEPA	Single Euro Payments Area
SGD	Singapore Dollar
SGS	Singapore Government Securities
SIC	Swiss Interbank Clearing
TEU	Treaty on European Union
TFEU	Treaty on the Functioning of the European Union
UK	United Kingdom
US	United States of America
USB	Universal Serial Bus

USD	United States Dollar
VAN	Value-Added Network
VAR	Value at Risk
VAT	Value-Added Tax
ZIRP	Zero interest rate policy

Chapter 1
On the Role of Cash in East Asia

Frank Rövekamp, Moritz Bälz, and Hanns Günther Hilpert

Abstract While due to technological development, the notion of cash is changing, the function and future of cash is entering the monetary debate. Proponents of a cashless society point to cost considerations, the prospect of widening anti-deflationary monetary policy into the realm of negative interest rates, as well as the chances of repressing the shadow economy. As such expectations are being contested, the discussion of the pros and cons of a cashless society is in full swing. Against this backdrop, the contributions to this volume analyse the use of cash in various East Asian economies or examine specific aspects of cash usage. Taken together, the contributions show that many issues related to cash still remain without a solid research foundation. Any top-down moves to reduce the role of cash or to head towards a "cashless society" should therefore be taken with great care and only gradually.

Not long ago, cash—here defined in the narrow and physical sense as banknotes and coins—played no role in monetary policy discussions or in the considerations of monetary economists. Cash was a given, the manifestation of money itself. Its administration and logistics have certainly been a complex undertaking, but a purely technical one, which could be left to the specialists in this field. Other methods of payment evolved more and more, but were built on the fundament of cash. Even if cash became the smaller part of the monetary base or monetary aggregates like M1 a long time ago, people considered the use of debit and credit

F. Rövekamp (✉)
East Asia Institute, Ludwigshafen University of Applied Sciences, Ludwigshafen, Germany
e-mail: Roevekamp@oai.de

M. Bälz
Faculty of Law/Interdisciplinary Centre for East Asian Studies, Goethe University, Frankfurt, Germany
e-mail: baelz@jur.uni-frankfurt.de

H.G. Hilpert
Research Division Asia, German Institute for International and Security Affairs (SWP), Berlin, Germany
e-mail: Hanns-Guenther.Hilpert@swp-berlin.org

F. Rövekamp et al. (eds.), *Cash in East Asia*, Financial and Monetary Policy Studies 44, DOI 10.1007/978-3-319-59846-8_1

cards just as a convenient means not to carry their money, i.e., their cash, around all the time, but to leave it in a safe place. This has been most visible in times of financial uncertainties or crisis, when people regularly lined up at banks to withdraw their money as banks were no longer considered safe.[1]

This notion of cash has been challenged in recent years, and, as a result, the function and future of cash entered the monetary policy debate and also slowly came under academic scrutiny. One reason for this has been technological development. Cash plays virtually no role in the important and growing area of e-commerce. Even in person-to-person transactions, cashless payments—using debit cards, credit cards, prepaid cards and electronic wallets—are ever more convenient and easy to use. Hand in hand with this development, public authorities have embarked on influencing the use of payment methods. Cashless payment is being promoted and, in some cases, even required—the payment of taxes in Germany for example—despite cash still being the only legal tender in most countries. Many countries have also moved towards putting caps or strict reporting requirements on cash payments beyond a certain amount.[2]

Out of this development, the vision of a "cashless society" has emerged. As the use of cash decreases naturally, this trend can—and maybe should—be enforced by various incentives and regulations. In the end, cash can be abolished altogether. A prominent academic proponent of this idea is Kenneth Rogoff.[3] Explicitly embarking in this direction are countries such as Sweden, Denmark and India, although the latter case also shows the pitfalls of moving too quickly, too abruptly, and largely unprepared in this direction.[4]

Proponents of a "cashless society" regularly refer to its three main benefits:[5]

(1) The supply and the use of cash are costly. Non-cash electronic payment methods not only reduce the transaction time at the point of sale, but also allow for a gradual dismantling of the physical infrastructure for handling cash. Non-cash payment methods, including more recent instruments such as electronic wallets and digital currencies, are rapidly evolving, thereby offering ever more choice and convenient handling.

    The assumption behind this argument is that the cost of non-cash payment and its supporting infrastructure is lower than that of cash.

[1]Laeven and Valencia (2008).

[2]Letzing (2017).

[3]Rogoff (2016).

[4]On 8 November 2016, Indian Prime Minister Narendra Modi made the surprise announcement that all 500- and 1000-rupee notes, amounting to more than 85% per value of the cash in circulation, would be withdrawn in order to fight illicit activities, corruption, terrorism, and to lead India to a modern pathway of a cashless society. Most Indians, however, do not have bank accounts and the newly designed 500- and 2000-rupee notes as substitutes were not sufficiently available yet. Social unrest occurred and the economy was damaged by slowing sales and production already in the two months following Prime Minister Modi's announcement; see Frankfurter Allgemeine Zeitung (2017) and The Economist (2016).

[5]Beer et al. (2015, p. 1).

(2) Cash is the preferred means of payment for all kinds of shadow economy dealings enabling tax evasion, crime and even terrorism, as it allows the anonymity of all the parties involved. Non-cash payment methods, on the other hand, are recorded and traceable.

The assumption behind this argument is that, with the restriction of the use of cash or its abolition, such illicit activities could be pushed back.

(3) Cash can become a hindrance in the proper conduct of monetary policy. Once the so-called zero lower bound is being approached, lowering interest rates further ceases to be a valid option, because people might withdraw their money to avoid paying negative interest rates.[6] However, negative interest rates might be the best way to fight deflationary tendencies or even deflationary contractions. This argument has gained traction by the notion of a "secular stagnation", which implies a negative equilibrium real interest rate.[7] The massive programmes of quantitative easing devised by several major central banks with all their side-effects of blurring the line between monetary and fiscal policy might not be necessary if interest rates could be reduced significantly below zero.

This argument implies that the setting of negative interest rates is just a natural extension of the conventional monetary policy, which has been artificially restrained by the existence of cash. In this view, the zero lower bound is not a natural barrier against unsound financial repression, but simply a hurdle which can and should be overcome by technical progress.

These arguments proposing a "cashless society" are being countered in two ways. On the one hand, critics doubt whether the asserted benefits could prove true in reality. On the other, they fear negative consequences once cash is abolished.[8] The critics expect that the benefits of a "cashless society" would be accrued, above all, by the financial industry, whereas private citizens would only face higher costs, less choice, less security, less ease and less privacy.[9] In addition, the seigniorage of central banks, the profit accrued by creating cash, would shrink. Furthermore, critics are sceptical of the alleged containment of criminal and black market activities, since the incentives for illegal behaviour remain the same and cash substitutes would be available soon. What is more, negative interest rate payments could be avoided or at least mitigated by various acts of arbitration or speculation,

[6]Rogoff (2016, pp. 119–146), for an overview and Agrawal and Kimball (2015) for a method of breaking the zero lower bound despite the existence of cash.

[7]"Secular stagnation" describes a situation of prolonged low to negative growth. Recent discussions have focused on the possibility of an oversupply of savings. Such an oversupply could only be brought to an equilibrium with investments, if the real interest rate—which can be derived at by deducting the rate of inflation from the nominal interest rate—becomes negative; see Summers (2014), and Weizsäcker (2015).

[8]See, for example, Rösl and Seitz (2015, pp. 525–528).

[9]Häring elaborates on the potential misuse of data gained by the use of electronic payment methods. Häring (2016, pp. 85–111).

for example, advance payments of taxes and invoices, or the flight into central bank money substitutes such as Amazon vouchers, Bitcoins or tradeable money market certificates. Last, but not least, negative interest rates could have various detrimental side-effects such as waste of capital and the creation of financial or real estate bubbles.

The debate on the pros and cons of a "cashless society" is in full swing. It is noteworthy, however, that the controversially and ideologically led discussion is lacking a solid empirical foundation. It is against this background that this volume is looking into "Cash in East Asia". Being aware that cash is much more than a technical issue, the contributions in this book analyse the use of cash in various East Asian countries and examine specific aspects of cash usage. The East Asian experience is furthermore contrasted with some European cases.

Masaaki Shirakawa takes the example of Japan in order to analyse the role of cash in a modern economy. He starts off from two observations: Firstly, the cash to GDP ratio has been on the rise in various economies, most notably in Japan. Secondly, there are marked differences in the use of cash and in the tendency to hold cash between countries.

Important reasons for the increased cash to GDP ratio in general include the low level of interest rates in most industrialised countries, which reduces the opportunity costs of holding cash, and precautionary motives. In times of financial turbulence and crisis, people resort to holding significant amounts of cash as a presumably secure store of value.

There is a mixture of reasons for why Japan appears to be the country with the highest *cash to GDP ratio* in international comparison. Japan is a very safe society with a low crime rate and low risks of theft and robbery. The high population concentration furthermore arguably induces many direct person-to-person interactions, which are still most easily settled by cash. This is further corroborated by the demographic change, as elderly people tend to be more reluctant to change their habits, i.e., to switch from cash to cashless payment methods. A dense network of ATMs supports the *status quo*. Finally, a strong drive to preserve privacy among the Japanese people in view of recent technological change is assumed to be an important reason for the unwavering use of cash.

From these cultural features, it can be concluded that the use of cash is strongly influenced by the characteristics of a specific society. In all societies, however, cash is the only means for private individuals to access central bank money directly and thus remain independent of the private banking industry. In times of systemic banking failure caused by a financial crisis, natural disasters or large-scale terrorist attacks, it may thus have an important bearing on the protection of individuals and on financial stability in general.

Against this background, Shirakawa moves on to assess the major arguments for the abolition of cash:

- The benefits of negative interest rates remain fuzzy at best, whereas the forced reduction of the use of cash may cause major disruptions in society.

- There is no proven link between the usage of cash and illicit activities. Japan is a prime example of a safe society with overall low levels of crime and high cash holdings.
- The Bitcoin and other digital currencies based upon new technologies such as the blockchain technology still have a long way to go before they may be widely accepted as a general substitute for cash.

Shirakawa concludes that cash will continue to play an important role in most countries and that moves towards reducing the use of cash should be carried out only gradually.

Friedrich Schneider provides estimates for the relative sizes of the shadow economies of eleven Asian countries: Bangladesh, Cambodia, China, Indonesia, Japan, Laos, Malaysia, the Philippines, South Korea, Thailand, and Vietnam. Using the multiple indicator multiple causes (MIMIC) approach,[10] his econometric model shows a wide range in the size of Asian shadow economies in relation to the official GDP in the period of 2000–2014, starting at 9% in Japan and reaching up to 45% in Cambodia.

The shadow economy plays an important role in the discussion about cash, as an estimated 80% plus share of all shadow economy transactions are conducted in cash. It can be argued, therefore, that a cashless society would limit and restrict shadow economy activities.[11] According to Schneider, however, cash is not a cause of the shadow economy. Cash is just an indicator of the level of shadow economy activities in a similar way as the labour force participation rate or the growth rate of the official GDP *per capita*. The real causes of the shadow economy in Asia are rather different, in particular tax and social security contribution burdens, the intensity of regulations, the quality of public sector services and public institutions, as well as the state of the official economy.

To reduce shadow economy activities, several incentive-oriented policy measures are suggested, such as a reduction of indirect tax rates and the deregulation of the official economy. Moreover, the promotion of the use of credit cards can also work in this direction. The abolition of cash, however, would only increase the transaction costs for shadow market activities and would not work to diminish them significantly. Simulations for European countries indicate that, with the abolition of cash, the shadow economy would be reduced by no more than roughly 10%.

Rüdiger Frank takes up the monetary history of North Korea, focusing in particular on the process of re-monetisation within the last two decades. The extreme case of North Korea shows that both de-monetisation (by political design) and re-monetisation (by economic necessity) are technically feasible. Further lessons can be deduced: first, the way a monetary system is organised and managed has a profound influence on the behaviour of people whatever the cultural and political circumstances. Second, "shadow market activities", which are illegal and

[10]Kirchgässner (2017) provides an overview and critique of this and other approaches for estimating shadow economies.

[11]See, for example, Rogoff (2016, pp. 58–79).

considered morally improper in democratic countries, can be the only means of basic well-being or even survival in repressive states.

From the 1950s to the mid-1990s, North Korea could be characterised as a widely de-monetised country in the sense that, although money existed, it was severely restricted in its functions. Goods and services were provided by the state-run distribution system upon the basis of allocations and quotas. Prices were centrally regulated and had no signalling function. Access to goods and services thus depended on political and social capital, and not on money.

This system broke down in North Korea's great famine in the mid-1990s. The central distribution systems virtually collapsed and even staple food could not be provided for the populace, thereby putting their physical survival at risk. To preserve stability, the government tolerated the resurgence of the previously sidelined private farmers' markets, where goods could more or less be freely traded. Money started to matter again with the domestic *won* functioning as the main means of exchange and storage of value alongside foreign currencies.

The ever growing importance of markets supported by the cautious economic reform of 2002 induced modest economic development over the last two decades and even provided opportunities to give rise to a middle class. Fearing a loss of control, the government tried to scale back market activities by means of a currency reform in 2009: the old currency was replaced by a new one, and only a limited amount of cash was allowed for exchange. The main goals of this forced reduction of private cash holdings were to expropriate the middle class and curb inflation. However, since some traders managed to convert their savings into foreign currencies beforehand and the parallel wage increases resulted in an inflationary push, the reform turned out to be a complete failure. Markets continued to thrive and, as a consequence of the loss of trust for the *won*, private transactions were mostly conducted by the more trusted Chinese Yuan. Nowadays, domestic and foreign currencies exist in parallel and they are serving dual or even triple distribution structures. In addition, the North Korean government has introduced cash cards, but their functioning is dependent on critical infrastructure such as a stable supply of electricity and data connection.

Hwee Kwan Chow undertakes to analyse the relationship between domestic liquidity conditions and monetary policy in Singapore. As a very open economy depending on free trade and capital flow, Singapore has adopted an exchange-rate centred monetary policy framework.

Under this system, the value of the Singapore dollar (SGD) is monitored in terms of a currency basket. The Monetary Authority of Singapore (MAS), the central bank, is setting a target exchange rate and a policy band around it, within which the currency is allowed to float. Fluctuations beyond the band are avoided by currency market interventions. Under this framework, the SGD appreciated steadily, albeit in a controlled way, over the last decades, reflecting Singapore's strong economic performance.

Interventions by the MAS usually served to stem stronger appreciations of the SGD and thus tended to increase domestic liquidity, giving rise to potential inflationary pressures. A high national savings rate, however, which is rooted in contributions to a government administered compulsory saving scheme, and long-run state budget surpluses, are offsetting the effects.

Cash in circulation does not carry a high weight as a money market factor in Singapore. The ratio of cash to M1 dropped from about 50% in 1991 to around 20% in 2015. This trend has been supported and driven by the *National Campaign to Minimise Cash Transactions* launched in 1985 with the primary objective of saving manpower and increasing productivity.

Singapore thus seems to be heading towards a society with a minimum use of cash without strong coercive measures by the government in this direction. A track-record of prolonged economic growth, low inflation, strong institutions and, arguably, high trust between the government and its people appears to be very conducive for this trend.

Franz Waldenberger proposes a shift to a fully reserve-backed money regime (FRBM) in Japan as a solution to the countries fiscal and monetary challenges. An FRBM requires banks to keep the full amount of their depositors' funds as reserve money at the central bank. Such a change would also have the side-effect of reducing the private cash holdings resulting from safety considerations.

In the course of quantitative and qualitative easing (QQE), starting in April 2013, the Bank of Japan (BoJ) has increased its monetary base on a large scale. A massive purchasing programme for Japanese government bonds is supposed to suppress deflation and make a 2% inflation rate possible. The already high fiscal debt burden increased to a gross debt to GDP ratio of 230% by 2015. By mid-2016, the BoJ already owned 35% of all government bonds.

However, this situation appears to be unsustainable in the long run. It is unclear how the government will consolidate its debts and how the BoJ will exit from its ultra-expansive monetary easing policy. A severe trade-off between fiscal crisis and price stability might occur.

A solution might be the shift to an FRBM, in which all the money deposited in current bank accounts is subject to a 100% reserve requirement at the central bank. The main purpose is to deprive the private banking sector of the ability to create surplus liquidity, which is regarded as the crucial cause for the boom and bust of asset bubbles.

As a result of the large financial surpluses accrued by Japan's corporate sector, the demand for bank credit is very low, so that the commercial bank reserves held at the central bank already amount to a 47% share of the money in current account bank deposits. According to Waldenberger, this high share opens a window of opportunity for a shift to an FRBM system and the consolidation of government debt, too. Almost halfway of this route has already been accomplished. Further increasing the monetary base by purchasing government bonds would thus be a necessary step to complete the system change and, at the same time, alleviate the fiscal woes of the government. Under the FRBM system, demand deposits in current bank accounts would be as safe as cash, thereby reducing the demand for cash out of safety considerations.

The far-reaching proposal of shifting to an FRBM regime in Japan will certainly induce a vigorous discussion. It also underlines, however, that the use of cash is intimately related to the level of trust within a given society.

Woosik Moon focuses on the ongoing efforts in South Korea to realise a coinless society. The Bank of Korea (BoK) is seeking to eliminate coins as a payment instrument by the year 2020 for three reasons: first, it would reduce the social cost and the inconvenience related to the use of coins in economic transactions; second, the achievement of a coinless society can be seen as a test case for realising a cashless society; and third, the coinless project could finally pave the way for a smooth redenomination of the South Korean Won (KRW), which now stands at about 1200 KRW for 1 US Dollar.

In international comparison, South Korea is already one of the countries with the lowest cash usage ratios in the world. Important economic factors such as retail businesses are strongly in favour of eliminating coins, because of the high transaction cost associated with their handling. The case is also supported by the fact that coins account for less than 3% of the total cash in circulation, whereas banknotes account for more than 97%.

Various incentives to reduce the use of coins are employed based upon the good infrastructure for alternative payment methods in South Korea such as credit and debit cards, electronic cash receipts, prepaid cards and digital wallets. Small change for purchases can be credited to such devices, instead of being paid out in coins. This can furthermore be incentivised by granting bonus points or tax reductions.

Attaining a coinless society by 2020 may thus be a realistic target. This might have the important side-effect of also paving the way for a cashless society. Eliminating coins is expected to face much less fundamental resistance than eliminating all cash. In the meantime, the necessary infrastructure is being prepared and the necessary changes in the behaviour of people is being induced and encouraged for significant advances into the cashless society.

Patrick Hess analyses the evolution of payment instruments in China and the role of the central bank in this regard. Electronic means of payment have seen a steep increase since 2011, whereas the use of cash has been in steady decline. Regulatory steps to accelerate the deployment of point-of-sales equipment at retail level, the integration of payment functions into social media, low cost smartphones and the rapid growth of e-commerce have all been behind the continued growth of non-cash payments.

The growth of e-commerce has, in particular, been driven by the fierce competition for customers between the three Internet giants *Alibaba*, *Tencent* and *Baidu*, which are likened to the Three Kingdoms warring with each other in the period following the end of the Han dynasty (220–280 AD). This competition furthermore spurs financial innovation in various ways. In the course of these developments, the People's Bank of China (PBoC) is assuming a pivotal role, both as an active promoter and as a supervisor to assure the safety and reliability of non-cash payment systems. As a promoter, the PBoC operates five domestic interbank payment systems, and, as a regulator, it requires mandatory licences for all providers of non-cash payment services, for example. The PBoC furthermore regulates the use of Bitcoin, which has gained high popularity in China.

Although China embarked comparatively late on the use of non-cash payments, the actual development appears to be much more dynamic than in most other countries. Hess concludes, however, that cash is nonetheless unlikely to disappear in the foreseeable future and that the PBoC will continue to support the use of banknotes and its underlying infrastructure.

Erwin Gladisch provides an overview of the use of cash in Germany, where the issue is discussed broadly and often emotionally. The German case may thus serve as an interesting point of reference for other countries.

The chapter starts with the observation that the amount of cash issued by the Eurosystem has been rising continuously since 2002. Cash is still the most common means of payment in Germany. According to the *Bundesbank*'s empirical survey, almost 80% of all payment transactions, amounting to 53% of the payment value, are settled in cash at the point-of-sale. What is more, in times of financial crises such as in 2008 in the wake of the Lehman bankruptcy, the demand for cash tends to rise significantly in Germany.

As for the cost of cash, there is no indication that it is more expensive than other payment instruments. According to a study carried out by the European Central Bank (ECB), cash costs 0.42 € per transaction on average, which is much less than debit or credit cards with 0.70 € and 2.39 € respectively. EDEKA, one of the largest retail chains in Germany, reports costs for the whole cash handling of 0.14% of turnover as compared with 0.47% for debit cards.

There is only faint evidence of a direct link between cash, on the one hand, and tax evasion, crime and terrorism, on the other. For tax evasion mostly cashless instruments are of relevance as evidenced by an estimated 5.8 trillion euros worth of private assets in so-called tax havens. Chinese authorities even claim that cash is the simplest way to uncover illegal activities as it leaves traces and is easy to find, contrary to other payment methods.

Gladisch finally asserts that private industry groups have an interest in the drive for a "cashless society" hoping to earn fees and collect valuable data on consumer behaviour. Such a move, however, would not necessarily be a benefit to consumers. However, the latter may cherish a generally accepted, simple means of payment that can be used without any technical set-up, requirements that are still best fulfilled by cash.

Helmut Siekmann draws attention to the fact that cash is not just defined by its economic function as medium of exchange, a unit of account and a store of value. Legally, it also assumes the role of legal tender in the sense that it has to be accepted for settlement of any kind of monetary obligation, whereas other means of payment may be rejected by the creditor. The legal tender role is further supported by the fact that cash does not discriminate, is easy to handle, does not imply the risk of insolvency for the issuer, protects privacy and is still efficient in many situations.

Restricting or abolishing the use of cash in the European Union (or elsewhere) is closely-connected with the issue of legal tender. It has to be asked whether there are legal ways to restrict the function of legal tender or to define a new entity as legal tender, which to date is unknown. Based upon an analysis of primary and secondary European Union law, Siekmann comes to the conclusion that the elimination of cash would be an infraction of the law. In principle, albeit to a lesser degree, this also applies to mere restrictions on the use of cash such as maximum amounts for the use of cash in business transactions.

The lesson to be drawn for countries in Asia and elsewhere, which adhere to the rule of law, is that any consideration of the abolition or massive restriction on cash needs to take the legal tender aspect into account. Despite all technological progress, it is still not easy to identify a monetary instrument that is as suitable as cash is for legal tender.

*****

What lessons can be drawn from the contributions in this volume as far as the function and the use of cash are concerned?

One important point to note is that the diversity of the use of cash and cashless instruments between countries does not stem so much from technological factors, but from social and cultural habits, instead. Whereas cashless payments in South Korea are advancing smoothly up to the point that the "coinless society" is concretely envisioned for 2020, people in Japan still hold cash dearly even with a growing trend which is comparable to that of Germany and Switzerland on the other side of the world. Singapore appears to be more similar to South Korea, whereas the case of China is driven by special factors such as the economic latecomer status of the country and the important role of the three giant Internet companies.

Whereas the differences between the countries can be observed, described and researched, the knowledge of the universally valid factors which govern the use of cash and other payment instruments in general are still scarce and limited. This suggests that a "one size fits all" approach for regulating the use of cash would be mistaken. At least for the time being, the specific circumstances of each country or culture need to be uncovered and to be taken into consideration.

The contributions do not explore the issue of the zero lower bound of interest rates and its relation to private cash holding in depth. At various points, however, they do confirm that cash is linked to financial stability.[12] In times of financial crisis, people invariably increase their cash holdings out of fear of losing their assets. Such flights into cash can be observed universally spanning countries and cultures. Such interdependencies between cash and financial stability suggest that the abolition of cash to enable deep forays into the realms of negative interest rates may not just simply be an extension of regular monetary policy. Restrictions or even the abolition of cash usage may generate compensating behaviour by various

[12]Potential effects of negative interest rates on financial stability are pointed out by Beer et al. (2015, pp. 4–6).

economic actors and might result in unforeseeable negative effects for the financial system.[13] In this area, too, research appears to be not very advanced yet.[14]

Although shadow economic activities are significant in Asian countries to varying degrees, the contributions in this volume only briefly touch the, at times, politically-asserted link between cash usage and shadow market activities or even crime and terrorism. An important reason for this may be the high likelihood that, with the restriction of the use of cash or even its abolition, such activities will not be reduced to a large extent; they are profitable enough to allow for other hard to detect payment methods, even if they incur much higher transaction costs than cash.[15] In contrast, the extreme case of North Korea shows that, under certain circumstances, "shadow market activities" might be the only source of well-being for a people. North Koreans would certainly not welcome the abolition of Chinese or American cash.

Taken together, the contributions in this volume can only offer a glimpse of the role of cash in selected Asian countries, thereby pointing to the fact that many areas of this subject still remain without a solid research foundation. Any top-down moves to reduce the role of cash or to head towards a "cashless society" should, therefore, be taken with great care and only gradually.

References

Agrawal R, Kimball M (2015) Breaking through the zero lower bound. IMF working paper 15/224, Oct 2015

Beer C, Birchler UW, Gnan E (2015) Cash without future? Future without cash? A wider view. SUERF Policy Note Issue No. 3, December

Frankfurter Allgemeine Zeitung (2017) Indiens 50-Tage-Wunder ist gescheitert, 3 Jan 2017, p 17

Häring N (2016) Die Abschaffung des Bargelds und die Folgen – Der Weg in die totale Kontrolle. Quadriga, Cologne

Kirchgässner G (2017) On estimating the size of the shadow economy. Ger Econ Rev 18 (1):99–111

Krüger M (2016) Pros and cons of cash: the state of the debate. In: Beer C, Birchler UW, Gnan E (eds) Cash on trial. SUERF conference proceedings 2016/1

Laeven L, Valencia F (2008) Systemic banking crises: a new database. IMF working paper 08/224, Nov 2008

Letzing J (2017) Swiss Frankly Love Cash. Wall Street J, 4 Jan 2017, B7

Rogoff KS (2016) The curse of cash. Princeton University Press, Princeton

[13] Krüger points out that a bank run can have stabilising effects, if people are able to withdraw their money. A bank run thus can work like a "safety valve". Without the possibility of non-banks to withdraw funds however frantic buying and selling of assets might occur with further destabilising effects. Krüger (2016, pp. 61–63).

[14] Several potential effects of negative interest rates on financial stability like an impairment of the monetary policy transmission mechanism, a build-up of price bubbles and a misallocation of resources are indicated by Beer et al. (2015, pp. 4–6).

[15] Schneider and Linsbauer (2016, p. 92).

Rösl G, Seitz F (2015) Warum Bargeld *nicht* abgeschafft werden sollte – Effizienz-, Praktikabilitäts- und Implementierungsaspekte, Wirtschaftsdienst 2015/5, pp 525–528

Schneider F, Linsbauer K (2016) The financial flows of transnational crime and tax fraud. In: Beer C, Birchler UW, Gnan E (eds) Cash on trial. SUERF conference proceedings 2016/1, pp 83–107

Summers LH (2014) US economic prospects: secular stagnation, hysteresis and the zero lower bound. Bus Econ 49(2):65–73

The Economist (2016) Modi's bungle, 3 December 2016, p 10

von Weizsäcker CC (2015) Kapitalismus in der Krise? Der negative natürliche Zins und seine Folgen für die Politik. Perspekt Wirtsch 16(2):189–212

Part I
Cash and Its Impact on Society

Chapter 2
The Use of Cash in Europe and East Asia

Masaaki Shirakawa

Abstract This is an opportune time to think about cash. First, some academics are arguing for the abolition of cash in order to make monetary policy more effective by enabling a further decline in interest rates into the negative zone. Second, the rapid development of retail electronic payment and the emergence of digital currencies are making us rethink seriously the future of cash. Third, there is a growing discussion about whether to abolish high denomination banknotes and limit the maximum value of cash transactions on the grounds that cash is often used in illicit activities. My belief is that money is more important than monetary policy. An optimum response differs both across countries and over time. When it comes to the various proposals on cash, we should carefully and thoroughly perform a cost-benefit analysis and, even if it proves favourable, we should then proceed only gradually, while nonetheless remaining open to new technology and ideas.

2.1 Introduction

Why are we discussing cash now? There are many good reasons. First, some academics are arguing for the abolition of cash in order to make monetary policy more effective by enabling a further decline in interest rates into the negative zone. This is proposed on the grounds that the existence of cash sets the effective lower bound of interest rates.[1] Second, the rapid development of retail electronic payment and the emergence of digital currencies such as Bitcoin underpinned by blockchain technology are making us rethink seriously the future of cash. Third, there is a growing discussion about whether to abolish high denomination banknotes and limit the maximum value of cash transactions on the grounds that cash is often used in illicit activities. In this regard, the ECB governing council has recently decided to stop the issuance of the 500 € note.

[1]Rogoff (2016).

M. Shirakawa (✉)
Aoyama Gakuin University, Tokyo, Japan
e-mail: shirakawa@sipeb.aoyama.ac.jp

F. Rövekamp et al. (eds.), *Cash in East Asia*, Financial and Monetary Policy Studies 44, DOI 10.1007/978-3-319-59846-8_2

So, this is an opportune time to think about cash, one in which many questions arise:

- Is cash outdated?
- What is the intrinsic role of cash?
- How will the role of cash evolve in the future?
- Should we eventually abolish cash?

2.2 Two Basic Facts About the Use of Cash

Cash is something which provokes emotional reactions among people. And yet cash is perceived so differently. Here are some examples of such perceptions: cash is a symbol of freedom; cash is money used in illicit activities; cash is an outdated form of money which will eventually be replaced by more advanced forms of money, such as digital currency. As this shows, people have different reactions towards cash. When I read various speeches by central bank governors or research papers by the senior staff and economists at central banks, I am struck by the non-negligible difference in the nuances of the perceived role of cash in each society.[2]

Keeping these perceptions and viewpoints in my mind, I will start my remarks by observing two basic facts about the use of cash. Here, I used the word "use" loosely. Cash to GDP ratio could serve as a proxy of the extent to which cash is used, although this number might not be an ideal indicator of the use of cash in a society. When we look at cash to GDP ratios, we find some intriguing statistical facts. The first fact concerns the time dimension. Despite the popular talk of the advent of a "cashless society" over the past decades, cash has not died in many countries to date (Fig. 2.1).

The second fact is about the cross-section, because the use of cash varies considerably across countries (Table 2.1).

As I will explain later, on both counts, Japan is quite distinctive. Given that most analysis and policy debate on cash is shaped by the experience in the US and, to a lesser extent, Europe, it may be useful to explain the use of cash in Japan. I hope that an explanation of the use of cash in Japan will widen the perspective of this debate.

2.2.1 Increased Cash to GDP Ratio

The Cash to GDP ratio has noticeably declined in some countries, of which Sweden is an example, but it has also been increasing in many countries (Fig. 2.1). The most notable case of the latter is that of Japan. Cash to GDP ratio in Japan had been very stable at 8% for many years until the early 1990s, but, since then, it has started to rise and now stands at 20%. It gives us some insights into the role played by cash

[2]Boel (2016), Liikanen (2016), and Weidmann (2016).

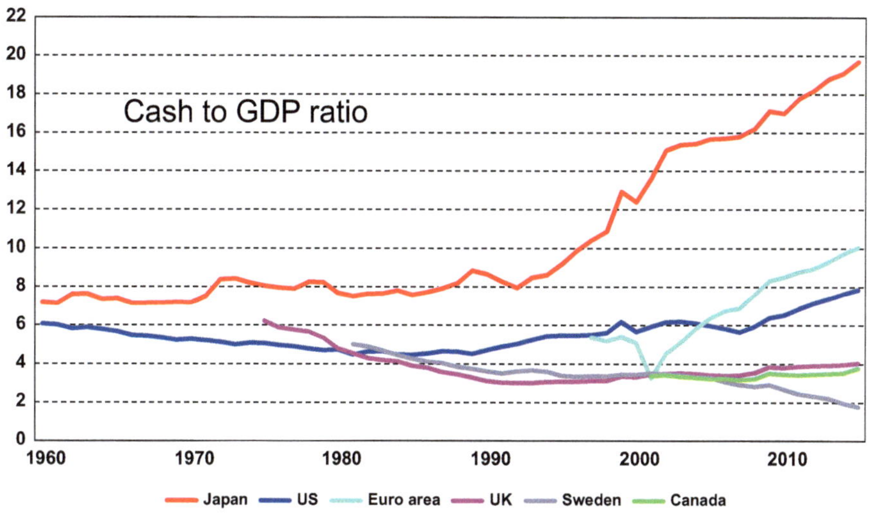

Fig. 2.1 Development of cash to GDP ratio in selected countries. Source: International Financial Statistics

Table 2.1 An international comparison of the stock of cash

	Value per inhabitant (US$)	Value as a percentage of GDP	Value as a percentage of narrow money
Australia	2459	4.4	24.2
Brazil	410	4	62.9
Canada	1839	3.8	9.8
Hong Kong	6272	15.7	31.6
India	180	11.6	66.1
Japan	6429	20.1	15.8
Korea	1350	5	12.7
Mexico	607	6.2	36.9
Russia	1084	12.4	57.5
Saudi Arabia	1567	6.5	15.8
Singapore	4762	8.8	21.4
South Africa	217	3.6	10.8
Sweden	1108	2.1	4.1
Switzerland	8655	11	12.4
Turkey	480	5	33.5
UK	1587	3.6	4.3
USA	4218	7.7	45.1
Euro-area	3734	10.3	17.5
CPMI courtiers	1564	8.3	20.7

Source: BIS Committee on Payments and Market Infrastructures (2015)

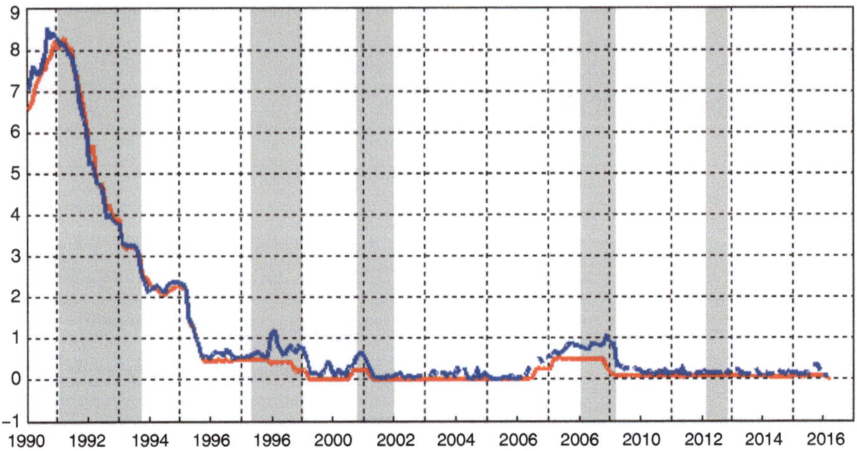

Fig. 2.2 Developments of short-term interest rates in Japan. *Red* denotes overnight interbank rate. *Blue* denotes 3-month interbank rate. Source: Bank of Japan

and makes us ask ourselves *why* it is increasing rather than decreasing. We can analyse the development of the cash to GDP ratio as an economic agent's decision on the selection of financial assets including cash holdings.

There are a couple of hypotheses which explain the increased cash to GDP ratio in Japan. First and foremost, the declining interest rate has definitely increased the demand for cash, since the opportunity cost of holding cash has decreased significantly (Fig. 2.2).

Second, the demand for cash as a safety precaution increased, although this was a temporary factor. Japan witnessed a heightened demand for cash in the financial crisis in the late 1990s (Fig. 2.3).

The same phenomenon was witnessed in the US and Europe during the global financial crisis in 2008 and 2009.

Third, demand for cash for motives of privacy seems to have increased. Specifically, it is said that recent changes in law regarding inheritance tax by lowering the exemption threshold and the commencement of the "My Number System"—an identity card of Japanese nationals—has created demand for privacy (anonymity) and thus demand for cash (Fig. 2.4).

Fourth, the inventory demand for cash at ATMs and vending machines is increasing, because the number of such terminals is increasing.

The above explanation is based upon the decision of economic agents to hold cash; the analysis is framed in terms of stock, rather than flow. But this way of analysis might not be able to explain fully the development of the cash GDP ratio in the era of a prolonged low-interest-rate environment. There is no strong incentive for people to rush to deposit cash in banks, once cash is withdrawn from bank accounts. They do not necessarily have a clear recognition that they have deliberately increased their cash holdings but, at macro level and over time, cash actually piles up, so to speak. Stock analysis and flow analysis are somewhat duplicated, but we need to complement stock analysis by flow analysis in the current extremely-

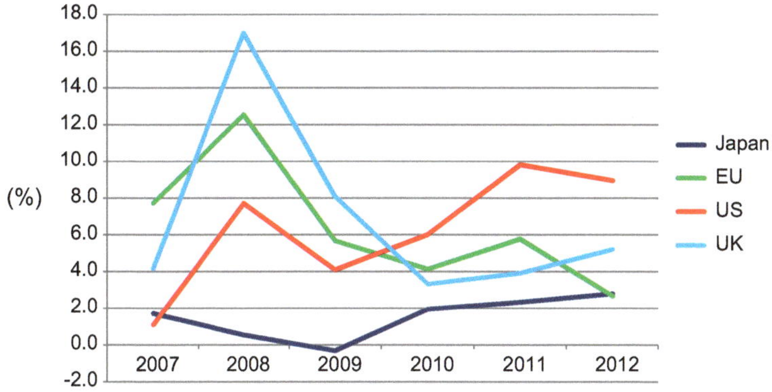

Fig. 2.3 Year-on-year change of cash outstanding in Japan's financial crisis (1997–1998). Source: Bank of Japan (Money stock statistic (notes and coins held by entities other than depository institutions)

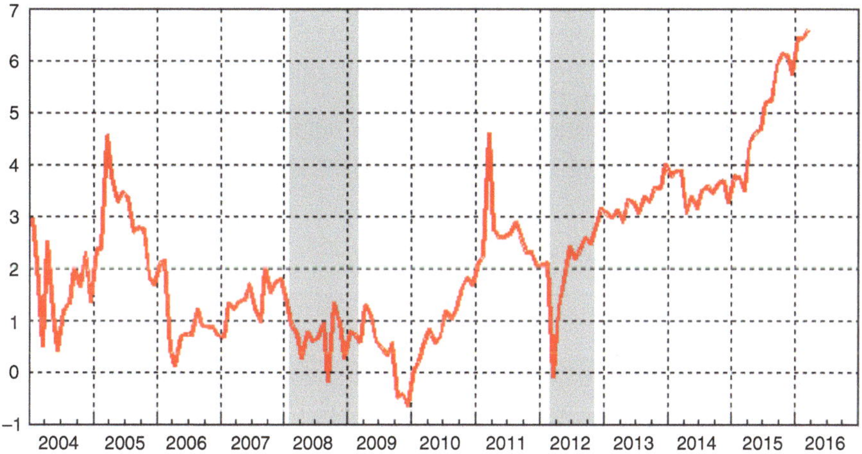

Fig. 2.4 Year-on-year change of banknotes in Japan. Source: Bank of Japan

low-interest-rate environment, given that the transaction costs involved delays in the adjustment to the stock equilibrium.

Aside from these analyses, it may be useful to ask ourselves why Japan is not witnessing the trend towards a cashless society that we can observe in Sweden. Cash is still convenient for small payments, especially in person-to-person transactions (hereafter, P-to-P transactions), even though bank transfers, credit cards, debit cards and e-money are increasingly being used. Payment habits are very difficult to change. One of the crucial factors determining the speed of embracing the new payment methods in society is the proportion of old people who are not necessarily knowledgeable about them. In this regard, the low penetration of new payment methods in Japan may be attributable to the fact that Japan is a country whose population is ageing rapidly.

2.2.2 *The Wide Variation of Cash to GDP Ratio Across Countries*

So far, I have analysed why the cash to GDP ratio has increased rather than decreased, despite the popular talk of the "advent of cashless society". Now, I will turn to the cross-section dimension of currency holdings. The situation regarding cash varies considerably across countries. For comparison, I will take three countries: Japan, Switzerland, and Sweden. What all three countries have in common is that they have adopted negative interest rates in recent years. However, the cash to GDP ratios for these countries remains in stark contrast; it is as high as 20.1% in Japan, and 11.0% in Switzerland, while, in Sweden, it stands at a mere 2.1%, decreasing not only in proportion to GDP, but also in absolute terms (Fig. 2.5).

Why is Japan's cash to GDP ratio so distinctively high? There are several hypotheses, although some of them are pure conjecture on my part.

First, Japan is very safe society, as is shown by its very low crime rate. In contrast, in a society where the crime rate is high, carrying banknotes, especially high denomination banknotes, is quite dangerous. Foreign visitors to Japan are often surprised when they see so many vending machines which accept large denomination banknotes on the streets.

Second, the high population density in Japan might have some bearing on the heavy use of cash. A form of transaction which is not easily replaced by the existing

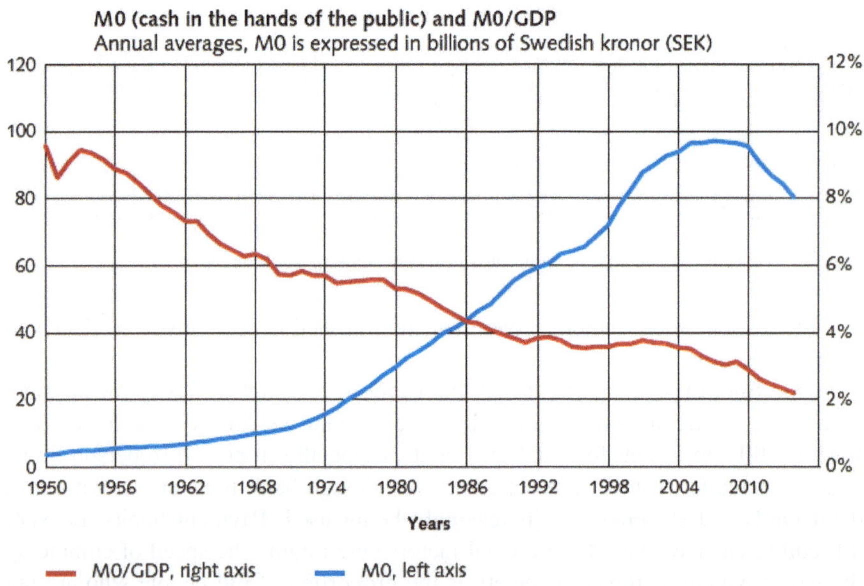

Fig. 2.5 The use of cash in Sweden. Source: Boel (2016, p.145)

payment methods is the P-to-P transaction, where cash still plays an important role. We can conjecture that the high concentration of the Japanese population in urban areas may contribute to the increasing use of cash.

Third, the strong pursuit of privacy or anonymity might increase the demand for cash. Even though Japan has recently introduced the "My Number System", we still do not have a US style Social Security Number system, which shows how strong the Japanese abhorrence towards violation of privacy is. Some might wonder whether the use of cash in illicit activities plays a role here. But, according to a study cited by Ken Rogoff (2016), the size of the underground economy as a percentage of the economy in Japan is quite low in comparison with other nations.[3]

Fourth, the resistance of the public against shifting to "the digital processing and payment platform" is very strong. People are always asking for the co-existence of payment platforms. Since cash payment is supported by a de-centralised system,[4] some sort of coercive measure might be needed if society really wants to make headway with the new payment methods quickly and on a significant scale. Generally speaking, Japanese society is not tolerant of such coercive measures. This is partly due to cultural reasons but it is also magnified by the rapid ageing of the population.

Fifth, against all these backgrounds, the density of ATMs and vending machines is quite high, which increases the demand for cash. Since a shortage of cash at ATMs is not tolerated by bank customers, banks are extremely cautious about running short of cash.

Sixth, old banknotes are honoured indefinitely. Japan has no fixed date beyond which an old banknote cannot be used legally or becomes very costly to convert into new banknotes.

Some of these factors are of a transitory nature but others are of a more structural nature, if not permanent. The reason why I have explained the situation regarding cash in Japan in detail is not because I think that the factors affecting the Japanese use of cash to be held universally, but because I want to emphasise that the use of cash is significantly affected by the characteristics of each society or economy. For example, when we analyse the use of the US Dollar in cash, we cannot ignore the fact that US Dollar banknotes are used heavily outside the country of issuance.

When it comes to the relationship between cultural and social background and cash holdings, we should go deeper into its causality. Which of the following propositions is correct?: "Use of cash dictates society" or "Society dictates use of cash". Since cash has a comparative advantage in P-to-P transactions, we cannot neglect social factors affecting people's behaviour, including how they choose to make payments. But, at the same time, we have to note that the opposite causality is working. The argument in favour of abolishing banknotes rests on the understanding that the very existence of high-denomination notes facilitates illicit activities. One of the issues here is to what extent central banks can and should, by their own

[3]See Rogoff (2016, p. 63).

[4]Ibid., p. 10.

judgement, intervene in the preferences or decisions of private individuals with regard to cash holdings. It is sometimes economically costly or politically unjustifiable to embrace some of such social factors, but is a central bank in a position to decide whether such factors are good or bad? This is a rather subtle issue. I will come back to this issue later.

2.3 What Is the Role of Cash?

Cash constitutes an important part of money. As the textbooks say, money plays three basic roles: (1) a medium of exchange; (2) a store of value; and (3) a unit of account. But this traditional typology based upon functionality, although quite correct, does not cover one important role that is played uniquely by cash, as opposed to bank deposits: cash provides private individuals with a legal alternative to private money. For private individuals, cash is the only form of central bank money to which they can get direct access, while private financial institutions can get access to central bank money through central bank deposits (reserves) as well. If it were not for cash, what would happen to private individuals? What are its implications for financial institutions and the financial system? At least, two issues immediately come to mind.

The first issue is the weakening of the disciplinary mechanism due to a change in the competitive balance between the central bank and private banks. When private individuals judge that the bank with which they have deposited their money is not safe, they will be able to shift their deposit to other banks which they regard as safe, even in the event that cash is abolished. This mechanism imposes a discipline on banks to run their institutions properly. Even though cash is not available for private individuals in this hypothetical world, they still have the option of shifting their deposits to good private banks just in case. So, we can count on the disciplinary mechanism. But, if the problem of banks is not of an idiosyncratic nature, but of a genuine systemic nature, private individuals cannot protect themselves. This is because they do not have direct access to risk-free money. If risk-free central bank money is no longer available because of the abolition of banknotes, it could have some long-term consequences on the financial system by weakening the disciplinary mechanism.

The second issue is that of contingencies. We cannot be confident that payment using bank accounts is always and everywhere available in the event of severe damage to the online network of banks due to natural disasters, terrorist attacks or other serious accidents. Japan has been hit hard by a tragic earthquake recently: the Great East Japan Earthquake in 2011. The online payment system continued to function well, but, in certain areas where branches and ATMs had been destroyed, cash became the most important method of exchange, especially for small retail payments. This experience makes us feel that a financial system which leaves us without an alternative means of exchange for bank deposits is not robust enough.

2.4 Arguments in Favour of the Abolition of Cash

Now, I will move on to the arguments about whether to abolish banknotes in more detail. People in favour of abolishing cash cite two reasons. One is that the existence of cash limits the effectiveness of monetary policy.[5] If central banks really press to obtain low negative interest rates, people will withdraw cash from their bank deposits. Thus, central banks cannot lower interest rates deeply below zero. The other reason is that cash facilitates illicit activity and tax evasion.[6] I will take up these two arguments in turn.

2.4.1 "The Existence of Cash Limits the Effectiveness of Monetary Policy"

If cash is abolished, central banks can lower interest rates deeply into the negative without worrying about dis-intermediation. But, if cash is abolished, can central banks achieve the intended goal of monetary policy? In order to answer this question, we have to think about the mechanism through which monetary easing, be it QE or a negative interest rate or any combination of both, becomes effective in the face of the zero lower bound of the interest rate. Essentially, there are two kinds of mechanisms for monetary easing to be effective.

One is to bring future demand to the present. Economic agents consider that now is the time to spend, simply because very accommodative monetary conditions prevail. This works. Households consume more and save less. Firms invest more. This essentially shifts the of timing of expenditure from tomorrow to today. In this process, debt increases. But when tomorrow becomes today, we have to bring demand from the day after tomorrow. So, we need further monetary easing. Again, this works and debt increases further. But we cannot count on this mechanism indefinitely. After all, the demand that is brought forward from the future is determined by the potential growth of the economy. If expenditure continues to increase, it means that the level of debt becomes unsustainably high relative to the income-generating capacity (potential growth rate), which ultimately damages the stability of the financial system. The other mechanism is to bring demand from somewhere else to the home country by devaluing the exchange rate of the home currency. It works when a single country is hit by a demand shock. But if many countries are hit by a demand shock simultaneously, the exchange rate channel does not work collectively.

So, is there a case for abolishing banknotes on the grounds that it makes monetary policy more effective? I do not diametrically rule out this possibility,

---

[5]Rogoff (2016).

[6]Sands (2016).

but I do not consider the abolition of banknotes to be a solution to the problems that many countries are now actually facing. After all, the advanced economies have been resorting to unconventional monetary policies for many years. A case in point is Japan, where the short-term interest rate has been practically zero since the mid-1990s. The more demand we bring forward from the future, the less demand we are faced with. Some argue that lower or negative interest rates are needed, because the natural rate of interest is itself declining. This argument sounds plausible at first blush, but lowering the interest rate for an extended period of time also induces a decline in the natural rate of interest simply because demand has already "borrowed". Monetary easing is effective and meaningful, but it is essentially a measure to buy time. It is not a solution to the underlying problem of the gradual decline in the potential growth rate which many countries are now faced with. Nevertheless, if central banks are bestowed with new capacity to engineer a deep negative rate by abolishing cash, I wonder how society and politics will respond. In order to extract a very marginal benefit, if any, should we pay the price by abolishing the basic infrastructure of cash? I am very sceptical.

2.4.2 "Cash Facilitates Illicit Activity and Tax Evasion"

There are three issues that need to be discussed. First, we have to define what is "illicit activity". Second, we have to establish clearly what constitutes a high denomination banknote. Third, we have to assess quantitatively to what extent high denomination banknotes are used in illicit activities. These three issues are all interrelated.

When critics say that cash is used in illicit activities, it envisages such activities as tax evasion, the drug trade, extortion, bribes, human trafficking and money laundering. These are outright illegal activities. The distinction between such outright illegal activities and human behaviour motivated by natural anxiety or fear that privacy is being violated is clear in theory, but it is sometimes difficult for outside observers to distinguish between the two. On top of this, there is a grey area in between.

As for the issue of the definition of a high denomination banknote, the notion of "high" varies across countries. In the US, a 100 USD note is really a "high" denomination banknote. A study by economists at the Boston Fed says the following:

> On a typical day in the United States, 5.2 percent of consumers have a $100 bill in their pocket, purse, or wallet. But only 22 percent of U.S. consumers have at least $100 in their wallet, pocket, or purse.[7]

In contrast, the situation in Japan is quite different. Although I do not know of a rigorous comparable study based upon Japanese data, the proportion of Japanese

[7] Greene and Schuh (2016).

consumers carrying a 10,000 Yen banknote in their wallet is much higher. This is because the cash system is well developed. This also means that it is difficult to define high denomination banknotes independently from how well the cash system is developed and how the average citizen in the street uses banknotes in his or her everyday life. This also means that the usage of cash might change over time. As time passes, the IT savvy generation, who are now young, will become dominant in society and the usage of cash might drastically change.

Finally, with regard to quantitative assessment, the information about the extent to which cash is used compared with the bank accounts of those involved in illicit activities is very limited. It may be that a prolonged period of extremely low interest rates is just masking the underlying situation regarding the use of cash.

All told, I can understand the argument in favour of abolishing high-denomination banknotes conceptually, but I feel that the actual implementation has to be decided upon the basis of a careful study in each country.

2.4.3 *"Digital Currencies such as Bitcoin Replace Cash"*

Now, I will move on to the argument that digital currencies will replace banknotes. Again, I do not diametrically rule out the possibility that digital currencies such as Bitcoin will replace cash in the future, given the history of paper banknotes, which are now the traditional means of payment, and were once a miraculous innovation when they were invented. The question here is one of a projection of what will occur in the next 20–30 years to come. I do not think that the possibility of moving completely to digital currencies is high. Even if digital currencies replace existing money as a medium of exchange, society will still need money to perform as a store of value and as a unit of account. Since a mechanism for keeping the value of digital currency stable is not incorporated, the space for it to be used as a store of value and as a unit of account is limited for the time being. One important issue here is whether central banks should issue digital currencies which allow private individuals to obtain direct access to credit risk-free money in a world where cash is replaced by digital currencies. There are many interesting issues to be studied and central banks should be open-minded about blockchain technology.

2.5 Final Thoughts and Conclusions

The monetary system is a crucially important form of infrastructure for both the economy and society. Even though we are gradually heading towards a cashless society, cash will still play an important role. When we think of whether we should deliberately reduce the role of cash and eventually whether we should actually abolish it, one thing we have to note is that the use of cash is run by a de-centralised system. Clearly, the central bank plays a crucial role as an issuer of money. Banks play an important role in the distribution of cash. Both branches and the ATMs network are key forms of infrastructure, which definitely include the printing and minting of money (banknotes and coins). Given the rapid progress of computers and copying machines, co-operation between central banks and the producers of copying machines is critical in order to avoid the counterfeiting of banknotes in this age of technological change. In terms of the shipment and warehousing of cash, companies offering logistics services are also important. The point is that cash is built on the de-centralised network of trust of the many parties mentioned above, so to speak. This is in stark contrast to a wholesale or large-value system which is more of a centralised system. So, there is a possibility that the cash system will gradually deteriorate in an unnoticed manner. Once the cash system is destroyed, it will be quite costly to rebuild it. As I have discussed above, the loss of the availability of credit risk-free payment-means might have potentially significant implications in the long run. Moreover, an additional decline in interest rates enabled by the abolition of cash might lead to over-reliance on monetary easing without society addressing the problems that the economy is facing. History shows that tinkering with the monetary system in order to solve structural problems is very costly. Money is more important than monetary policy. And an optimum response differs both across countries and over time. So, my conclusion is rather simple: when it comes to the various proposals on cash, we should carefully and thoroughly perform a cost-benefit analysis and, even if it proves favourable, we should proceed gradually, while nonetheless remaining open to new technology and ideas.

References

BIS Committee on Payments and Market Infrastructures (2015) Statistics on payment, clearing and settlement systems in the CPMI countries

Boel P (2016) Thinking about the future of money and potential implications for central banks. Sver Riksbank Econ Rev 1:147–158

Greene C, Schuh S (2016) U.S. consumers' holdings and use of $100 bills, Research Data Reports No 14-3, Federal Reserve Bank of Boston

Liikanen E (2016) Cash and the central bank, opening remarks at the Bank of Finland Conference on going cashless

Rogoff K (2016) The curse of cash. Princeton University Press, Princeton

Sands P (2016) Making it harder for the bad guys: the case for eliminating high denomination notes, M-RCBG Associate Working Paper Series, No 52

Weidmann J (2016) Opening speech at the Deutsche Bundesbank's third cash symposium

Chapter 3
New Estimates for the Shadow Economies of 11 Asian Countries from 2000 to 2014

Friedrich Schneider

Abstract The chapter presents estimations of the size of the shadow economies of Bangladesh, Cambodia, China, Indonesia, Japan, Laos, Malaysia, the Philippines, South Korea, Thailand and Vietnam over the period 2000–2014. According to my estimation the average size (over 2000–2014) of the shadow economy of Bangladesh is 33.7%, of Cambodia 45.4%, of China 12.0%, of Indonesia 29.0%, of Japan 9.2%, of Laos 27.5%, of Malaysia 28.9%, of the Philippines 32.6%, of South Korea 15.1%, of Thailand 39.0%, and of Vietnam 15.2%. I find that an increase in the burden of indirect taxation and the unemployment rate and less business freedom are the driving forces of the shadow economies of these eleven countries.

3.1 Introduction

Information about the extent of the shadow economy, who is involved in it, the frequency of these activities, and their magnitude, is crucial for making effective and efficient decisions regarding the allocations of a country's resources in this area. For policy-makers, in particular, it is very crucial to know the size and the development of the shadow economy, because their decisions, for example, to reduce unemployment, quite often depend on figures from the official economy, and these figures may be misleading if there is a sizeable shadow economy. If a country has a shadow economy greater than 10–15% points, at least a third or even 40–50% of the officially registered unemployed may have a job in the shadow economy, and, due to this, the government might be spending more tax revenues in fighting unemployment than is actually necessary. Also, in order to obtain a realistic estimate of the tax losses caused by the shadow economy, the size and development of it is crucial. It is one thing to have a shadow economy of only around 8–10%, in which the tax losses are not so severe, it is quite another to have a shadow economy of between 18% and 20%, in which the tax losses are quite sizeable. Unfortunately, it is very difficult to obtain accurate information about shadow economy activities

F. Schneider (✉)
Johannes Kepler University of Linz, Linz, Austria
e-mail: friedrich.schneider@jku.at

F. Rövekamp et al. (eds.), *Cash in East Asia*, Financial and Monetary Policy Studies 44, DOI 10.1007/978-3-319-59846-8_3

on the goods and labour market, because all the individuals engaged in these activities do not wish to be identified. Hence, doing research in this area can be considered as a scientific passion for knowing the unknown.

The goal of this chapter is twofold: (i) to undertake the challenging task of estimating the shadow economy for the 11 Asian countries: Bangladesh, Cambodia, China, Indonesia, Japan, Laos, Malaysia, the Philippines, South Korea, Thailand, and Vietnam from the year 2000 to 2014; and (ii) to provide some preliminary insights into the main causes of the shadow economy.

In the following Sect. 3.2, some theoretical considerations about the shadow economy are made, including a short literature review. In Sect. 3.3, the size of the shadow economy of the 11 Asian countries, mentioned above is calculated. Finally, in Sect. 3.4, a summary and policy conclusions are given.

3.2 Some Theoretical Considerations About the Shadow Economy

3.2.1 Short Literature Review

Using the MIMIC[1] approach, there are only a few papers trying to estimate the size and development of the shadow economy of Asian countries. In a paper by Schneider et al. (2010), the authors present estimates of the shadow economies for 162 countries. According to their estimates, the average size and development of the shadow economies over 1999–2007 (in % of GDP), is 35.9% in Bangladesh, 48.7% in Cambodia, 12.7% in China, 18.9% in Indonesia, 11.7% in Japan, 29.6% in Laos, 30.9% in Malaysia, 41.6% in the Philippines, 16.1% in South Korea, 50.6% in Thailand, and 15.1% in Vietnam. Similar results of these countries are reached in Schneider and Williams (2013). Bajada and Schneider (2005) also measure the size and development of the shadow economies of 17 Asia Pacific countries.

In another study, Vo and Ly (2014) estimate the size of the shadow economy and its trend for countries in the Association of the South East Asian Nations (ASEAN), excluding Singapore and Brunei, for the period from 1995 to 2014. In their study, a MIMIC approach is adopted to estimate the size of the shadow economy and its trend for the ASEAN nations. In general, the figures of Vo and Ly are quite high for these countries, and, for some countries, they have a similar size to my results in this chapter.

---

[1]The Multiple Indicator Multiple Causes (MIMIC) Approach is a latent estimation procedure for the size and development of a shadow economy. It is briefly explained in Sect. 3.3.1, entitled Econometric Methodology. The MIMIC method is based upon a statistical theory of unobserved variables, which considers the multiple causes and multiple indicators of the shadow economy to be measured. The MIMIC model uses multiple indicators and multiple causes in a structural equation model (SEM) with the latent variable shadow economy. The cause variables influence the shadow economy and the shadow economy activities are reflected in the indicator variables.

3.2.2 *Definition of the Shadow Economy*

One commonly used working definition of the shadow economy is that of *all* currently unregistered economic activities that contribute to the officially calculated (or observed) Gross Domestic Product.[2] Smith (1994, p. 18) defines it as "market-based production of goods and services, whether legal or illegal, that escapes detection in the official estimates of GDP". In this chapter, the following more narrow definition of the shadow economy is used: the shadow economy includes all market-based production of goods and services that are deliberately concealed from the public authorities to avoid the payment of income, value added, or other taxes; to avoid the payment of social security contributions; having to meet certain legal labour market standards, such as minimum wages, maximum working hours, safety standards, etc.; and complying with certain administrative procedures, such as completing statistical questionnaires or administrative forms.

3.2.3 *Causes of the Shadow Economy*

Given this definition, the most important causal determinants of the shadow economy are described in the following sub-sections: I want to emphasise clearly that, while the following causal factors are mostly relevant for Asian countries, other factors might also be important, such as the political structure of a country (a strong federalist *vs.* a strong non-federalist country). However, as I am concentrating on the Asian countries in this chapter, only the following ones are put forward.

3.2.3.1 Tax and Social Security Contribution Burdens

It has been ascertained that the overall tax and social security contribution burdens are among the main causes of the existence of the shadow economy.[3] The bigger the difference between the total cost of labour in the official economy and the after-tax earnings (from work), the greater the incentive is to avoid this difference and to work in the shadow economy. Since this difference depends broadly on the social security payment and the overall tax burdens, the latter are the key features of the actual existence and the increase of the shadow economy. As indirect taxes, and

[2]This definition is used, for example, by Feige (1989, 1994), Schneider (2005, 2010, 2015), Feld and Schneider (2010), Schneider and Williams (2013), Buehn and Schneider (2012), Schneider et al. (2010) and Williams and Schneider (2016). Do-it-yourself activities are not included. For estimates of the shadow economy and the do-it-yourself activities for Germany, see Buehn et al. (2009).

[3]See Schneider (1986, 2005, 2010, 2015), Johnson et al. (1998a, b), Tanzi (1999), Giles (1999), Giles and Tedds (2002), Feld and Schneider (2010), Schneider and Williams (2013), Williams and Schneider (2016), Buehn and Schneider (2012), and Schneider et al. (2010).

especially the value added tax (VAT), is charged on all components of a bill, indirect taxation also plays a role when calculating this total tax gap.

The concrete measurement of the tax and social security contribution burdens is not easy to define, because the tax and social security systems are vastly different among the countries. In order to have some general comparable proxies, I use the following causal variables: (1) indirect taxes as a proportion of GDP (positive sign expected); and (2) share of direct taxes including social security payments: direct taxes and social security payments as proportion of GDP (positive sign expected).

3.2.3.2 Intensity of Regulations

Increased intensity of regulations is another important factor that reduces the freedom (of choice) for individuals engaged in the official economy. One can think of labour market regulations such as minimum wages or dismissal protections, trade barriers such as import quotas, and labour market restrictions for foreigners such as restrictions regarding the free movement of foreign workers. Johnson et al. (1998b) find significant overall empirical evidence of the influence of (labour) regulations on the shadow economy; and this impact is clearly described and theoretically derived in other studies, for example, in Schneider and Williams (2013). Regulations lead to a substantial increase in labour costs in the official economy. Their empirical evidence supports the model of Johnson et al. (1997), which predicts, *inter alia*, that countries with more general regulation of their economies tend to have a higher share of the unofficial economy in total GDP.

To measure the intensity of regulation or the impact of such regulation on the decision of whether to work in the official or unofficial economy is a difficult task, and I try to model this by using the following two causal variables: (1) business freedom: it is a sub-component of the Heritage Foundation's economic freedom index; it measures the time and efforts of business activity. It ranges from 0 to 100, in which 0 is least business freedom and 100 is maximum business freedom (negative sign expected); and (2) regulatory quality: the World Bank's regulatory quality index, which includes measures of the incidents of market-unfriendly policies, such as price controls or inadequate bank supervision, as well as perceptions of the burdens imposed by excessive regulation in areas, such as foreign trade and business development. It scores between −2.5 and +2.5 with higher scores corresponding to better outcomes (negative sign expected).

3.2.3.3 Public Sector Services

An increase in the shadow economy can lead to reduced state revenues, which, in turn, reduce the quality and quantity of publicly provided goods and services. Ultimately, this can lead to an increase in the tax rates for firms and individuals in the official sector, quite often combined with a deterioration in the quality of the public goods (such as the public infrastructure) and of the administration, with the consequence of even stronger incentives to participate in the shadow economy. The provision and, in particular, the quality of the public sector services is thus also a crucial causal variable for people's decision to work or not work in the shadow economy. If a government does not provide a high quality of public goods and services, such as poor infrastructure, the incentive for people to pay taxes and not to work in the shadow economy, is considerably lowered because people ask themselves why they should honestly pay so many taxes when they do not receive good quality services from the government in return. To capture this effect, I use the following variable: Government Effectiveness from the World Bank's Worldwide Governance Indicators. It captures the quality of public services, the quality of the civil service and the degree of its independence from political pressures, the quality of policy formulation and implementation, and the credibility of the government's commitment to such policies. The scores of this index lie between −2.5 and +2.5 with higher scores corresponding to better outcomes (negative sign expected).

3.2.3.4 Quality of Public Institutions

The quality of public institutions is another key factor for the development of the informal sector. In particular, the efficient and discretionary application of the tax code and other regulations by the government plays a crucial role in the decision to work underground, an even more important role than the actual burden of taxes and regulations. In particular, bureaucracy with a high level of corrupt government officials seems to be associated with larger unofficial activity, while effective rule of law which secures property rights increases the benefits of formal, legal activity through stability. A certain level of taxation, mostly spent in productive public services, characterises efficient policies. In fact, production in the formal sector benefits from higher provision of productive public services and is negatively affected by taxation, while the shadow economy reacts in the opposite way. An informal sector developing as a consequence of the failure of political institutions to promote an efficient market economy leads to the consequence of entrepreneurs going underground.[4] The quality of public institutions is captured by two variables: the first is the control of corruption (percentile rank among all countries; 0 — lowest, 200 = highest) and the second is the rule of law (percentile rank among all countries; 0 = lowest, 200 = highest).[5]

[4]Compare here Schneider (2010), Buehn and Schneider (2012), Schneider and Williams (2013).

[5]These indices are compiled by the Heritage Foundation, Washington D.C., various years. The control of corruption ranks between 0 (lowest no-corruption) and 200 (highest possible corruption) and the rule of law ranks between 0 (no rule of law) and 200 (best rule of law).

3.2.3.5 Official Economy

As has been shown in a number of studies (Enste and Schneider 2006; Feld and Schneider 2010), the situation of the official economy also plays a crucial role in the decision to work or not to work in the shadow economy. In a booming official economy, people have many opportunities to earn a good salary and "extra money" in the official economy. This is not the case in an economy facing a recession, when more people try to compensate their losses of income from the official economy through additional shadow economy activities. In order to capture this, I will use the following two variables: (1) unemployment rate defined as total unemployment in percentage of total labour force (positive sign expected); and (2) inflation rate: GDP deflator (annual rate in percent); inflation is measured by the annual growth rate of the GDP implicit deflator, and shows the rate of price changes in the economy as a whole (positive sign expected).

3.2.4 Indication of the Shadow Economy

Because the shadow economy cannot be measured directly, I have to use indicators in which shadow economy activities are reflected. Here, I use the following ones:

3.2.4.1 Monetary Indicators

Given that people who engage in shadow economy transactions do not want to leave traces, they conduct these activities in cash. Over 80% of all shadow economy transactions are done by cash. Hence, most shadow economy activities are reflected in an additional use of cash (or currency). To take this into account, I use the following indicator: M1/M2. M1 corresponds to the currency outside the banks plus deposits; the usual definition for M2 is M1 + savings.[6]

[6]Cash is the most popular and frequent means for paying people in the shadow economy. Cash does not leave any traces (the opposite of a cheque or an electronic transfer) and, due to this, cash is the most easy means of payment for shadow economy transactions. In most countries, cash is used for shadow economy transactions in up to 80% of the cases. If one were to abolish cash, the transaction costs for shadow economy activities would rise, but they would not diminish because the causes of why people work in the shadow economy would not diminish. If one were to abolish cash, the first simulations for European countries show that the shadow economy would be reduced by roughly 10%.

3.2.4.2 Labour Market Indicators

Shadow economy activities are also reflected in labour market indicators. I use the following one: labour force participation rate: this is the proportion of the population that is economically active, supplying labour for the production of goods and services during a specified period.

3.2.4.3 State of the Official Economy

In addition, shadow economy activities are reflected in the state of the official economy. For this reason, I include the following indicator: growth rate of GDP *per capita*, i.e., the annual growth rate of the GDP *per capita*.

3.3 The Size of the Shadow Economy of 11 Asian Countries

3.3.1 Econometric Methodology

Estimating the size and trend of a shadow economy is a difficult and challenging task. Methods—designed to estimate the size and trend of the shadow economy—such as the currency demand approach, or the electricity approach, consider just one indicator that "must" capture all the effects of the shadow economy.[7] However, it is obvious that the effects of shadow economy show up simultaneously in the production, labour, and money markets. A shadow economy directly increases the production of an economy because the shadow-economy produced GDP can, at least partly, be added to the official GDP; a shadow economy uses mostly labour, hence, the official labour market is actually higher with a shadow economy. And, finally, a shadow economy is also reflected in the money markets as most shadow-economy transactions are paid in cash.

The empirical method used in this chapter is based upon the statistical theory of unobserved variables, which considers the multiple causes and multiple indicators of the phenomenon to be measured, i.e., it explicitly considers the multiple causes leading to the existence and growth of the shadow economy, as well as the multiple effects of the shadow economy over time. In particular, I use a Multiple Indicators Multiple Causes (MIMIC) model—a Structural Equation Model (SEM) with one latent variable—for the empirical analysis.[8] The main idea behind a SEM is to

[7]In this chapter, a detailed discussion about the various measurement methods is not attempted. See Schneider and Enste (2000), Feld and Schneider (2010), Schneider and Williams (2013) and Schneider (2015).

[8]The pioneers of this approach are Frey and Weck-Hannemann (1984), who applied this approach to cross-section data from the 24 OECD countries for various years.

examine the relationships among unobserved variables in terms of the relationships among a set of observed variables by using the co-variance[9] information of the latter. In particular, a SEM compares a sample co-variance matrix, i.e., the co-variance matrix of the observed variables, with the parametric structure imposed on it by a hypothesized model. The relationships among the observed variables are described in terms of their co-variances, and it is assumed that they are generated by (a usually smaller number of) unobserved variables. In the MIMIC model presented in this chapter, the shadow economy is the unobserved variable and is analysed with respect to its relationship to the observed variables using the co-variance matrix of the latter. For this purpose, the unobserved variable is, in a first step, linked to the observed indicator variables in a factor analytical model, also called a measurement model. Second, the relationships between the unobserved variable and the observed explanatory (causal) variables are specified through a structural model. Thus, a MIMIC model is the simultaneous specification of a factor model and a structural model. In this sense, the MIMIC model tests the consistency of a "structural" theory through data, and has two goals: (i) estimating the parameters (co-efficients, variances, etc.); and (ii) assessing the fit of the model. Applying this to shadow economy research, these two goals mean: (i) measuring the relationships of a set of observed causes and indicators in the shadow economy (latent variable); and (ii) testing whether the researcher's theory or the derived hypotheses, as a whole, fit the data used.

3.3.2 Econometric Results

Table 3.1 presents four different specifications for estimating the size and development of the Bangladesh, Cambodian, Chinese, Indonesian, Japanese, Laos, Malaysian, Filipino, South Korean, Thai, and Vietnamese shadow economies.[10]

I use a MIMIC estimation procedure over the period 2000–2014 (yearly data). If I first consider the cause variables, I realise that the variable indirect taxes have the expected sign and the estimated co-efficient is highly statistically significant for all four specifications. The variable direct taxes and social security contributions have

[9]The co-variance (cited from Wikipedia, the free encyclopedia, www.wikipedia.org, September 2016) is a measure of how much two random variables change together. If the greater value of one variable mainly corresponds with the greater value of the other variable, and the same holds for lesser values, i.e., the variables tend to show similar behaviour, the co-variance is positive. In the opposite case, when the greater values of one variable mainly correspond to the lesser values of the other, i.e., the variables tend to show the opposite behaviour, the co-variance is negative.

[10]These 11 Asian countries were chosen because I could compile a consistent data-set of the causal and indicator variables for them.

Table 3.1 MIMIC Model Estimations for 11 Asian Countries (standardised solution): Bangladesh, Cambodia, China, Indonesia, Japan, Laos, Malaysia, the Philippines, South Korea, Thailand, and Vietnam, Period 2000–2014

Specification	1	2	3	4
Cause variables				
Indirect taxes (% of GDP)	+0.38*** (4.04)	+0.30*** (3.33)	+0.32** (2.53)	+0.34*** (2.82)
Direct taxes and social security contributions (% of GDP)	0.26** (1.86)	0.28(*) (1.75)	–	–
Unemployment rate	0.20* (2.06)	0.21* (2.40)	0.28* (2.06)	0.29* (2.07)
Regulatory quality	−0.06 (0.59)	–	–	+0.10 (1.39)
Government effectiveness	–	−0.13 (1.49)	−0.20(*) (1.90)	−0.10 (1.50)
Control of corruption	–	–	−0.15(*) (1.86)	−0.23(*) (1.74)
Rule of law	0.05 (0.35)	−0.06* (0.73)	–	–
Business freedom	–	−0.16** (2.06)	−0.16** (2.02)	−0.17** (2.03)
Indicator variables				
Ratio M1 to M2	1.00	1.00	1.00	1.00
GDP growth	−0.26** (2.36)	−0.31* (1.94)	−0.42* (1.70)	−0.20 (1.46)
Labour force participation rate	−1.07*** (3.51)	−1.05*** (3.46)	−1.23*** (2.62)	−1.17*** (2.93)
Observations	165	165	165	165
Degrees freedom	73	73	73	73
Chi-square	18.50	15.65	17.59	19.65
RMSEA	0.10	0.13	0.14	0.15

Note: Absolute z-statistics in parentheses. *, **, *** indicate significance at the 10%, 5%, and 1% level, respectively
Source: Own calculations

the theoretically expected positive sign and are just statistically significant.[11] The unemployment rate is also highly statistically significant and has the expected positive sign in all four specifications. The estimated co-efficients of regulatory quality are not statistically significant and have switching signs. The estimated co-efficients of government effectiveness have the expected negative sign, but are not statistically significant except for equation 3. Control of corruption has the expected negative sign and is just statistically significant. The estimated co-efficients of the variable "business freedom" have the expected negative sign and are statistically significant in equations 2, 3 and 4. If I turn to the indicator

[11]As these two tax variables are highly correlated in equations 3 and 4, the direct tax variable is left out, as the direct tax burden variable is of minor importance in these countries.

variables, the variables M1 to M2, GDP growth and labour force participation have all the theoretically expected signs and GDP growth and labour force participation are statistically significant.

To summarise: these are the MIMIC results for these 11 Asian countries over the period 2000–2014. They certainly could be improved, and, if one could add more countries, the results would most likely become more stable. However, I clearly realise that I have a more or less consistent and statistically significant result for most causal variables, but let me again explicitly mention that these results are somewhat unstable, because only 11 countries are captured and the estimation period from 2000 to 2014 is rather short.

3.3.3 The Size of the Shadow Economy of 11 Asian Countries (Bangladesh, Cambodia, China, Indonesia, Japan, Laos, Malaysia, the Philippines, South Korea, Thailand and Vietnam)

The estimated MIMIC co-efficients allow me—only relatively—to determine the estimated sizes of the shadow economy, which describe the pattern of the shadow economy in a particular country over time. In order to calculate the size and trend of the shadow economy, I must convert the MIMIC index into "real world" figures measured in percentage of official GDP or in currency units. This final step requires an additional procedure: the so-called benchmarking or calibration. Unfortunately, no consensus exists in the literature of which benchmarking procedure to use. The methodology that we use was promoted by Dell'Anno (2007) and Dell'Anno and Solomon (2008). In the first step, the MIMIC model index of the shadow economies is calculated by multiplying the co-efficients of the significant causal variables with the respective time series.

Secondly, this index is converted into absolute values of the shadow economies, taking a base value in a particular base year. The base values necessary for this final step of the calibration procedure are from the year 2007 and are taken from Schneider et al. (2010), who estimated the shadow economies in 162 countries around the world using the MIMIC and the currency demand approach. Thus, the size of the shadow economy $\eta\hat{}_t$ at time t is given as:

$$\eta\wedge = \frac{\eta_t}{\tilde{\eta}_{2007}} \eta^*_{2007}$$

where $\eta\tilde{}_t$ denotes the value of the MIMIC index at t according to the above equation, $\eta\tilde{}_{2000}$ is the value of this index in the base year 2007, and η^*_{2007} is the exogenous estimate (base value) of the shadow economies in 2007. Applying this benchmarking procedure, the final estimates of the shadow economies of these countries can be calculated.

The size and development of the shadow economies of the 11 Asian countries (Bangladesh, Cambodia, China, Indonesia, Japan, Laos, Malaysia, the Philippines, South Korea, Thailand and Vietnam) are shown in Table 3.2.

Let me clearly state that these are preliminary results and again I explicitly want to mention that, in my opinion, the MIMIC estimations shown in Table 3.1 are the first ones to be used for the calculations. If I discuss the size of the shadow economy of Bangladesh, it has a value of 35.6% in the year 2000, which more or less decreases up to the year 2014 to 31.6%. In Cambodia (China[12]), I have a value of 50.1% (13.1%) in the year 2000, which decreases to 41.5% (to 12.5%) in the year 2014. Indonesia has a size and development of its shadow economy of 29.4% in the year 2000, which increases to 37.0% in 2010 and then decreases back to 28.4% in 2014. In Japan (Laos), I have a size of the shadow economy in the year 2000 of 11.2% (30.6%), which decreases to 8.8% (27.3%) in 2008 and then decreases again to 8.2% (24.8%) in 2014. If I next consider Malaysia, it has a shadow economy of 31.1% in 2000, which decreases to 28.7% in 2008, increases to 29.1% in 2010, and then decreases to 26.4% in 2014. The shadow economy of the Philippines was 35.4% in 2000, decreases to 31.4% in 2010, and then decreases further to 29.0 in 2014. The shadow economy in South Korea was 17.5% in 2000, decreases to 15.1% in 2008, increases to 16.2% in 2009 and then again decreases to 12.4% in 2014. The shadow economy of Thailand was 42.6% in 2000, decreases to 37.1% in 2010 and then increases again to 40.9% in 2014. The shadow economy in Vietnam was 15.6% in 2000, decreases to 14.3% in 2008 and then increases again to 16.8% in 2014. In general, here we see no unique pattern of the size and development of the shadow economy. For most countries, we observe a decrease from 2000 to 2008, but, for the Philippines, Thailand, Vietnam and China, we observe later on, from 2010 to 2014, a renewed increase. The largest average shadow economy over this period was Cambodia with 45.4%, followed by Thailand with 39.0%, then Bangladesh with 33.7% and the Philippines with 32.6%. The lowest shadow economy was Japan with 9.2%, followed by China with 12.0%.

The empirical results can be summarised as follows: the OECD countries, Japan and South Korea, have the lowest shadow economy, which is not astonishing because they are highly developed countries, where, for most people, the official economy offers sufficient opportunities to work and to earn a high salary. In particular, Thailand, Cambodia and the Philippines, and maybe also Bangladesh and Indonesia, are countries with a stronger developing country "status" and where the official economy is not large or efficient enough to offer sufficient opportunities to earn a decent salary, and, hence, a lot of the people are engaged in shadow economy activities. To measure the size and development of the former Communist countries of China and Vietnam (and partly Laos) is quite difficult, because these countries are in the middle of a transformation process from a Communist system to

[12]China is an extremely difficult case, due to the fact that China is a mixture of a planned and market economy; these figures have to be interpreted with great care and may be not reliable.

Table 3.2 Size and development of the shadow economies in some Asian countries from 2000–2014 (in % of GDP)

Country	2000	2005	2006	2007	2008	2009	2010	2011	2012	2013	2014	*Average*
Bangladesh	35.6	35.1	34.5	34.1	33.7	34.2	33.8	33.2	32.7	32.2	31.6	*33.7*
Cambodia	50.1	47.8	46.8	46.0	45.2	45.6	45.0	44.2	43.8	43.2	41.5	*45.4*
China	13.1	12.5	12.2	11.9	11.8	12.1	11.4	10.8	11.3	11.9	12.5	*12.0*
Indonesia	29.4	28.6	28.3	27.9	27.6	27.4	27.0	27.5	28.2	28.1	28.4	*28.0*
Japan	11.2	10.3	9.4	9.0	8.8	9.5	9.2	9.0	8.8	8.1	8.2	*9.2*
Lao PDR	30.6	28.9	28.4	28.0	27.3	27.6	27.7	27.1	26.3	25.4	24.8	*27.5*
Malaysia	31.1	30.4	30.0	29.6	28.7	29.3	29.1	28.4	27.8	27.2	26.4	*28.9*
Philippines	35.4	33.4	32.8	32.3	31.9	31.6	31.4	32.0	32.1	32.6	32.9	*32.6*
South Korea	17.5	16.3	15.9	15.6	15.1	16.2	15.6	14.8	13.6	13.0	12.4	*15.1*
Thailand	42.6	39.0	38.5	38.2	37.7	37.5	37.1	38.4	39.3	40.1	40.9	*39.0*
Vietnam	15.6	14.7	14.6	14.4	14.3	14.6	14.4	15.1	16.0	16.3	16.8	*15.2*
Average	*29.3*	*27.9*	*27.4*	*27.0*	*26.6*	*26.9*	*26.5*	*26.4*	*26.4*	*26.2*	*26.0*	*26.0*

Source: Own calculations, April 2016

a market system, so that it is not only the statistics that are misleading but also what type of economy is really captured here. Hence, the size and development of these three countries have to be interpreted with great care and should be taken as rough estimates.

3.4 Summary and Policy Conclusions

Writing this chapter, I realise that there are many obstacles to overcome when measuring the size of the shadow economy of these 11 Asian countries of Bangladesh, Cambodia, China, Indonesia, Japan, Laos, Malaysia, the Philippines, South Korea, Thailand, and Vietnam. However, this chapter shows that I have made some progress. I provide estimates of the size of the shadow economy, of these 11 Asian countries over the period 2000–2014 by using the MIMIC procedure for the econometric estimation and the benchmarking procedure for calibrating the estimated MIMIC into absolute values of the size of the shadow economy of these 11 countries.

These new insights gained with regard to the size and trend of the shadow economies for these 11 Asian countries lead us to the following two conclusions:

The *first* conclusion from these results is that, for all 11 countries investigated, the size of the shadow economy is quite large, with an average value for Bangladesh of 33.7%, for Cambodia of 45.4%, for China of 12.0%, for Indonesia of 28.0%, for Japan of 9.2%, for Laos of 27.5%, for Malaysia of 28.9%, for the Philippines of 32.6%, for South Korea of 15.1%, for Thailand of 39.0%, and for Vietnam of 15.2%. Except for Japan, which is a highly developed OECD country, the sizes of the other Asian countries are considerably higher than that the United States, 9%, or in Central Europe, where the average size is between 10% and 12%. However, the size of the nine developing Asian countries is not higher than those in South America or Central Africa.

The *second* conclusion is that the shadow economies are a complex phenomenon that is present to an important extent in these 11 Asian countries. People engage in shadow economy activities for a variety of reasons. Among the most important are government actions, most notably taxation, regulations and the quality of public (government) services.

Considering these two conclusions, it is obvious that one of the big challenges for every government is to undertake efficient and incentive-orientated policy measures in order to make work in the shadow economy less attractive. And, hence, to make work in the official economy more attractive, successful implementation of such a policy may lead to a stabilisation or even a reduction in the size of the shadow economy, as can be seen in these eleven countries.

Finally, I offer six suggestions of incentive-oriented policy measures to reduce shadow-economy activities:

(1) Reduction of indirect tax rates;
(2) An exemption of the value-added tax on labour-intensive economic activities, such as the re-construction of old houses;
(3) The firms which do demand or supply shadow-economy activities, should be excluded for 4–5 years from all public contracts;
(4) Incentives to use credit cards for transactions (e.g., to reduce fees or taxes);[13]
(5) Strong punishment if shadow economy activities are linked to organised crime (such as prostitution);
(6) Good governance and a deregulation of the "official" economy.

References

Bajada C, Schneider F (2005) The shadow economy of the Asia Pacific. Pac Econ Rev 10/3:379–401
Buehn A, Schneider F (2012) Shadow economies around the world: novel insights, accepted knowledge and new estimates. Int Tax Public Financ 19(1):139–171
Buehn A, Karmann A, Schneider F (2009) Shadow economy and do-it-yourself activities: the German case. J Inst Theor Econ 164(4):701–722
Dell'Anno R (2007) The shadow economy in Portugal: an analysis with the MIMIC approach. J Appl Econ 10:253–277
Dell'Anno R, Solomon OH (2008) Shadow economy and unemployment rate in USA: is there a structural relationship? An empirical analysis. Appl Econ 40:2537–2555
Enste D, Schneider F (2006) Wie groß ist die Schattenwirtschaft? Des Rätsels Lösung, Wirtschaftsdienst—. Z Wirtsch 86(2):185–191
Feige EL (1989) The underground economies. Tax evasion and information distortion. Cambridge University Press, Cambridge
Feige EL (1994) The underground economy and the currency enigma. Suppl Public Financ/Financ Publiques 49:119–136
Feld L, Schneider F (2010) Survey on the shadow economy and undeclared earnings in OECD countries. Ger Econ Rev 11(2):109–149
Frey BS, Weck-Hannemann H (1984) The hidden economy as an unobserved variable. Eur Econ Rev 26(1):33–53
Giles DEA (1999) Measuring the hidden economy: implications for econometric modelling. Econ J 109(456):370–380
Giles DEA, Tedds LM (2002) Taxes and the Canadian underground economy. Canadian Tax Foundation, Toronto
Johnson S, Kaufmann D, Shleifer A (1997) The unofficial economy in transition. Brook Pap Econ Act 2:159–221

[13]Such an incentive would lead to more credit card transactions. The use of credit cards would provide us with a better documentation of the payment system because card payments are more visible and one clearly sees the type of payment that is used for a certain service or good. If credit cards were used more, this would certainly have a dumping effect on the size and development of the shadow economy.

Johnson S, Kaufmann D, Zoido-Lobatoìn P (1998a) Regulatory discretion and the unofficial economy. Am Econ Rev 88(2):387–392

Johnson S, Kaufmann D, Zoido-Lobatoìn P (1998b) Corruption, public finances and the unofficial economy, World Bank Policy Research, Working Paper Series No. 2169. The World Bank, Washington, DC

Schneider F (1986) Estimating the size of the Danish shadow economy using the currency demand approach: an attempt. Scand J Econ 88(4):643–668

Schneider F (2005) Shadow economies around the world: what do we really know? Eur J Polit Econ 21(3):598–642

Schneider F (2010) The influence of public institutions on the shadow economy: an empirical investigation for OECD countries. Eur J Law Econ 6(3):441–468

Schneider F (2015) Schwarzarbeit, Steuerhinterziehung und Korruption: Was ökonomische und nicht ökonomische Fehler zur Erklärung beitragen. Perspekt Wirtsch 16(4):412–425

Schneider F, Enste D (2000) Shadow economies: size, causes, and consequences. J Econ Lit 38 (1):77–114

Schneider F, Williams CC (2013) The shadow economy. Institute of Economic Affairs, London

Schneider F, Buehn A, Montenegro CE (2010) New estimates for the shadow economies all over the world. Int Econ J 24(4):443–461

Smith P (1994) Assessing the size of the underground economy: the statistics Canada perspectives. Can Econ Observer 7:3.16–3.33

Tanzi V (1999) Uses and abuses of estimates of the underground economy. Econ J 109 (456):338–340

Vo DH, Ly TH (2014) Measuring the shadow economy in the ASEAN nations: the MIMIC approach. Int J Econ Financ 6(/10):139–148

Williams CC, Schneider F (2016) Measuring the global shadow economy: the prevalence of informal work and labour. Edward Elgar, Cheltenham

Chapter 4
De-monetisation, Re-monetisation, and Parallel Currencies in North Korea

Rüdiger Frank

Abstract North Korea has been, and arguable still is, an extreme case of a state socialist system. Due to ideological and economic reasons, by the late 1980s, the country had been largely de-monetised in the sense that money existed but was unable to fulfil its basic functions. A massive economic shock resulting from the collapse of the global socialist system after 1990 contributed to a re-monetisation including a reform of the domestic currency from the mid-1990s. Individuals have reacted in a predictable way, thus weakening the power of the state. Currently, North Korea is, in some aspects, more monetised than, for example, East Germany was in 1989, thanks to the de facto existence of parallel currencies. This chapter analyses the process of re-monetisation, its impact on society, and the state's efforts to curb these effects, which we are only beginning to comprehend fully.

4.1 Introduction

The Democratic People's Republic of Korea, or North Korea, did not emerge on a blank spot. When it was founded in 1948, it succeeded a country that had existed for a long time as a close ally of the Chinese Empire and had been colonised by Japan for 35 years from 1910 to 1945. This is important to note because we can assume that the Koreans have had centuries of experience with a central government and decades of experience with a modern, monetised industrial economy in a Western sense. In particular, the colonial pre-1945 economic system essentially adhered to market principles including relatively[1] free market entry and exit, private ownership of the means of production, and de-centralised price setting according to the interplay of demand and supply. During the period of Japanese colonisation, money

[1]The Japanese authorities initially discouraged investment in particular areas such as industry, and promoted investment in agriculture. After a brief period of moderate liberalism, the beginning of the World War 2 in East Asia marked a transition to a military economy with strategic investments in heavy and chemical industry. The participation of Koreans was possible, but limited to collaborators. See D. McNamara (1990).

R. Frank (✉)
University of Vienna, Vienna, Austria
e-mail: ruediger.frank@univie.ac.at

F. Rövekamp et al. (eds.), *Cash in East Asia*, Financial and Monetary Policy Studies 44, DOI 10.1007/978-3-319-59846-8_4

was largely able to fulfil its functions as a medium of exchange, of storage and of transfer of value, and as a unit of account.

In the first decade after the country was liberated from Japan in 1945, the Soviet Union exercised significant influence on the economic system of North Korea (Armstrong 2003). This did not mean the abolition of money, but it led to severe restrictions in its functions, as has been widely documented in the literature on state socialist systems (Kornai 1992). The absence of the threat of market exit led to a soft budget constraint on the side of producers and a decision to a focus on quantity instead of quality. Most importantly, price-setting was centrally regulated, and access to goods and services depended, to an increasing degree, on political capital, not on the ability or willingness to pay. As a result, the reaction of supply to changes in demand was disturbed, if not completely disconnected. State-set prices remained nominally stable despite a chronic shortage, and inflation was hidden (French 2005).

Individuals reacted to this situation. Their career decisions were not driven by concerns over job security, because there was no unemployment; and they were only weakly related to the size of their salaries, because wages were standardised and money had very limited buying power. Instead, individuals aimed at improving their *access* to goods and services. They did so through acquiring Party membership, by other measures to improve their status in the eyes of the state, or by getting jobs that would allow them to interact with foreigners. Improving access to goods and services became the dominant motive of economic activity, as opposed to a maximisation of funds, as would be typical for a market economy.[2]

Enterprises reacted, too. With a focus on nominally fulfilling the plan, access to inputs had to be maximised, and since the latter was difficult to achieve under the conditions of a chronic shortage, output had to be minimised through plan bargaining. Neither prices nor money or cash played a major role here. Rather, political and social capital was used to secure supplies and to reduce output requirements (Eberstadt 2009). These mechanisms are typical for state socialist systems and were among the reasons for the near collapse of East Germany's economy after a sudden change of the "rules of the game" following the parliamentary elections in March 1990, monetary union with West Germany in July 1990, and after actual unification in October 1990 (Ritter 2007). The level of empirical detail available on this kind of development in North Korea is lower than in the case of Eastern Europe, but it has nevertheless been sufficiently documented to provide us with a fair understanding of the situation.[3]

However, as of 2016, North Korea is, in some aspects, more monetised than East Germany was in 1989, thanks to the de facto existence of parallel currencies. The aim of this chapter is to analyse the process of re-monetisation that has taken place

[2]For a glimpse on the life of North Koreans in the early years after 1945, see S. Kim (2013).

[3]An excellent study of the mechanisms of business-to-business relations in North Korea, based upon a thorough analysis of North Korean publications such as *Kŭlloja* or *Kyŏngje Yŏn'gu* can be found in P.H. Park (2016, p. 115).

in the last two decades, its impact on society, and the state's efforts at curbing these effects, which we are only beginning to comprehend fully.

Major sources used in the secondary literature on this field are North Korean defectors and outside visitors who have been residents in North Korea, including occasional business people (Abt 2014). In addition, given the scarcity of fieldwork on North Korea, I dare to use the insights which I have systematically collected during my numerous visits to the country since 1991 as supplementary empirical information to generate a more tangible image of the effects of de- and re-monetisation.

4.2 De-monetised North Korea

De-monetisation in North Korea after 1948 took place as a process. The role of markets for the distribution of goods and services was gradually reduced. Simultaneously, rationing was expanded from the provision of staple food to textiles, consumer electronics and alcoholic beverages. In addition to the extension of the range of rationed goods, the amount that was distributed by the state also rose. In the case of staple food in North Korea, it did, at some point, reportedly reach as much as 700 g per day, although, in reality, the rations consisted of grains of different quality and were often downsized (Lankov 2007). The aim of the state was clear: to realise a vision of Communism as a moneyless society in which constant and reliable oversupply would make money, including cash, unnecessary. Considering the cases of Lenin and Mao, it is rather typical that the realisation of such a vision was attempted in a socialist economy that was by no means as highly developed as Karl Marx had in mind for his image of a Communist society.[4]

By the late 1980s, North Korea was described as "perhaps the modern world's most demonetized economy" (Kihl and Kim 2006). When I spent one semester in North Korea as a student in 1991–1992, the situation which I could observe corresponded perfectly with this characterisation. Three currencies existed in parallel with one another: a domestic currency, called "our money" (*uri hwa*) which was only to be used by North Koreans; "red" foreign exchange certificates[5] (*pulgun ton*) to be used by non-Koreans who came from socialist countries such as China, Cuba or Vietnam; and "blue" foreign exchange certificates (*purŭn ton*) that were to be used by foreigners from capitalist countries.[6]

[4]Marx argued that economic development takes place in stages and according to objective laws. There is no room for shortcuts in this way of thinking. A society first had to go through a full capitalist stage before it could move on. This simple rule has been ignored or bent massively by the leaders of states that had hardly moved beyond feudalism, not to speak of capitalism, but nevertheless wanted to use the brand image of "Marxism" for ideological and legitimacy purposes.

[5]The official term was "*woehwawa pakkun ton*" (foreign exchange money).

[6]It should be noted that other socialist countries including Cuba and East Germany had used foreign exchange certificates. In China, these certificates were abolished only in 1994.

The three currencies were not interchangeable, and their use was severely restricted. To purchase products in regular stores or restaurants, local currency was required. For such purpose, foreign exchange certificates could not be used at all. In hard currency shops, however, only "blue" capitalist foreign exchange certificates could be spent. In hotels, both kinds of certificates were accepted; the owners of "red" certificates, however, were de facto charged a lower price because they had to pay relatively less in their own currency to obtain the certificates, while the prices remained the same regardless of the type of certificate used.

The political context is interesting to note. The main reason for the existence of "blue" Won at that time was the regular inflow of Japanese Yen, sent by relatives who lived there as part of the Zainichi community.[7] Until 2002, Japan was also North Korea's main trading partner. In order to avoid the hoarding of large amounts of hard currency cash, and to have immediate access to this valuable resource, the state demanded that the transferred money be exchanged into certificates. We know little about how this was received by North Koreans. In East Germany, the introduction of the so-called "*Forumscheck*" in 1979 in combination with the ban on the use of *Deutschmarks* was not very popular, and the restriction was often ignored.

In North Korea, dissatisfaction, if it existed, was not openly expressed. However, there were occasional irregularities. I was, for example, able to benefit from the system of multiple exchange rates as described above by illegally exchanging a few US Dollars into "red" socialist certificates from fellow Chinese students to buy a train ticket to Beijing. The ticket price was the same in red or in blue Won, but, due to the different exchange rates, it was more expensive if bought with capitalist currency.

This example hints at a few opportunities for profit through the creative utilisation of the various currencies, but it was a complicated and potentially risky endeavour. I could only purchase the train ticket with the "wrong" type of (red) forex certificates because I was able to present my East German passport,[8] and the railway officer was sufficiently confused even though he had heard about German unification.

However, when I attempted to buy an ice cream from a vendor on the street in 1991, neither "blue" forex certificates nor US Dollars or *Deutschmarks* were accepted, although one would assume that they would have been valued much higher than the non-convertible domestic currency. The vendor obviously had no use for this kind of cash because money alone, without some kind of political capital, would not be able to buy her anything. On the other hand, I was not allowed to possess domestic currency. I got the ice cream because a friendly person bought

[7]For more detail on the Zainichi, see C. S. Lee and G. De Vos (1981). The pro-North Korean part of this group is organised in the Chōsen Sōren (ch'ongryŏn).

[8]Despite German unification that had taken place a year before, the GDR (East German) passport was still valid for another five years. This was a technical regulation to avoid the need to convert over ten million East German passports into new documents immediately.

it for me; the same happened when I needed local currency to use public transportation including the subway, which also required "our" money.

My most memorable experience with the de-monetised North Korean economy was my attempt to buy a coffee mug in Pyongyang's Department Store No. 1 in October 1991. On the first floor of the store, there was a pyramid of about 50 or more such cups. But the saleswoman plainly refused to sell me a single one of them, first saying "we don't have any", and then just running away. I was left flabbergasted and thus found out the hard way that a product on display did not mean a product for sale. Following a government directive, which was allegedly based upon an on-the-spot-guidance from Kim Il-sung, the few existing shops and department stores always had to be fully equipped, but the goods on display turned into mere decorations whenever nothing to restock the shelves was available.

The chronic shortage in combination with the limited utility of money led to an extreme version of a typical feature of state socialist systems: the distribution sector was largely neglected. Shops and restaurants were rare in numbers and hardly recognisable. Advertisements and commercials did not exist, neither in public nor in the media. The behaviour of sales personnel in shops and restaurants did not indicate any interest in selling. Goods for actual sale were usually not unpacked but sold out of packages that were sitting on the ground. The availability of something was indicated by the actual process of selling, which instantly attracted a large crowd until the stocks were depleted.

To sum it up, the interest in selling and in making money was very underdeveloped. For the whole of the 5 months that I stayed in the country at that time, beyond the state organised collection of fees, there was not a single attempt by individual North Koreans to extract money from me. The high political risk of doing so would hardly have been counter-balanced by the questionable gain of money that would have been difficult to spend and was thus more or less useless.

Accordingly, phenomena such as corruption were not as rampant as one would expect in a system with a chronic undersupply and a strong bureaucracy. In fact, there are various reports about corruption in North Korea even from that time, but it took different, non-monetary forms.[9] Since money was not useful as a means of exchange or storage of value, access to goods and services became more crucial. Such access was based not only upon superior information, but also on membership in certain groups including the military, the Party, or the citizenry of Pyongyang.

Many goods were distributed for free. Clothing, for example, was handed out on the occasion of major holidays such as the leader's birthdays. Other goods, such as staple food, were sold at extremely low subsidised prices. The so-called public distribution system was operated in buildings that were hard for outsiders to recognise. Such distribution centres were only accessible to local residents who

[9]In a long conversation with a North Korean (anonymity of this source is kept for safety reasons) in 1992, I was, for example, told about some young women using their physical attractiveness to obtain Party membership. Men often "volunteered" to serve in the military for up to one decade in order to get Party membership after deobilisation. Smaller favours could be bought with a bottle of liquor.

were registered there. The administrators of each of these centres kept a book with the names of the residents and the amount of rice or other food that they were entitled to receive. For goods such as television sets, Koreans received coupons that could be redeemed once the desired good was available. Money had to be paid for these goods, but it only played a secondary role in this process.

All this is important to note in order to comprehend the magnitude of the transformation that happened from around 1994.

4.3 Re-monetisation since the Mid-1990s

The major game changer in this situation was the collapse of the foreign trade structure of North Korea as a result of the implosion of the Communist *bloc*. Goods and services had, for decades, been imported from socialist countries based upon long-term low-interest loans or barter trade. North Korea is rich in minerals and thus could offer valuable inputs for the COMECON[10] economies, although contracts were often not respected and the minerals were bartered at unrealistic values (Frank 1996). The background for such practices were the Cold War as well as bilateral competition between the Soviet Union and China, which made it politically desirable for Moscow and Beijing, and their respective allies, to maintain trade relationships with North Korea that were economically not profitable.

In addition to advanced technology, the most crucial material inputs that had been acquired through such preferential trade were crude oil, which North Korea does not produce, and chemical fertilisers. Both are essential for North Korea's agriculture which, due to geographic and climatic conditions, needs to be highly intensive in order to feed the country's growing population (Haggard and Noland 2007). Oil was processed into fuel for machines and pumps for irrigation systems and to produce fertilisers and other important chemicals, but was also directly used to generate electricity.

The relatively sudden conversion of the Soviet Union's and later Russia's trade to hard currency and world market prices resulted in the virtual stop of imports by North Korea. Crude oil imports from Russia dropped from 640,000 t in 1988 to 190,000 t in 1992, while those of coking coal dropped from over 1 million tons in 1988 to zero in the same period (Park 2016, p. 115). China was not yet a major trading partner, and, anyway, had its own difficulties after the shock of the Tiananmen Square protests of 4 June 1989, known in China as the June Fourth Incident. Other trading partners such as Poland or Hungary followed the Russian example, while the German Democratic Republic, another important trading

[10]The Council for Mutual Economic Assistance (COMECON) was a formal organisation to co-ordinate the economic activities of the Soviet Union's socialist satellite states. The basic idea was the same as for every domestic socialist economy: the conviction that competition through parallel production facilities was a waste of resources, and that economic efficiency could be maximised through a centrally organised division of labour. See Springer Gabler Verlag (2016).

partner with a long-standing bilateral relationship (Kang-Schmitz 2010), simply disappeared.

This sudden shock happened in addition to the long-standing structural problems of North Korea's socialist agriculture and regularly occurring natural disasters, some of which have been exacerbated through man-made deficiencies, such as de-forestation. As a result, agricultural production dropped dramatically and fell below subsistence level, which is estimated by the FAO to be around 4.5 million tons of rice equivalent annually. Production of rice fell from 4.5 million tons in 1992 to 1.4 million tons in 1996, output of maize fell from 3.7 million tons to 0.8 million tons in the same period (FAOSTAT 2016). The distribution system collapsed in most parts of the country except Pyongyang and even in the capital life became harder (Smith 2005).

This is when distribution of goods via so-called "farmer's markets" (*nongmin sijang*, also *changmadang*) started to gain a hitherto unseen level of importance. Such markets had been present in North Korea throughout its existence; their size and the scope of the available goods was, however, both strongly regulated and curbed by the government. They typically opened only three times a month (on days with a "1", such as the 11th, the 21st, and the 31st) and offered a limited range of local products, fruits, wild plants, etc. Farmers had to submit almost all of their production to the state and thus had little left to sell individually, which would have been a relatively pointless endeavour anyway because of the limited utility of money. The private economy, as much as it existed, did so at a low level of equilibrium.

With the collapse of public distribution, the previously sidelined farmer's markets suddenly became the major distribution channel for food and anything else of either domestic production or of Chinese origin, entering through the only superficially guarded border. Almost overnight, money started to matter in North Korea. As far as we know, domestic currency was used at the beginning, later in parallel with Chinese Renminbi, Japanese Yen[11] and, to a lesser degree, US Dollars.

Around the mid to late 1990s, Western interest in North Korea began to grow due to the news of a major famine. Images of hungry children appeared in mainstream news, and aid organisations were allowed to become active in North Korea (Smith 2005). Reports from defectors, which had previously been accessible mostly to South Korean intelligence circles alone, made their way into the media spotlight, and thus the collapse of the public distribution system and the spontaneous upgrading of the farmer's markets in North Korea became known in South Korean and Western academic circles. As soon as South Korea had overcome the worst of the Asian Financial Crisis of 1997/1998, and facilitated both by compassion for the suffering of fellow Koreans and the election of a progressive president

[11]The role of Japanese currency can be explained by the close economic relationship between North Korea and the pro-North Korean group of Zainichi Koreans in Japan who regularly sent money to relatives. In fact, trade relations were brisk; at the time of my studies in North Korea, most products in the hard currency stores were obviously imported from Japan including Coca Cola, shoes, stationery, etc.

in Seoul, South Korea's co-operation with North Korea achieved a few milestones including Mt. Kŭmgang tourism in 1999 and the first inter-Korean summit in June 2000 (Moon and Swenson-Wright 2014).

Clearly pushed by the experience of the famine and pulled by the new, forthcoming attitude of South Korea, perhaps also impressed by the evermore visible success of the cases of China and Vietnam, Kim Jong Il, since 1994 the new leader in North Korea, decided to legalise the spontaneous developments that had occurred during the chaotic years of the famine. He restored the state's control over distribution by partly re-establishing the public distribution system, but left the markets intact and even legalised the trade of goods other than food, renaming them officially from "farmer's markets" into "markets". The number of such markets in the whole country was reportedly around 380 by the end of 2015 (Silberstein 2015).

The July 2002 reforms harmonised prices, eliminated subsidies, introduced wage differentiation and devalued the domestic currency *vis-à-vis* the US Dollar. The foreign exchange certificates were scrapped, and the country now had only one currency. State prices were multiplied to match the market prices, thereby acknowledging, for the first time, a phenomenon called inflation (Frank 2005).

In various training seminars both in Pyongyang and in other countries including Switzerland, I was asked again and again by the North Korean participants from the Party, the Central Bank, and universities, about how best to fight inflation, which seemed to be the major concern of the leadership. Considering that right before the Tiananmen Square protests in China, inflation there had reached double-digit levels, and given that inflation in North Korea was estimated to be even higher, this focus was understandable.

It became clear that the North Korean government had, to a certain extent, decided to turn away from direct administration and was endeavouring to use macroeconomic and monetary instruments to achieve its goals. Not all these measures were successful; the introduction of People's Life Bonds in 2003, the first such attempt since the issuance of war bonds in the early 1950s, was designed to reduce liquidity in North Korea in order to curb inflation.

Meanwhile, North Korea's society underwent a change of little less than epic dimensions. When I visited Pyongyang in 2005, I was stunned to see hand-written signs on the door of a watch shop inviting customers to benefit from discounted prices on the occasion of the 60th anniversary of the Party foundation. Avoiding empty shelves did not seem to be a priority anymore. Rather, sales had to be maximised, and discounts were used to incentivise potential buyers. A few blocks down the street, I passed by a textile shop that, again in hand-written posters on its doors, invited customers to enter and enjoy a cup of tea or a glass of beer. A semi-legal cafe had been set up to attract more visitors and to make more money. The contrast to my experience a decade before was stunning.

A few days later, I visited a cultural heritage site in one of the provinces and wanted to buy an aquarelle as a souvenir. I asked for a discount if I bought four pieces but the vendor either did not understand the concept or was unwilling to reduce the price further. I insisted, and, in the end, he agreed. When I unpacked what I expected to be four paintings in my hotel room in the evening, I found that the vendor had cheated me; he had wrapped up only three paintings. My initial anger made room for the recognition that the goal of profit maximisation had trumped the very real fear of serious repercussions; defrauding a foreigner would almost certainly have been punished severely by the state if I had reported the incident.

Similar anecdotes appeared from various sources. It became clear that, within a few years, the attitude of most North Koreans towards profit had changed completely. This was possible through the resuscitation of money as a means of exchange and of the storage of value. The resulting behaviour, as such, was what is regarded as normal elsewhere and thus escaped the attention of most Western visitors. But compared to my experience a little more than a decade earlier, North Korean society had changed almost beyond recognition.

One visible expression of the re-monetisation was the emergence of cash cards.[12] As soon as money started to matter, some individuals were able to acquire so much of it that carrying cash was simply too cumbersome. The phenomenon of cashcards was a first proof of the emergence of a new middle class; I suggest using the number of mobile phone subscribers as a rough estimate for the size of this group (Frank 2012). It is important to note that this does not include the upper class in North Korea, who live in secluded areas and rarely interact with the ordinary population. Rather, the new middle class is an integral part of society. Differences in external appearance such as clothes became apparent; even the body language changed. Some North Koreans were seen with dyed hair or pet dogs, indicating the growing influence of South Korean fashion about which they learned from illegal DVDs or USB sticks.

The re-introduction of money had changed a formerly highly egalitarian society. Signs of different levels of affluence became obvious. The state's power was weakened through the ever-growing role of the markets for the distribution of goods and for price-setting. Political capital, which was once the only decisive factor to acquire almost any good or service was pushed into the background by money. In conversations with North Koreans, I rarely heard the desire to become a Party member or to spend a decade in the military anymore. Rather, learning English or Chinese, and doing something with "business" was what parents desired for their children, and what young people wanted to do.

[12]They function as a pre-paid card. They can be charged with cash and then used with a password at designated shops, even taxis. The most popular cash card in North Korea is the red-blue "Narae Card", issued by the Foreign Trade Bank.

4.4 The Currency Reform of 2009

It is not surprising that such changes raised concerns among parts of the leadership about regime stability. The result was a phase that I have called "socialist neo-orthodoxy",[13] lasting roughly from 2005 until 2009, but having been in preparation from about 2003.

The domestic driver of this policy shift has most likely been the seismic change within North Korean society as described above, and the resulting fear, on the part of the state, of losing control of society through the loss of its function as the sole provider of everything, and the growing individual self-confidence resulting from increasing economic autonomy. However, there was also a major external factor, namely, the uncompromising "War against Terror" of the George W. Bush administration after the 9/11 attacks on 11 September 2001. North Korea had been branded as a member of the "Axis of Evil" in January 2002 (Bush 2002). With the invasion of Iraq in March 2003, it became likely that such rhetoric might be followed by action. Economic reform including re-monetisation is risky for an authoritarian system that seeks to maintain stability. It is understandable that such a risk will only be taken, if it is taken at all, if the security of the regime is not otherwise threatened. Accordingly, reforms were stopped, and the state even attempted to repeal some of them.

The number of reports about the state's efforts to reduce the influence of private, money-based economic activities increased. They included the rumour that new regulations had been passed requiring a minimum age for women to be granted a license as a market trader. I was unable to verify this particular information during my visits, but a systematic study of the official media revealed a return to pre-reform wording (Frank 2010b).

The neo-orthodox turn lasted for a few years and culminated in an ill-fated attempt at curbing rampant inflation in 2009. On 30 November 2009, it was announced that, within one week, old banknotes would have to be exchanged for new ones. Only a limited amount of cash could be converted. Initially, this was only 100,000 Won, equivalent to about 40 kilograms of rice at the markets. The amount was later expanded to be 150,000 Won in cash and 300,000 Won in bank savings (Moon 2009). The rate of exchange from old to new money was 100:1 for cash and 10:1 for savings (Yonhap 2009). While prices and savings were reduced, wages remained at the previous nominal level, thus resulting, for a brief period, in a real wage increase of 10,000%. This should, however, be contrasted with the fact that, in the decade before, wages had remained rather stable while market prices had soared. It could thus be argued that, by the currency re-valuation, the state had intended to make regular work financially attractive again.

[13]In fact, I had initially used "socialist neoconservatism", but this led to confusion among American colleagues who had a very specific understanding of the term "neocon". See Frank (2010a).

North Korea has had a number of currency reforms before, including the reforms in 1959, 1979, and 1992 (Lankov 2013). The goal had usually been to re-establish the state's control over cash holdings in the country, and to eliminate excessively high savings, including those accumulated by sideline economic activities. For this purpose, however politically questionable, the replacement of an old currency with a new one was a sensible instrument. In 1979, the year of the introduction of domestically printed bills, there was the additional political motive of reducing dependency on the Soviet Union, which, until that time, had printed North Korean banknotes, and thus gathered valuable information about the amount of cash in circulation (Hunter 1999, p. 185).

In 2009, however, one of the main goals seems to have been not only to expropriate the middle class, but also to curb inflation. As indicated above, North Korean officials have repeatedly approached me over a number of years regarding this issue. The re-monetisation since the late 1990s, and, in particular after the 2002 reforms, had magnified the problem of skyrocketing prices, to reach dimensions that had not been known before in North Korea. There are no official figures, but my own estimate of annual inflation between 2003 and 2005, based upon a small basket of goods and services, was in the range of 200% (Frank 2005).

Politically, the state wanted to regain its control over the lives of its people by bringing them back into employment in the state sector. The markets had helped the country to overcome the famine but now had to be curbed again. A North Korean economist, clearly speaking on behalf of the state, explained in an AP interview in March 2010 that "Markets will be removed in the future, by reducing their numbers step-by-step, while continuously expanding the planned supply through state-run commercial networks" (Boston.com 2010).

One effect of the currency re-valuation was a massive expropriation of those who, in the past years, had been able to generate huge amounts of cash through the classic technique of selling products at a price above their costs. The term "confiscatory currency reform" (Haggard and Noland 2010) is thus well deserved. Once again, we lack solid data, but anecdotal evidence suggests that the big players were mostly unaffected by this measure because they had habitually converted their earnings into foreign currencies, mainly Chinese Yuan. Those who saw their savings de-valued were the smaller traders and private households (Park 2016, p. 199).

The public reacted with protest, something that is very unusual for North Korea. Reports of minor skirmishes with the authorities as well as of suicides emerged (Lee 2009). As a consequence, the government again increased the amount of cash that could be exchanged to 500,000 Won and savings to 1,000,000 Won or even more, if the origin of the money could be properly explained.

Andrei Lankov has argued that "the person who suggested this [the currency measure] was unbelievably naïve, not to say ignorant, about the fundamental workings of an economy" (Lankov 2013, p. 218). He implied that Kim Jong Il himself could have given the order. Whether or not this was the case, being the top leader includes responsibility. A scapegoat had to be found. As far as we know from defector reports, the currency measures were later declared to have been an attempt by a pro-American individual to undermine the dignity of the state. Pak Nam-gi, a Department Director of the Korean Worker's Party, was presented as the culprit and disappeared, in the true sense of the word (Branigan 2010). In North Korean newspaper articles, his name was edited out.

After the failed reforms, the neo-orthodox phase was over. Most restrictions on markets were lifted, and their activities were tacitly acknowledged as part of ordinary North Korean life. The currency revaluation of 2009 was followed by the re-emergence of explicit claims on the part of the state that it aimed to improve the consumer economy by focusing on light industry and agricultural production (Abrahamian 2011). Within a few months, prices returned to pre-reform levels, which means that the originally very substantial real wage increases were reduced to zero.

From a strictly economic point of view, the 2009 currency measure suddenly reduced the money supply, especially the amount of cash in circulation, which, in North Korea, plays a central role.[14] If all wages and all other sources of income were reduced by the same rate, not much would have happened except for the above stated expropriation or a forced disclosure of hidden cash reserves. But this was not the case; in addition to the above-mentioned 100-fold real wage increase and the tenfold increase in the value of bank savings, cash holdings in other currencies were not affected. The wage-earning and bank-saving part of North Korea's society saw its purchasing power jump up, which resulted in growing demand while supply remained stable or even decreased due to a shortage of cash among wholesale merchants, at least in the short run. This led to an upward pressure on prices and thus to massive inflation that further devalued savings and cash holdings.

The logical reaction of individuals in any society would be to abandon local money and to conduct business in alternative currencies. In the post-war economies of the twentieth century, cigarettes have often played this role. In North Korea, those traders and their clients who had not yet done so switched to foreign exchange such as Chinese Yuan, US Dollars, or the official main foreign currency[15] in North Korea, the Euro.

The state reacted by banning the use of foreign cash in the country. In January 2010, the Foreign Trade Bank informed foreigners residing in Pyongyang, including diplomatic missions, NGOs, and businesses, that the use of foreign currency in North Korea was no longer permitted, and that all transactions had to take place in North Korean Won at a nominal conversion rate of 1 € to 140 KPW as of 2 January

[14]I once asked a North Korean friend what she does with her monthly salary. She replied that she takes it home, in cash, and keeps it there. When I explained that, in my country, wages would typically be transferred to a bank, she gazed at me in bewilderment, and, over the next days, kept asking about the reasons why we considered the use of a bank to be a good idea.

[15]During a closed door meeting with North Korea's Vice Minister of Foreign Affairs in Brussels, the participants including myself were informed as early as 14 October 2002, that North Korea would stop using the US Dollar and introduce the Euro as its official currency for hard currency operations. This measure was officially implemented on January 2003. In reality, however, the US Dollar did not disappear from North Korea, and the Chinese Yuan became stronger.

2010. Payments including for accommodation, electricity, salaries etc. had now to be made in the form on non-cash cheques or bank transfers and denominated in KPW (Foreign Trade Bank 2010).[16]

It is unclear whether the ban on the use of forex in North Korea is still technically valid. In reality, it is definitely not. It is even difficult to get a quick reply when asking traders at North Korean markets about the prices of their goods in North Korean Won. This is not because they are reluctant to answer; they simply do not know, because they conduct their transactions mainly in "*Inminbi*" (Chinese Yuan). The currency disaster of 2009 taught North Koreans that they cannot trust their government when it comes to monetary stability, and, as a result, they found alternatives. Remarkably, the government seems to have accepted this, showing once again a degree of pragmatism that does not correspond with its stereotypical image in the West.

4.5 The Symbolism of North Korean Banknotes

Money is usually seen as having mainly economic functions. It is, however, also an important carrier of ideology. The *Euro* notes, for example, are decorated with images of bridges to symbolise the connecting function of the common currency, and none of these images is drawn after an actual original to avoid harming national feelings (Schmid 2001).

In North Korea, the images on banknotes have long been used for mainly three purposes: to promote leader Kim Il Sung; to symbolise the various strata in society, such as the farmers, the scientists, the workers, the military, etc.; and to display national symbols such as the national flower, the Chuch'e Tower, or the Kaesŏnmun (Arch of Triumph).

In 2002, the emergence of significantly higher denominations of up to 5000 Won accompanied the July measures and the resulting price adjustments. In December 2009, two major changes could be observed on the new banknotes that implicitly foreshadowed the solution of a major problem—the succession of power (Frank 2010c).

The 50, 10 and 5 Won bills of the new North Korean currency showed the people of North Korea. The Workers Party (50 Won) was valued higher than the military (10 Won), and the farmers were missing altogether; the 5 Won bill honoured the technical intelligentsia. This provided some food for thought for those who interpreted the Military First Policy as the expression of the dominance of the military over the Party.[17]

[16]Foreign Trade Bank of the DPRK (2010) Document No. DC03310-004. 29 January 2010.

[17]This is a view that I emphatically do not share. The Party and the military are both instruments of power, and are closely interconnected; each high-ranking officer is also a Party member. Dividing lines in North Korea's élite certainly exist. However, they run between families and regions, not between (but inside of) institutions.

The truly significant message was to be found on the three highest denominated bills. Not unexpectedly, on the 5000 Won note, we find the Eternal President Kim Il Sung. Comparing this to the bills issued in 2002 with the somewhat timeless pictures on which he had black hair and seemed to be in his fifties, he was now depicted as an elder man, with grey hair, glasses, and a smile on his previously stern face.

The 2000 Won banknote was the most remarkable piece of the new currency: it complemented the message of the 5000 Won banknote by showing the second generation, providing a symbolic reference to Kim Jong Il. Never before had this been done in North Korea. Kim Jong Il's portrait was still missing, but the banknote showed the log cabin at the "secret camp" beneath Jong Il Peak, where Kim Jong Il was born in February 1942, according to official North Korean mythology. Kim Jong Il's close connection to his father was symbolised by the 1000 Won banknote, which shows the birthplace of Kim Jong Il's mother, Kim Jong Suk, in Hoeryŏng.

Two things became obvious: by changing the age of Kim Il Sung, room was created for upgrading the status of his eldest son Kim Jong Il. He had ruled the country since 1994, and his image was hanging inside office buildings and apartments next to that of his father. But he had avoided replacing Kim Il Sung as the primary national symbol, as well as the erection of statues of himself, or bestowing his name upon streets, universities, or plazas. Kim Jong Il's image was also conspicuously missing on coins and banknotes.

By adding his birthplace as well as that of his mother, in 2009 Kim Jong Il effectively changed the message on the banknotes from "this country is ruled by Kim Il Sung" to "this country is ruled by the family of Kim Il Sung". This opened the way for the introduction of the next successor, Kim Jong Un, who was presented to the public less than 1 year later in September 2010.

4.6 The Choco Pie Mystery and Two Competing Currencies

The ups and downs in North Korea's monetary system and the existence of parallel currencies can be rather confusing, especially for *ad hoc* observers. The difficulties in understanding this complex situation are reflected by what I call the "Choco Pie mystery".

This phenomenon emerged when South Korean employers in the now closed Kaesong Industrial Zone (Frank 2016a) sought for ways to motivate their staff materially. Wages were negotiated and collected by the North Korean state on behalf of the workers, so the standard way of providing an incentive to work harder through wage discrimination was not available. The employers therefore introduced in-kind incentives. The latter included snacks the size of a flattened golf ball consisting of two small round layers of cake with marshmallow filling and covered with chocolate. They were wrapped in foil and were thus non-perishable. This made them popular among Kaesong workers because these Choco Pies could be taken out of the compound and either given as presents to those at home or even be sold.

Apparently, news about the latter reached the South Koreans, either directly through Kaesong workers or, more probably, through China. The price of one Choco Pie on North Korean markets was about 1000 North Korean Won. Someone who was not familiar with the North Korean economy divided this amount by the "official" conversion rate for foreign shoppers as it is displayed in international hotels in Pyongyang, which is 100 Won per US Dollar. This is how the idea emerged that one Choco Pie sells for a whopping 10 (!) US Dollars on the North Korean market.

The problem is that North Korea still has different kinds of distribution systems: facilities in which payment can be made either in local currency *or* in hard currency, converted at the market exchange rate; and facilities in which payment can *only* be made in Euros, US Dollars, Japanese Yen or Chinese Yuan. In the latter case, to avoid having price tags with four different prices or using one of the foreign currencies as the official accounting unit, prices are provided in a fictitious currency which is, confusingly, also called Won. But the exchange rate here does nothing but reflect the value of these four foreign currencies in relation to each other. It is often called the "official exchange rate" but this is technically not correct. North Korean currency cannot be converted into hard currency at this rate, and *vice versa*. In other words, if someone enters a shop in Pyongyang and the price tag on a can of soda says that it costs 100 Won, it means he or she will not be able to pay with Won, but only with hard currency, which is, in this case, about 1000 Chinese Yuan. If a foreigner wants to buy an "Eskimo" ice cream from one of the kiosks on the streets of Pyongyang, the price will be around 2000 Won and can be paid either in local currency or in hard currency, typically one or two Chinese Yuan depending on the seller's salesmanship.

Against this background, it is obvious that the assumption that a single Choco Pie costs 10 US Dollars in North Korea is absurd. The actual price is 80 times less, because the market rate is in the range of 8000 Won per US Dollar. One 1000 Won Choco Pie thus costs about 12 US Cents, which is only slightly above the price at which this product sells in China.

Even without knowledge of the complex situation which determines North Korea's exchange rates, it would be easy to discover that a price of 10 US Dollars would simply be unrealistic. All it requires is that we recall that North Korea is a country where food supply is not secure for most people. It is very unlikely that they would spend the equivalent of several kilograms of rice on a small 120 calorie snack. It is also not realistic to assume that the North Korean population would indeed possess the enormous purchasing power for buying millions[18] of Choco Pies at that price.

[18]We are indeed talking about millions. If each of the 50,000 Kaesong workers received only two Choco Pies per day, this would amount to about 35 million such snacks annually.

It is thus somewhat surprising that a major news company such as CNN (Park et al. 2014) carried the story about the 10-Dollar-a-piece Choco Pie, and it is disturbing that the former National Security Advisor for North Korea to US President George W. Bush repeated the story in his memoirs (Cha 2012).

4.7 Present Status and Outlook

Despite all the recent changes, the state maintains its grip on the economy. Traders on markets need a licence, and the authorities control the markets to make sure that no illegal trading is taking place. Prices on the markets are freely set through the forces of demand and supply, using China as a benchmark with a premium for transportation and other transaction costs. The currency used by traders and their clients is mostly the Chinese Yuan, but domestic currency is also in use, in particular, in areas that are not close to the Chinese border. Exchange rates are calculated based upon the market rate which is on display in some banks and shops.[19] Thus, calling either the markets or the exchange rate "black" is not justified. Instead, we should speak of a dual, or actually triple, distribution structure, consisting of public distribution at state set prices, market distribution at freely set (but state controlled) prices, and hard currency facilities.

The currency re-valuation of 2009 was, in many regards, a remarkable event. It demonstrated how well money now functions in the previously de-monetised society of North Korea. Its failure marked a stop of the neo-orthodox push, even though it has not been reversed. As of 2016, it is fair to say that North Korea's economy is, in many ways, more monetised than those of countries like East Germany ever were. The state has tacitly accepted the existence of markets and, for the time being, does not try to curb them further; on the contrary, they are now being integrated into the official distribution system.

Since the currency re-valuation, the situation has been relatively stable. Prices including exchange rates have developed up and down according to demand and supply. No new experiment has taken place. There are still hard currency stores where goods and services can only be purchased with foreign money, and elsewhere domestic and foreign currencies exist in parallel.

The North Korean economy has effectively been re-monetised. Currently, there is no indication that this will be undone, even though the overall trend in economic policy under Kim Jong Un points at an attempt to normalise the operation of the national economy. This includes the strengthening of centralised control through the Cabinet.

It is clear that there are strong forces in Pyongyang that are trying to reduce the role of markets and to strengthen central control again. But their chances of success

---

[19] Among those that I have personally seen are the Golden Triangle Bank in Rasŏn and the Kwangbok Area Supermarket in Pyongyang.

are limited, given the low efficiency of a state administered economy, on the one hand, and the necessity for Kim Jong Un to provide a visible and sustainable improvement in the people's living conditions, on the other. In his speech at the 7th Party Congress on 8 May 2016, Kim showed no sympathy for a further marketisation and de-centralisation, but instead repeated a number of concepts that had been popular in the 1980s when North Korea very guardedly modernised its socialist economic system to make the operations of its enterprises more efficient (Frank 2016b). The general tenor seems to be that exceptions had to be made in order to cope with the mid-1990s crisis, but that now is the time to return to a normal operation along the lines of the *status quo ante*. This does not, however, mean a return to the 1950s, but rather to the 1980s when North Korea was attempting its own, much more cautious and often overlooked Chinese-style adjustment of the obviously unsustainable post-Stalinist economic model.

It remains to be seen how the economic sanctions of March 2016 (Gladstone and Sanger 2016), and, in particular, the designation of the whole country as a jurisdiction of primary money-laundering concern under Section 311 of the US Patriot Act in June 2016 will affect the monetary economy of North Korea (Treasury 2016). It is difficult not to see the connection between monetisation and marketisation; allowing the use of foreign currencies within the country was a decisive factor to make the spread and growth of markets in North Korea possible, because it provided a trusted and stable means of payment. Friedrich von Hayek would have called this competitive money supply (Hayek 1990); in particular, the Chinese Yuan is challenging the Korean Won.

Economic pressure on North Korea is among the few peaceful options on the table to respond to the continued expansion of the nuclear programme and is thus understandable from a short-term security perspective. However, sanctions will significantly limit foreign trade and the circulation of money in North Korea and thus suffocate the very forces that provide the best chance for a long-term solution to a number of issues including the nuclear problem. If the financial side of trade cannot be handled by banks, the remaining options are barter trade and payment in cash. The former has its limitations, especially if the trading partners are single enterprises, not states that represent multiple trading partners. Payment in cash has been used by North Korea in the past but the limitations here are of a technical nature: it is simply too cumbersome, and, in some cases, it is forbidden by foreign authorities to carry bags with large amounts of clean 100 Dollar bills.

The changing role of money and of cash in North Korea presents an interesting case. A more or less modern economy had first been almost completely and deliberately de-monetised on order to strengthen the immediate role of the state in the distribution of goods and services for producers and consumers, and was then re-monetised as a method of coping with a severe economic crisis. We might now see attempts at undoing this again. These ups and downs turned North Korea into a gigantic economic experiment. The fly in the ointment for scholars was and is the limited access to study the actual effects of these measures, but we can nevertheless make a number of interesting observations.

A minor point that gains in importance if we consider the ongoing general debate in the West about the abolition of cash is the dependence of electronic means of payment on a stable supply of electricity and data connection. North Korea has introduced at least four different cash cards, but they often do not work due to problems with the infrastructure. From a broader perspective, the North Korean case shows that the de facto de-monetisation of a modern economy is technically possible, but that it will remain hollow unless scarcity is eliminated, too. It further demonstrates how a foreign currency can step in if the domestic currency is unable to fulfil its functions, and how opening the economy to trade resulted in the importation not only of goods and services, but also of habits and currencies.

References

Abrahamian A (2011) North Korea's 2009 currency reform in the context of national narrative. North Kor Rev 7(1):64–77

Abt F (2014) A capitalist in North Korea: my seven years in the hermit kingdom. Tuttle Publishing, North Clarendon

Armstrong C (2003) The North Korean revolution 1945–1950. Cornell University Press, Ithaca

Boston.com (2010) Economist says NKorea to phase out private markets. boston.com, 1 April 2010. http://archive.boston.com/business/articles/2010/04/01/economist_says_nkorea_to_phase_out_private_markets/?page=2. Accessed 30 June 2016

Branigan T (2010) North Korean finance chief executed for botched currency reform. Guardian, 18 March 2010. http://www.theguardian.com/world/2010/mar/18/north-korean-executed-currency-reform. Accessed 30 June 2016

Bush GW (2002) State of the Union Address. CNN, 29 January 2002. http://edition.cnn.com/2002/ALLPOLITICS/01/29/bush.speech.txt. Accessed 30 June 2016

Cha V (2012) The impossible state: North Korea, past and future. Ecco, New York

Eberstadt N (2009) The North Korean economy: between crisis and catastrophe. Transaction Publishers, London

FAOSTAT (2016). http://faostat3.fao.org/download/Q/QC/E. Accessed 29 June 2016

Foreign Trade Bank of the DPRK (2010) Document No. DC03310-004, 29 January 2010

Frank R (1996) Die DDR und Nordkorea. Der Wiederaufbau der Stadt Hamhung 1954–1962. Shaker, Aachen

Frank R (2005) Economic reforms in North Korea (1998–2004): systemic restrictions, quantitative analysis, ideological background. J Asia Pac Econ 10(3):278–311

Frank R (2010a) Socialist neoconservatism and North Korean foreign policy in the nuclear era. In: Park K-A (ed) New challenges to North Korean foreign policy. Palgrave Macmillan, New York

Frank R (2010b) North Korea: domestic politics and economy. In: Frank R, Hoare J, Köllner P, Pares S (eds) Korea 2010: politics, economy, and society. Brill, Leiden, pp 29–53

Frank R (2010c) New N.K. currency holds symbolism of note. The Korea Herald. 30 March 2010. http://www.koreaherald.com/view.php?ud=20091207000060. Accessed 30 June 2016

Frank R (2012) North Korea after Kim Jong Il: the Kim Jong Un era and its challenges. Asia-Pac J 10(2), 9 January 2012. http://japanfocus.org/-Ruediger-Frank/3674. Accessed 30 June 2016

Frank R (2016a) The Kaesong closure: punishment or shot in the foot? 38North, 12 February 2016. http://38north.org/2016/02/rfrank021216. Accessed 30 June 2016

Frank R (2016b) The 7th party congress in North Korea: an analysis of Kim Jong Un's report. Asia Pac J 14(8), July 2016. http://apjjf.org/-R--diger-Frank/4927/article.pdf

French P (2005) North Korea. The Paranoid Peninsula. London, Zed Books

Gladstone R, Sanger D (2016) New sanctions on North Korea Pass in Unified U.N. Vote. NY Times, 7 March 2016. http://www.nytimes.com/2013/03/08/world/asia/north-korea-warns-of-pre-emptive-nuclear-attack.html?_r=1. Accessed 30 June 2016
Haggard S, Noland M (2007) Famine in North Korea. Markets, aid, and reform. Columbia University Press, New York
Haggard S, Noland M (2010) The winter of their discontent: Pyongyang attacks the market. Peterson Institute for International Economics Policy Brief 10-01
Hunter H-L (1999) Kim Il-song's North. Praeger, Korea
Kang-Schmitz L (2010) Nordkoreas Umgang mit Abhängigkeit und Sicherheitsrisiko am Beispiel der bilateralen Beziehungen mit der DDR. http://ubt.opus.hbz-nrw.de/volltexte/2011/636/pdf/Nordkorea_DDR.pdf. Accessed 30 Jun 2016
Kihl YW, Kim HN (eds) (2006) North Korea: the politics of regime survival. Routledge, London
Kim S (2013) Everyday life in the North Korean revolution, 1945–1950. Cornell University Press, Ithaca
Kornai J (1992) The socialist system: the political economy of communism. Princeton University Press, Princeton
Lankov A (2007) North of the DMZ. Essays on daily life in North Korea. McFarland, Jefferson
Lankov A (2013) The real North Korea: life and politics in the failed Stalinist Utopia. Oxford University Press, New York
Lee S-J (2009) Chaos reigns after currency trick. Daily NK, 1 December 2009. http://www.dailynk.com. Accessed 30 June 2016
Lee CS, De Vos G (eds) (1981) Koreans in Japan: ethnic conflict and accommodation. University of California Press, Berkeley
McNamara D (1990) The colonial origins of Korean enterprise, 1910–1945. Cambridge University Press, New York
Moon SH (2009) Public currency announcement broadcast. Daily NK, 1 December 2009. http://www.dailynk.com. Accessed 30 June 2016
Moon CI, Swenson-Wright J (eds) (2014) Crisis of peace and new leadership in Korea. Lessons from Kim Dae-jung's Legacy. Yonsei University Press, Seoul
Park PH (2016) Rebuilding North Korea's economy. IFES, Seoul
Park M, Cha F, Contreras E (2014) How Choco Pie infiltrated North Korea's sweet tooth. CNN, 27 January 2014. http://edition.cnn.com/2014/01/27/world/asia/choco-pie-koreas. Accessed 6 June 2014
Ritter G (2007) Der Preis der Deutschen Einheit. Die Wiedervereinigung und die Krise des Sozialstaates. C.H. Beck, Munich
Schmid J (2001) Etching the notes of a new European Identity. NY Times, 03 August 2001. http://www.nytimes.com/2001/08/03/news/03iht-euro_ed3_.html?pagewanted=all. Accessed 29 June 2016
Silberstein BK (2015) Growth and geography of markets in North Korea. New evidence from satellite imagery. US-Korea Institute, Washington, DC
Smith H (2005) Hungry for peace. International security, humanitarian assistance, and social change in North Korea. US Institute of Peace Press, Washington, DC
Springer Gabler Verlag (2016) COMECON. Gabler Wirtschaftslexikon. http://wirtschaftslexikon.gabler.de/Archiv/122461/comecon-v4.html. Accessed 13 Sept 2016
Treasury (2016) Treasury takes actions to further restrict North Korea's access to the U.S. financial system. U.S. Department of the Treasury, 1 June 2016. https://www.treasury.gov/press-center/press-releases/Pages/jl0471.aspx. Accessed 30 June 2016
von Hayek F (1990) Denationalization of money: the argument refined. The Institute of Economic Affairs, London
Yonhap (2009) North Korea belatedly confirms currency reform. Yonhap News, 10 December 2009. http://english.yonhapnews.co.kr. Accessed 30 June 2016

Part II
Cash and Monetary Policy

Chapter 5
Domestic Liquidity Conditions and Monetary Policy in Singapore

Hwee Kwan Chow

Abstract Singapore has an unusual exchange rate-centred monetary policy framework that has served the economy well over the past decades. Monetary policy operations are carried out by the central bank through the management of the Singapore dollar against a currency basket. As is well recognised, such foreign exchange interventions do have an impact on domestic liquidity conditions. However, in the case of Singapore, this tends to be counteracted by the liquidity impact of public sector operations related to the fiscal position and the national pension scheme. The central bank takes into account the net liquidity impact of these and other autonomous money market factors as well as banks' demand for funds when performing money market operations to regulate the amount of domestic liquidity in the financial system. We conclude with an explanation of the negligible liquidity impact of currency in circulation as reflecting Singapore's gradual transformation towards a cashless society.

5.1 Introduction

Singapore operated a currency board system when the Monetary Authority of Singapore (MAS) was first established in 1971. With the collapse of the Bretton Woods system in the early 1970s, instabilities in the world currencies led Singapore to develop its own exchange-rate policy framework. Since 1973, the Singapore dollar has officially been on a managed float. An exchange-rate centred monetary policy framework was formally adopted by 1981, reflecting the small and open nature of the economy. Singapore's high degree of openness to trade is captured by its trade to GDP ratio, which has been greater than three since the early 1970s. As a major financial centre, Singapore has free capital mobility. Almost all forms of capital restrictions and foreign exchange controls have been eradicated since 1978. Even the restrictions on the non-internationalisation of the Singapore dollar, imposed to deter currency speculation, have been progressively removed over the

H.K. Chow (✉)
Singapore Management University, Singapore, Singapore
e-mail: hkchow@smu.edu.sg

F. Rövekamp et al. (eds.), *Cash in East Asia*, Financial and Monetary Policy Studies 44, DOI 10.1007/978-3-319-59846-8_5

years in order to facilitate the development of Singapore's capital markets (Ong 2003).

Given Singapore's open capital account, it follows, from the open-economy trilemma,[1] that the central bank needs to choose between interest-rate targeting *vis-à-vis* exchange-rate targeting. The MAS has chosen to use the exchange rate as opposed to the more conventional benchmark policy of interest rate as its policy-operating tool since the early 1980s (MAS 2000). The rationale behind this decision is revealed when we consider the structure of the Singapore economy as well as its monetary transmission mechanism. Firstly, Singapore is highly dependent on external demand, notwithstanding the economy's gradual shift towards the services industry. Exportable services, including financial, information technology and professional services, along with externally-orientated manufacturing, account for more than half of the aggregate output in Singapore. Secondly, domestic consumption has a high import content—out of every Singapore dollar spent in Singapore, approximately 60 cents go to imports. Being a price-taker in international markets, Singapore is highly susceptible to imported inflation. Hence, the highly open and trade-dependent nature of the economy implies that the exchange rate is the most effective tool for controlling inflation.

By contrast, the Singapore economy is less interest-rate sensitive, notwithstanding its status as a financial hub. The MAS does not focus on the interest rate variable or a monetary aggregate in its conduct of monetary policy due to a lack of control over them—a reflection of Singapore's openness to capital flows and a very liberal policy towards foreign direct investment. As a result of the exchange rate-centred monetary policy framework and free capital mobility in Singapore, domestic short-term interest rates are significantly determined by foreign interest rates. Findings from a monetary VAR analysis in Chow (2005) suggest the exchange rate is, indeed, more influential than the interest rate as a source of macroeconomic fluctuations. With the support of flexible factor markets and strong institutions, the past track-record of low inflation[2] and prolonged economic growth attests to the effectiveness of using the exchange rate as a key monetary-policy instrument.

In the next section, we discuss the operation of Singapore's monetary policy framework. The implications of this framework on domestic liquidity conditions, and how this is counteracted by the liquidity impact of public sector operations related to the fiscal position and the national pension scheme is examined in Sect. 5.3. We conclude, in Sect. 5.4, with the evolution of one of the money market

[1] Obstfeld et al. (2004) summarises the open economy trilemma by saying that monetary policy can only achieve fully two of the following three dimensions: monetary policy independence, fixed exchange rates, and open capital accounts.

[2] Chow et al. (2014) showed, through a DSGE-VAR, model that export price shocks were a major source of output volatility in Singapore and, consequently, the exchange rate system at work had a comparative advantage over Taylor rule in terms of reducing inflation volatility. Indeed, CPI inflation in Singapore averaged around 2.3% since 1980, which is relatively lower than in the advanced countries.

factors, that of currency in circulation, which reflects Singapore's gradual transformation to a cashless society.

5.2 Singapore's Monetary Policy Framework

Monetary policy operations are carried out by the MAS through managing the Singapore dollar under a basket-band-crawl (BBC) system (Khor et al. 2004). Under this system, the MAS monitors the value of the domestic currency in terms of a currency basket (S$NEER: Singapore dollar nominal effective exchange rate) which is a trade-weighted average of the currencies of Singapore's major trading partners and competitors. These represent the various sources of imported inflation and competition in the export markets, with the periodically updated basket weights in order to reflect their degree of importance. Neither the constituent currencies nor their assigned weights in the basket are publicly disclosed. In view of Singapore's diversified trade pattern, targeting a currency basket, instead of a single foreign currency, results in a more stable effective exchange rate.

The MAS uses a prescribed policy band centred at a parity that is the target exchange rate for the S$NEER. The target rate reflects the long-run equilibrium exchange rate and is allowed to adjust gradually over time, keeping the policy band in tandem with Singapore's slowly changing long-term economic fundamentals. The crawl circumvents the emergence of a situation in which the currency becomes significantly misaligned. It thereby reduces the incentive for speculative attacks against the currency. The S$NEER is allowed to float within the prescribed policy band in order to allow for short-term fluctuations in the foreign exchange markets. The undisclosed policy band is sufficiently wide so that market participants cannot be sure of making a profit even when they correctly speculate on an impending change. Nevertheless, too wide a band is avoided in order to prevent the Singapore dollar from overshooting. The Singapore dollar is frequently used as a proxy for broader Asian currency risk, which means that changes in the fundamentals of other regional currencies could lead to the overshooting of the Singapore dollar.

The MAS can directly influence the value of the currency and defend the band by carrying out intervention operations in the foreign exchange markets. Sometimes, interventions are carried out within the band to smooth out short-term exchange rate volatility since the latter could impair confidence in the currency. In addition, when the S$NEER approaches or exceeds the boundaries of the policy band, the MAS may intervene to "lean against the wind", which means resisting the recent trend of the exchange rate thereby preventing the bounds from being breached. Such intervention operations resist misalignments and push the S$NEER towards its estimated equilibrium value.[3] The MAS monitors the S$NEER closely and

[3]MacDonald (2004) estimated the equilibrium level of Singapore's real effective exchange rate and found the Singapore dollar to be close to equilibrium in the early 2000s. Nonetheless, as

manages the currency upon a daily basis, even though it "refrains from intervening unnecessarily and allows market forces to determine the level of the Singapore dollar within the policy band" (MAS 2013).[4]

In comparison, monetary policy formulation takes place twice a year. In its semi-annual monetary policy formulation cycle, the MAS announces the exchange rate policy stance through a Monetary Policy Statement. Appropriate changes are made to the level, slope and width of the policy band if these are deemed necessary through an assessment of the prevailing economic and market conditions as well as their outlook. For instance, the MAS widened its policy bands with heightened volatility in the foreign exchange markets during the Asian crisis and subsequently narrowed them when a degree of calm had returned to the regional markets. In response to the global financial crisis (the direct effect of which was less severe), the MAS flattened its policy band and re-centred it at a lower level. Apart from being a counter-cyclical tool in the short term, the primary objective of monetary policy is to provide an environment of price stability over the medium term, one which is conducive for sustainable economic growth. To this end, the MAS guides the path of the exchange rate to ensure that it remains consistent with Singapore's economic fundamentals.

5.3 Currency Management and Domestic Liquidity Impact

Countries with an export-led growth strategy would typically maintain a low international value of their domestic currency to prevent a loss of competitiveness. However, despite its openness and reliance on export growth, Singapore maintains a strong Singapore dollar policy. Figure 5.1 depicts a time plot of Singapore's nominal and real effective exchange rate as compiled by the IMF, denoted by NEER and REER respectively.[5] The exchange rate variables NEER and REER have been defined so that a rise in their value signals an appreciation of the Singapore dollar.

illustrated in Phillips et al. (2013), estimating the equilibrium exchange rate has become more complex. Apart from traditional fundamental variables, financial factors and policy variables have to be taken into consideration in determining the real exchange rate. The extent to which the central bank will intervene in the foreign exchange market in order to lean against misalignments will thus depend on how certain they are regarding their assessment of currency misalignment.

[4]Over the years, Singapore has maintained a conservative fiscal policy as well as a commitment to low inflation and a strong Singapore dollar, which has helped to build the central bank's credibility. Hence, market participants appear mostly convinced of the MAS' commitment to enforce the policy band, and they tend to keep within it. Such market discipline, in turn, alleviates the need for frequent central bank intervention operations in the foreign exchange markets (Krugman 1991).

[5]Due to the unavailability of more current data on the MAS' trade weighted index (S$NEER), we use the nominal exchange rate as computed by the IMF which is denoted by NEER. Both the NEER and REER time series are indexes whose values in 2010 are normalised to 100.

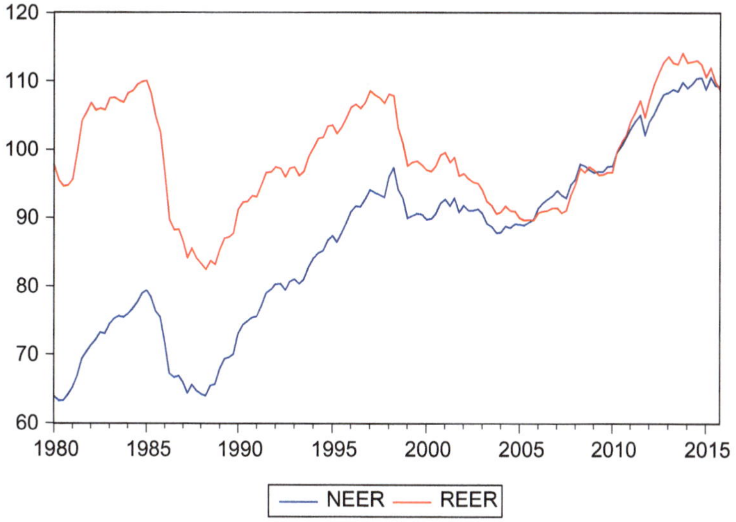

Fig. 5.1 Singapore's nominal and real effective exchange rates. Source: International Financial Statistics

It is clear from the secular upward trend of NEER in Fig. 5.1 that the Singapore dollar, in nominal terms, has been appreciating against its major trading partners over the past decades. We also note that REER remained strong, since the implementation of the exchange rate regime. The narrowing of the gap between NEER and REER after 1980 can be attributed to the relatively low inflationary environment in Singapore during this period. For instance, Singapore's consumer price index inflation averaged over the two periods of 1980–1989 and 1990–1999 are 2.8% and 1.9% respectively. These are lower than the corresponding numbers of 6.5% and 2.9% for the advanced countries; see Wilson (2015). Key considerations behind the strong Singapore dollar policy include the desire to maintain confidence in the domestic currency and to ensure price stability. After all, liberalised capital flows and a stable currency are important requirements for Singapore's role as an international financial sector and the development of a large offshore banking sector.

Although the exchange rate has not been used to safeguard competitiveness, Singapore's competitiveness does not seem to have been compromised by the strong Singapore dollar policy (Wilson 2015). In fact, Singapore has been registering recurrent current account surpluses over successive decades.[6] A plausible explanation for this is the appreciation of the Singapore dollar has been accompanied lower inflation, leaving Singapore's relative price competitiveness unaffected by the appreciation. Meanwhile, the secular appreciation of the domestic currency

[6]The overall balance of payments remained positive, except on rare occasions, in spite of the persistent export of capital abroad.

has the advantageous effect of pushing Singapore companies to move up the value chain to focus on higher value-added industries, thereby producing more technology-, skill- and capital-intensive exports. This, as well as its more moderate inflation, enables Singapore to maintain its international competitiveness despite the secular rise of its nominal exchange rate.

The upward trend in the domestic currency reflects the strong and improving fundamentals of the Singapore economy over the past decades. In particular, strong foreign capital inflows, consistent budget surpluses and high levels of domestic savings exert an upward pressure on the Singapore dollar to appreciate. Correspondingly, the foreign exchange intervention operations carried out by the MAS have mostly been to mitigate the appreciation of the domestic currency. Despite adopting a basket numeriare, it is not necessary to carry out intervention operations using all the component currencies of the basket. Not surprisingly, the MAS intervenes in the US dollar (USD) exchange market, as it is the most liquid (MAS 2013). When the MAS sells the Singapore dollar against the US dollar, there is an injection of Singapore dollars into the banking system which raises the level of domestic liquidity. There is a corresponding rise in foreign reserves and an increase in the monetary base.[7]

One macro-economic implication of defending appreciations is thus the increase in inflationary pressure, unless the MAS carries out sterilisation of its foreign exchange intervention. Nevertheless, there are domestic costs and risks associated with such sterilised intervention, especially when sterilisation is substantial and prolonged (Lavigne 2008). In the case of Singapore, the increase in the level of domestic liquidity due to foreign exchange intervention by the MAS tends to be offset by the withdrawal of liquidity due to the very high level of savings in the economy. Hence, the MAS does not necessarily have to sterilise its intervention operations if the banking system already has an appropriate level of liquidity.

Singapore's high level of savings is mainly due to the Central Provident Fund (CPF), which is a government administered compulsory savings scheme, and the government's strong fiscal position. As a result of prudent fiscal management, the government of Singapore has generally run persistent budget surpluses, averaging around 5% of GDP, since the early 1990s. Consequently, the Account-General Department (AGD) acting as the Government's accountant would normally transfer funds from its accounts with commercial banks to its deposit account with the MAS. The MAS, as the government's financial agent, is in receipt of deposits from the government. Such transfers are recorded as large sums in the item "Government Deposits" on the liabilities side of the MAS balance sheet, and they represent a liquidity drain from the domestic banking system.

[7]Foreign exchange reserves rose from 6.6 billion USD in 1980 to 248 billion USD in 2014 in Singapore. The high level foreign reserves, in turn, serve to deter currency speculators, as it grants the MAS the latitude to carry out intervention operations on a sufficiently large scale to defend the currency.

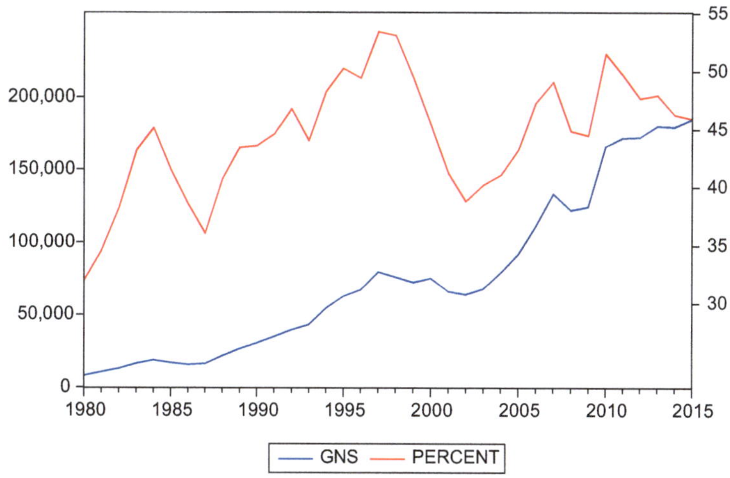

Fig. 5.2 Gross national savings rate (in millions of S$ and as % of GDP). Source: CEIC database

As for the CPF, this is a mandatory defined contribution pension fund scheme in which both employees and employers are required to contribute a certain percentage of the employees' income to the CPF.[8] Funds are disbursed to members by the CPF Board under various withdrawal schemes. As contributions tends to be in excess of withdrawals, the CPF Board usually transfers funds to the MAS by way of an advanced deposit with the MAS pending its purchase of special non-marketable Singapore Government Securities. These are issued specially to the CPF Board to meet its investment requirements and to mop up the surplus funds of the CPF. The net positive contributions to the CPF tend to be sizeable, and represent a withdrawal of funds from the banking system. Along with the fiscal surpluses, the CPF transactions contributed to a high gross national savings rate of above 40% for most of the past decades (see Fig. 5.2).

In summary, both the CPF Board and the Account-General Department tend to transfer funds to the MAS, which represents a drain on domestic liquidity. In order to overcome this liquidity drain, the MAS can conduct money market operations to ensure there is sufficient liquidity in the banking system. Other autonomous money market factors include the currency in circulation as well as the issuance, redemption and coupon payments of Singapore Government Securities (SGS) and Treasury Bills. The central bank takes the net liquidity impact of all these factors and the demand of banks for funds into account in order to assess the level of liquidity required in the banking system. The instruments used for money market operations include foreign exchange (reverse) swaps, direct lending to or borrowing from banks, and re-purchase agreements on SGS and MAS bills (MAS 2013). With the

[8]Employee and employer's CPF contribution rates are currently at 17% and 20% of gross salary for those earning above S$750 per month and below 56 years of age.

Table 5.1 Liquidity impact of money market factors and MAS' operations

	S$ million per Financial Year				
	2007/2008	2008/2009	2009/2010	2010/2011	2011/2012
Money market factors					
Public sector operations (AGD, CPF)	−40,008	−23,676	−12,185	−40,258	−38,069
Currency in circulation	−1111	−1323	−908	−962	−1793
SGS issuance, redemption, interest	−11,063	2643	−11,234	−494	−5662
Sub-total	−52,182	−22,356	−24,327	−41,714	−45,524
MAS foreign exchange and money market operations					
Foreign exchange operations, including swaps	65,983	8881	52,977	62,052	25,749
SGS repos and reverse repos	−1800	1800	−2300	−500	−1600
Direct borrowing and lending and net MAS Bills issuance and maturity	−11,800	13,000	−23,800	−13,600	17,234
Sub-total	52,383	23,681	26,877	47,952	41,383

Source: Monetary Authority of Singapore

use of market operations, the MAS has been able to regulate the amount of liquidity in the banking system.

While details of money market operations are made available in the Macroeconomic Review, time series data on public sector operations, MAS intervention operations, and MAS money market operations, are, in general, not publicly available. However, a monograph on money operations was published by the MAS in 2013, that showed a table of values on the various components of money market liquidity from 2007 to 2012. Part of this table is reproduced as Table 5.1, recording the liquidity impact of the various money market factors as well as that of monetary policy and money market operations.

Over this period, we can see from the table that public sector operations had a net negative impact on liquidity in the banking system and that the magnitude of the impact is larger than the other two money market factors, namely, currency in circulation as well as SGS issuance, redemption and coupon payment. In particular, we note from Table 5.1 that currency in circulation has a negligible impact on domestic liquidity. As recorded in the past issues of the MAS' Macroeconomic Review, public sector operations have consistently been the dominant negative money market factor over the successive years since 2003.

The item on foreign exchange operations in Table 5.1 combines direct foreign exchange interventions with money market operations using foreign exchange swaps. Although we are not able to distinguish monetary policy operations from money market operations, we can observe an injection of liquidity into the banking system through the combined foreign exchange operations in the various financial years. In terms of the distribution of the instruments used in money market operations, the MAS bills have gained importance since their introduction in 2011. As a share of the money market instruments used, they rose from 25% in

FY11/12 to 68% in FY14/15. There is a corresponding decline in the use of foreign exchange swaps from 73% to 43%.

Looking ahead, there are concerns that CPF net contributions could turn into net withdrawals as the population ages. After all, the CPF plays a key role as the fund for retirement income. In this event, the CPF transfers would be injecting, instead of removing, liquidity from the domestic banking system, which could potentially increase inflationary pressures (Yip 2005). Meanwhile, the Singapore economy is projected to experience a slower growth path associated with the decrease in its labour supply.[9] This suggests a likely fall in the tax revenue while government expenditure, especially on healthcare, rises. Such a scenario points to a decline in the government budget surplus, which also reduces the drain from domestic liquidity.

However, the attendant fall in the savings rate and the narrowing of current account surpluses implies that the Singapore dollar may no longer appreciate strongly upon a trend basis as in the past (Khor and Robinson 2005). This alleviates the need for intervention to moderate the strength of the Singapore dollar. In any case, when there is reduced offsetting liquidity impact from public sector operations, the central bank can still rely on the MAS bills in order to drain excess liquidity in the banking system. This way, the MAS could use money market operations to regulate the level of liquidity in the domestic economy in order to foster stable money market conditions and to keep the financial system functioning smoothly.

5.4 Cash in Circulation

As observed in the previous section, currency in circulation does not carry much weight as a money market factor in Singapore. Figure 5.3 displays the ratio of currency in circulation to M1 money supply in 1991–2016. It is evident from the figure that the ratio has been on a steady decline, falling from nearly 50% in 1991 to around 20% in 2011. The level seems to have stabilised at around 20% after 2011. The decline of currency in circulation can, in large part, be explained by policies undertaken in Singapore to move towards a cashless society.

In 1985, Singapore launched a National Campaign to Minimise Cash Trans actions to encourage Singaporeans to carry out their transactions electronically. The primary objective for reducing cash transactions was to save manpower costs, thereby increasing productivity. The three specific goals of the campaign were: (i) to urge receipt of wages through direct credit to the bank; (ii) to encourage the payment of bills electronically via General Interbank Recurring Order; and (iii) to promote payments through the Electronic Funds Transfer at Point of Sale system. In

[9]While the ageing workforce has been partially mitigated by immigration policies, the current political climate poses constraints on the intake of large numbers of foreign workers.

Fig. 5.3 Ratio of currency in circulation to M1 money supply (%). Source: Monetary Authority of Singapore

addition, steps were also taken to develop the related infrastructure, such as allowing commercial banks to place more Automated Teller Machines island-wide and the building of electronic networks. In particular, the setting up of the Network for Electronic Transfers in January 1986 was viewed as a milestone in Singapore's drive to become a cashless society. Efforts at transforming Singapore into a cashless society were gradual but effective.

Cashless transactions in Singapore started to become more commonplace from the mid-1990s with the expansion of the menu of electronic payment options. According to data from the Bank of International Settlements, transaction volumes in card-based electronic money shot up from 0.03 million to 2 billion between 1996 and 2010. The corresponding increase in the usage of debit cards, direct debits and credit transfers in the same period was 56 million to 203 million, 20 million to 57 million, and 14 million to 35 million, respectively. In terms of transaction value, there was a greater than four-fold increase for debit cards and direct debits to 25 billion SGD and 31 billion SGD in 2010, respectively. Meanwhile, the transaction value for credit transfers went up by 2.3 times to 179 billion SGD. Despite the surge in transaction volumes of card-based electronic money, the total value of transactions only went up to 2 billion SGD, suggesting that this form of cashless payment instrument was used mostly for payments in small transactions.

More recently, the advent of the digital revolution is transforming payment systems. For instance, physical wallets and credit cards are being replaced by payment solutions provided by non-financial players, such as Apple, Google, PayPal, Amazon and the like. Online payment is now a cheap and safe way of transferring funds, and can be effected through mobile devices such as smart phones and tablets that have become ubiquitous. Singapore has various characteristics identified by Haddad and Hornuf (2016) that pre-disposes it to more financial technology (FinTech) innovations. These include well-developed capital markets that provide FinTech start-ups with better access to capital to fund their business, the availability of the latest technology that enables new practices and business models to emerge, high mobile phone subscriptions that facilitate retail point of sale and mobile wallet transactions, as well as immigration policies that attract foreign talent to join its financial sector workforce.

In view of the dynamism that FinTech could inject into Singapore's financial industry, the MAS[10] committed 225 million SGD to support, over a 5-year span, the creation of a vibrant FinTech ecosystem, wherein the adoption of new payments technologies is a key emphasis. For instance, the MAS is currently working towards greater inter-operability across payment systems for more seamless payments across different platforms. The FinTech initiative is part of the Smart Nation programme launched in Singapore in November 2014 that has the vision of enabling better living through the extensive and systematic use of info-comm technology. However, the advent of FinTech start-ups which provide many financial services do disrupt some traditional financial institutions. In response, financial Institutions in Singapore are setting up in-house FinTech units such as "innovation labs" in the banks and insurance companies.

As is generally recognised, financial innovation alters the risk profile of financial institutions and makes risk assessment more difficult. The MAS as the regulator of the financial sector has to tread carefully when managing risks, and must do so without stifling innovation. To avoid over-regulation, the MAS eschews a one-size-fits-all approach and adopts a risk-based approach. Since payment services through the Internet are typically small payments related to e-commerce, they may not attract regulation. However, more significant players will be regulated under the Payment Systems Oversight Act or the Remittance Agents Act. These are modular regulations customised to address the specific risks or concerns that these payment systems pose.[11] In the words of the managing director of MAS, Mr. Ravi Menon, "The aim is to make payments swift, simple and secure. The vision is less cash, less cheques, fewer cards".[12] Going forward, cash will become a less common means of payment in Singapore as it continues its efforts to transform itself into a cashless society.

[10]Apart from its role as a central bank, the MAS is also responsible for the supervision and development of the Singapore financial services sector.

[11]See panel remarks made by MAS Managing Director Ravi Menon on *FinTech – Harnessing its Power, Managing its Risks* at the Singapore Economic Policy Forum held on 2 April 2016.

[12]In a keynote address titled "A Smart Financial Centre" by the MAS managing director, Mr. Ravi Menon, at the Global Technology Law Conference 2015 on 29 Jun 2015.

References

Chow HK (2005) A VAR analysis of Singapore's monetary transmission mechanism. In: Koh WTH, Mariano RS (eds) The economic prospects of Singapore. Addison Wesley, Singapore, pp 274–298

Chow HK, Lim GC, McNelis P (2014) Monetary regime choice in Singapore: would a Taylor rule outperform exchange-rate management? J Asian Econ 30:63–81

Haddad C, Hornuf L (2016) The emergence of the global Fintech market: economic and technological determinants. Available at SSRN: https://ssrn.com/abstract=2830124

Khor HE, Robinson E (2005) Exchange rates and price stability. Bus Times, August

Khor HE, Robinson E, Lee J (2004) Managed floating and intermediate exchange rate systems: the Singapore experience. MAS Staff Paper No 37

Krugman P (1991) Target zones and exchange rate dynamics. Q J Econ 106(3):669–682

Lavigne R (2008) Sterilization cost in emerging-market economies: trends, costs and risks. Bank of Canada Discussion Paper, 2008-4

MacDonald R (2004) The long-run real effective exchange rate of Singapore: a behavioural approach. MAS Staff Paper No.36, Monetary Authority of Singapore

Monetary Authority of Singapore (2000) A survey of Singapore's monetary history. MAS Occasional Paper no 18

Monetary Authority of Singapore (2013) Monetary policy operations in Singapore. MAS Monograph

Obstfeld M, Shambaugh JC, Taylor AM (2004) The Trilemma in history: tradeoffs among exchange rates, monetary policies, and capital mobility. University of California, Berkeley, Dartmouth College, Mimeo

Ong CT (2003) Singapore's policy of non-internationalisation of the Singapore Dollar and the Asian Dollar Market. In: China's capital account liberalisation: International perspective, pp 93–98

Phillips S, Catão L, Ricci L, Bems R, Das M, Di Giovanni J, Unsal DF, Castillo M, Lee J, Rodriguez J, Vargas M (2013) The external balance assessment methodology. IMF Working Paper No 13/272

Wilson P (2015) Monetary policy and financial sector development. Singap Econ Rev 60 (3):1550031. (25 p)

Yip SL (2005) The exchange rate systems in Hong Kong and Singapore, currency board vs. monitoring band. Prentice Hall, Singapore

Chapter 6
Fully Reserve-Backed Money: A Solution to Japan's Fiscal and Monetary Challenges

Franz Waldenberger

Abstract Modern monetary systems rely on two money creation channels: the issuance of new banknotes by the central bank and increases in loans by commercial banks financed by cash deposits. The latter are possible, because bank deposits that are meant as means of exchange by their holders are subject to very low minimum reserve requirements. For a long time, renowned economists have proposed to protect cash deposits fully by 100% reserve requirements, because depriving banks from creating new money would stabilise the financial system. The chapter argues that, under the prevailing fiscal and monetary conditions, Japan would greatly benefit from shifting to a 100% reserve-backed money regime. Such a move would not only take advantage of the benefits propagated by the supporters of a reserve-backed regime. The implied Bank of Japan's (BoJ) balance sheet expansion would allow the Bank to purchase further Japanese Government Bonds (JGB). As the expansion would be permanent, the regime shift would not only stabilise the government's fiscal condition, the BoJ, too, would no longer have to worry about exiting from its policy of quantitative easing. Both the government and the central bank could focus on their primary policy goals. The shift to a 100% regime would also very likely reduce Japan's very high ratio of cash to GDP.

6.1 Background and Outline

Japan faces two big macro economic challenges: a huge government debt and a historically equally record high monetary base (OECD 2015, pp. 112–115).[1] Neither one nor the other has been imposed by external factors, but are instead the outcome of explicit policy choices. They are also partly related because the expansion of the monetary base under the quantitative and qualitative easing (QQE) starting in April 2013 was brought about by massive purchases of Japanese

[1]The monetary base comprises coins and banknotes in circulation plus current account balances at the Bank of Japan (www.boj.or.jp/en/statistics/outline/exp/exbase.htm).

F. Waldenberger (✉)
German Institute for Japanese Studies, Tokyo, Japan
e-mail: waldenberger@dijtokyo.org

F. Rövekamp et al. (eds.), *Cash in East Asia*, Financial and Monetary Policy Studies 44, DOI 10.1007/978-3-319-59846-8_6

government bonds (JGBs) (Waldenberger 2014). The goal of QQE has been to escape from deflation and to reach 2% inflation. The inflation target has not been achieved to date. But QQE, nevertheless, had two positive side-effects. It supported the re-financing of government debt at a time when the amount of JGBs reaching maturity peaked, and it stabilised the financial system by reducing the exposure of private financial institutions to government debt (Waldenberger 2015).

However, QQE is basically designed to be only of a temporary nature. It does not finally answer, but only postpones, the fundamental questions pertaining to government debt and the future of monetary policy: When should the government consolidate its record high debt? Will it be able to do so? If not, what will be the consequences for the Japanese and the world economy? What will happen once the Bank of Japan (BoJ) achieves its inflation target? How can the BoJ exit from its policy of monetary easing? How will this affect the fiscal conditions of the government?

In the following, the shift to a fully reserve-backed money regime is proposed as a solution to both Japan's fiscal and monetary challenges. If implemented, the fundamental uncertainties surrounding both policy areas would be greatly reduced. The argument underlying the proposed solution makes use of two insights. One is the observation that, since the burst of the real estate and stock market bubble at the beginning of the 1990s, Japan's private corporate sector has been generating financial surpluses. Its internal cash flow exceeded its investment in non-financial assets by large amounts. As a result, demand for new credit has been very low, which means that commercial banks have had no outlet for the liquidity that they obtained from the BoJ, instead they invested in JGBs and deposited the money again with the BoJ.[2]

The second insight borrows from the discussions about fully reserve-backed money (Fisher 1936; Friedman 1960; Benes and Kumhof 2012; Jackson and Dyson 2012). In the present monetary regime, money as a means of payment is created by both central banks and commercial banks. This is possible because the money deposited with banks for the purpose of cashless transfers[3] does not have to be fully backed by central bank money. In fact, the minimum reserves for deposits that commercial banks have to maintain at the Bank of Japan are truly minimal in the range of 0.05–1.2%.[4] The portion of deposits not tied by reserve requirements can be used to finance loans or for the purchase of other asset. Proponents of a fully reserve-backed monetary regime, see money creation by commercial banks as one of the sources of the fragility and instability of modern economic systems (Benes and Kumhof 2012, pp. 4–5). They, instead, propose a 100% reserve requirement for

[2]Money that commercial banks deposit with the central bank will be referred to as "bank reserves" or just "reserves".

[3]Equivalent terms are "demand deposits", "transferable deposits", "cash deposits", "transaction deposits" or "current accounts".

[4]Ratios differ across types of institutions and types of deposits. For present requirements, see www.boj.or.jp/en/statistics/boj/other/reservereq/junbi.htm.

those deposits that are used for cashless transfers. The central bank would then be the only institution to create money.

The first insight tells us that Japan is de facto moving towards higher reserve ratios. For depository institutions, the ratio of BoJ reserves to transferable deposits was already at 47% at the end of June 2016 (see Fig. 6.10 and Table 6.3). This, however, represents no shift in regime. Commercial banks are not required to hold these reserves. They do so because they see no better investment opportunity. The second insight says that such a move might actually be beneficial and that even reserve ratios up to 100% might be desirable. However, they would then need to be obligatory and permanent.

The important aspect is that the expansion of the BoJ's balance sheet resulting from QQE would be permanent. Being permanent, the JGBs held by the BoJ would not have to be redeemed. The Bank would not have to worry about how to exit from QQE. QQE would, in the end, be the mechanism by which the transition to the new monetary regime is achieved. With a 100% reserve requirement, the BoJ could permanently accommodate more than half of the presently outstanding amount of JGBs (see Table 6.3). It would be a great leap towards consolidating Japan's government debt.

It will not be possible to elaborate in full detail on the optimal design of the proposed regime and the specifics of the transition process here. The main purpose of this chapter is to highlight the potential of a fully reserve-backed money regime as a solution for Japan's profound macro-economic challenges. Given the high uncertainties surrounding Japan's fiscal and monetary conditions, a regime shift is worth serious consideration and should be included in public policy discourses.

The next Sect., 6.2, will describe the fiscal and monetary policy challenges that Japan is facing. Next, the logic behind the 100% reserve-backed money regime will be elaborated. It will then be shown how a shift to such a regime, which is de facto already observable, could—if it were de jure made permanent—solve the fiscal and monetary challenge that Japan is facing. The last Sect., 6.4, considers the risks of such a move and also hints at some of the possible implications for the use of cash.

6.2 Japan's Fiscal and Monetary Policy Challenges

6.2.1 Government Debt

Japan's government sector, which comprises the central, prefectural and municipal, as well as the social security accounts, boasts a record high level of outstanding gross and net debt in comparison with other advanced economies. The gross debt to GDP ratio had reached 230% in 2015. Net debt was at 130% of GDP (Fig. 6.1).

Looking at this composition, we see that the increase in debt occurred at the central government level. The financial positions of local governments and of the social security system have remained relatively stable over the last two decades (Fig. 6.2).

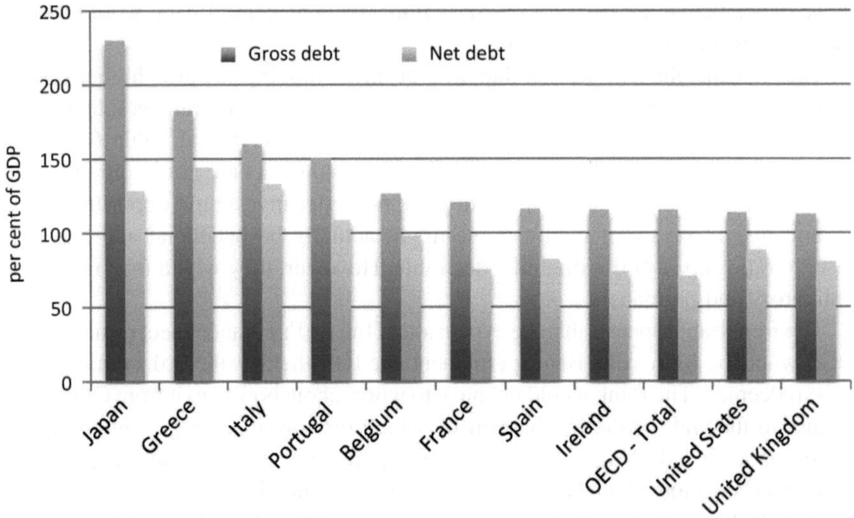

Fig. 6.1 Gross and net debt to GDP ratios of ten most indebted OECD governments, 2015. Source: OECD, Government at a Glance/Public finance and economics, stats.oecd.org

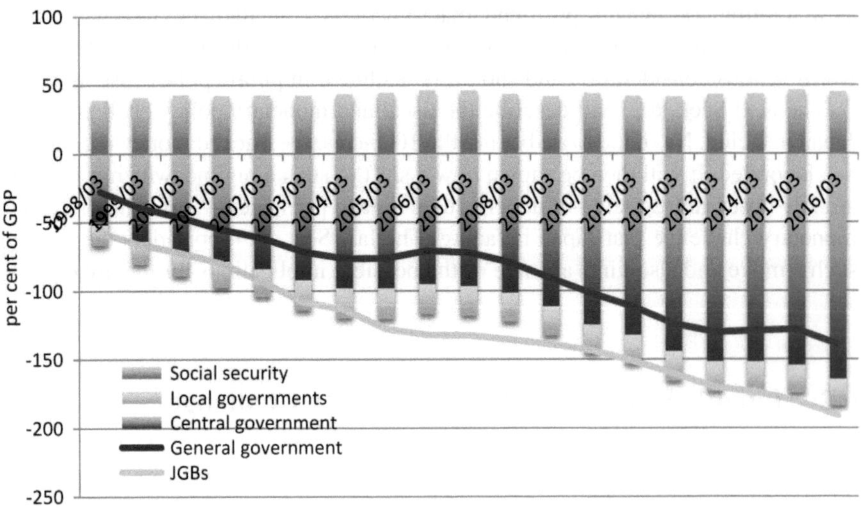

Fig. 6.2 Japan's government net financial position by sector and JGBs, FY 1997–2015. Source: Bank of Japan, Flow of Funds, www.stat-search.boj.or.jp; GDP data from Cabinet Office, Annual Report on National Accounts, www.esri.cao.go.jp

The outstanding amount of JGBs, on which most of the discussion of government debt focuses, surpasses the central government's level of net debt, though it does not reach the level of gross debt. The composition of the central government's outstanding gross debt is depicted in Table 6.1. "Normal", i.e., annual budget financing JGBs dominate. The Fiscal Investment and Loan Programme (FILP)

Table 6.1 Central government debt by financial instrument

Financing instrument	End of March 2013 trillion Yen (per cent)	End of March 2016 trillion Yen (per cent)
Government bonds	821 (83)	911 (87)
Normal bonds	705 (71)	805 (77)
Long term (>10 years)	463 (47)	575 (55)
Mid term (2–5 years)	196 (20)	194 (19)
Short term (<1 year)	47 (5)	36 (3)
FILP bonds	109 (11)	96 (9)
Other bonds	7 (1)	9 (1)
Loans	55 (6)	55 (5)
Treasury bills	115 (12)	84 (8)
Gross debt total	992 (100)	1049 (100)
Financial assets	220 (22)	234 (21)
Net debt	772 (78)	815 (79)

Ministry of Finance, Japanese Government Bonds/Data/Central Government Debt "Outstanding Bonds and Borrowings", www.mof.go.jp; financial assets are taken from Bank of Japan, Flow of Funds, www.stat-search.boj.or; net debt equals gross debt minus financial assets

and other bonds finance investments. They are expected to be redeemed by the returns generated by the respective investment projects. Only if such investments fail, will taxpayer money be needed. Over the last 3 years, the weight of long-term bonds has increased, extending the average maturity of the outstanding debt.

The build up of debt occurred over the last 25 years when expenditures rose steadily, while revenues remained flat (Fig. 6.3). The level of expenditure jumped twice, first in 1998 in response to Japan's banking crisis, then again in 2009 during the global financial crisis. However, the increase over time was mainly driven by outlays for social security necessitated by the fast ageing of Japan's population.

Overall, the government expenditure to GDP ratio is now in line with other OECD countries, whereas the revenue to GDP ratio remains still three percentage points below the OECD average (Fig. 6.4).

Japan's public debt is financed domestically, mainly through financial intermediaries (Fig. 6.5). However, massive purchases of JGBs by the BoJ under QQE propelled the Bank's share to 35% by the end of June 2016. However, the share of overseas investor's remained stable and well below 10%.

Net surpluses by households and non-financial corporations have, in sum, continuously surpassed the funding needs of the government sector. They have also been large enough to finance the further accumulation of net foreign assets, as indicated by the persistent net deficit position of the overseas sector (Fig. 6.6). Japan continues to be the world's largest supplier of capital.[5] Surprisingly, domestic financial surpluses have increasingly been generated by the corporate sector, while the household sector's contribution has declined, thereby reflecting the increasing share of older households, who are consuming formerly accumulated savings. The

[5]IMF, Balance of Payments and International Investment Position Statistics, (data.imf.org).

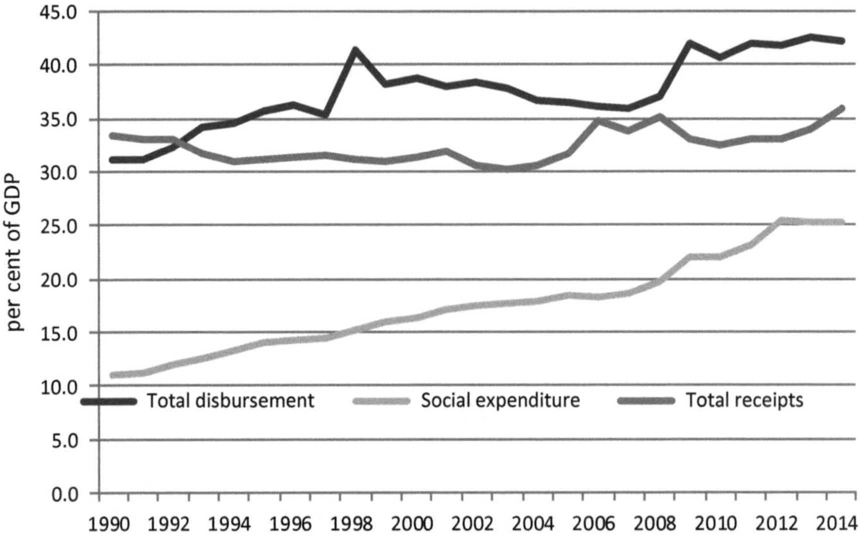

Fig. 6.3 Japan's government expenditure and receipts, FY 1990–2014. Source: OECD, Government at a Glance/Public finance and economics, stats.oecd.org

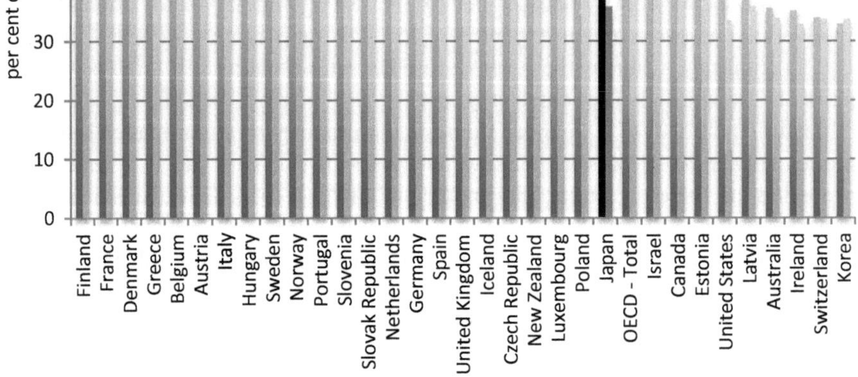

Fig. 6.4 OECD government expenditures and receipts, 2015. Source: OECD, Government at a Glance/Public finance and economics, stats.oecd.org

private corporate sector turned into a net supplier of funds after the burst of the asset price bubble in 1990/1991. The sharp decline in stock and real estate prices increased the sector's debt exposure. To improve their balance sheets, companies started to reduce their leverage. However, one sector in the economy can only

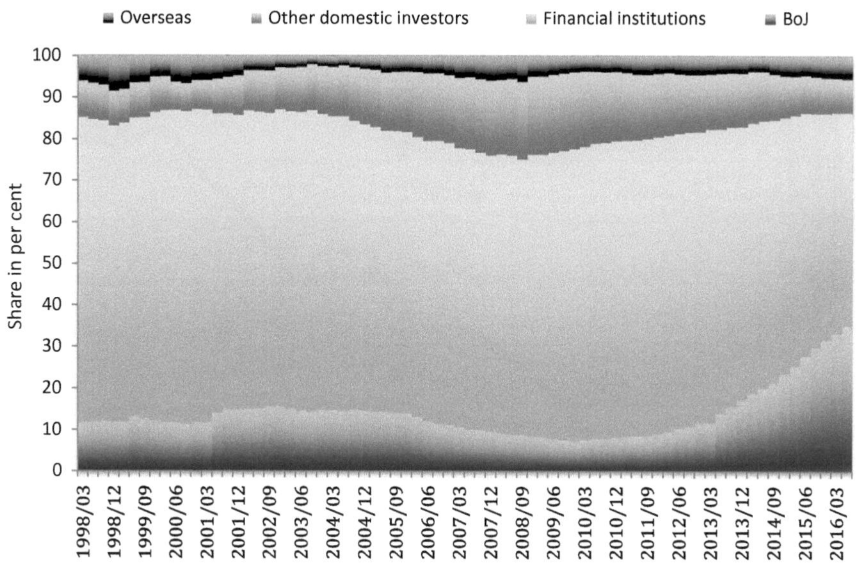

Fig. 6.5 Ownership structure of JGBs, March 1998–June 2016. Source: Bank of Japan, Flow of Funds, www.stat-search.boj.or.jp

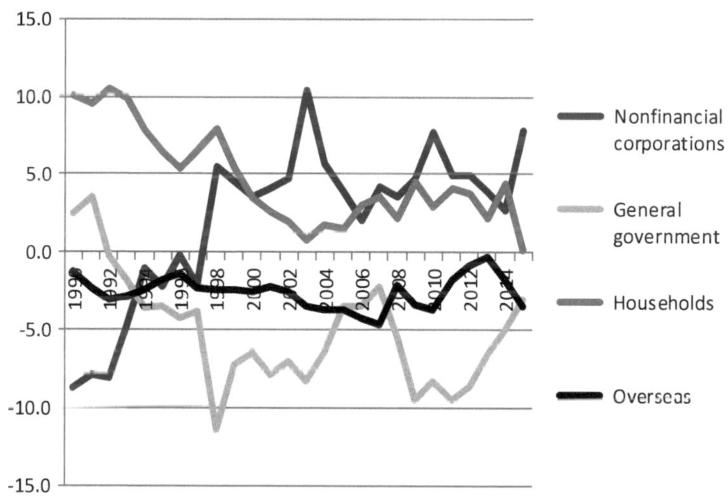

Fig. 6.6 Financial surpluses and deficits of main sectors in per cent of GDP, 1990–2015. Source: Bank of Japan, Fow of Funds, www.stat-search.boj.or.jp

improve its financial position if other sectors are willing to move in the opposite direction, because, in sum, the financial surpluses and deficits across all sectors—corporation, households, government and the outside world—will cancel each other out. It was mainly by the government sector's willingness to take on debt that the private corporate sector was able to de-leverage (Koo 2003). However, the private

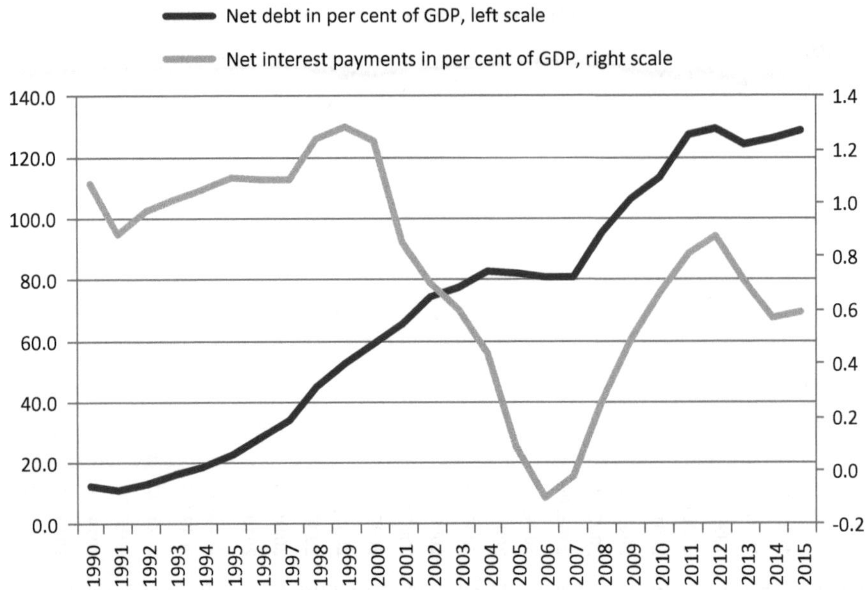

Fig. 6.7 Net debt and net interest payments, 1990–2015. Source: OECD, Government at a Glance/Public finance and economics, stats.oecd.org

corporate sector continued to generate saving surpluses even after balance sheets had been restored. Given the low growth prospects in a domestic market confronting a strong predictable decline in population, companies are understandably reluctant to expand production capacities at home.

The surplus situation depicted in Fig. 6.6 implies that deficit financing by the Japanese government did not crowd out private investment. The weak domestic investment demand combined with an increasingly expansionary monetary policy brought nominal interest rates to historically low levels. The government benefited from the extreme low interest rate environment. Although net government debt strongly increased, net interest payments, until 2006, declined rapidly, then increased in line with net outstanding debt, only to become decoupled again when QQE set in (Fig. 6.7).

All this gives the impression that we are in the best of all possible worlds. However, Japan's historically high level of outstanding debt raises serious concerns about whether or not it will be sustainable. But before turning to the issue of sustainability, it is first necessary to review Japan's monetary policy.

6.2.2 *Quantitative and Qualitative Easing*

After the burst of the bubble economy, the task of monetary policy was to relieve the private sector from the liquidity constraints caused by the sharp fall in asset prices, to stabilise the financial system, especially the banking sector, and to fight deflation. The measures used to achieve the economic objectives changed from the lowering of policy discount and lending rates, control of overnight call-rates for uncollateralised inter-banking loans, maximum limits for bank reserves, expansion of the monetary base, and, most recently, negative interest rates on bank reserves. Each shift in instruments or operational targets prompted policy-makers and commentators to attach a new name to the policy to characterise and market the new approach. Accordingly, the simple traditional classification as "expansionary policy" gave way to "zero-interest-rate policy" (ZIRP), "quantitative easing" (QE), "quantitative and qualitative easing" (QQE), and, most recently, "negative-interest-rate policy" (NIRP). In the end, policies relied mostly on open market purchases of assets by the BoJ—mainly, but not exclusively, Japanese government bonds (JGBs)—resulting in a steady expansion of the Bank's balance sheet, the monetary base and the Bank's holdings of JGBs and other assets (Fig. 6.8). By the end of FY 2015, i.e., end of March 2016, the monetary base had reached 72% of GDP. The BoJ held 33% of outstanding JGBs.

The final target of 2% inflation formulated under QQE has not been achieved to date (Fig. 6.9). Interest rates on newly contracted loans steadily declined. However, lending by financial institutions to private non-financial corporations picked up, albeit only slightly and briefly. Looking at the financial transactions balance over the 3-year period, we can see that the additional lending that corporations received from private financial institutions between April 2013 and March 2016 was, in sum, even less than the additional loans made by non-financial corporations (Table 6.2). This well reflects the surplus condition of the corporate sector referred to above.

As a result, transferable deposits grew at a much lower pace than bank reserves, implying a steep increase in the de facto reserve ratio from 11 to 47% (Fig. 6.10).

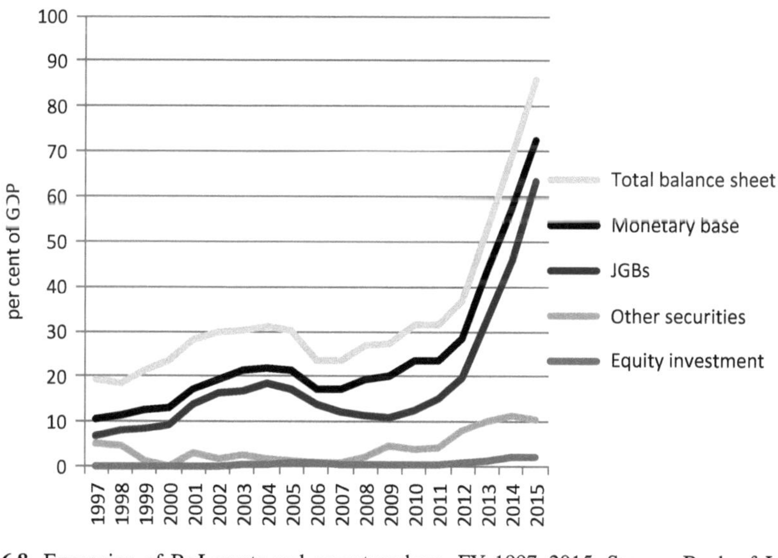

Fig. 6.8 Expansion of BoJ assets and monetary base, FY 1997–2015. Source: Bank of Japan, Bank of Japan Statistics, www.stat-search.boj.or.jp

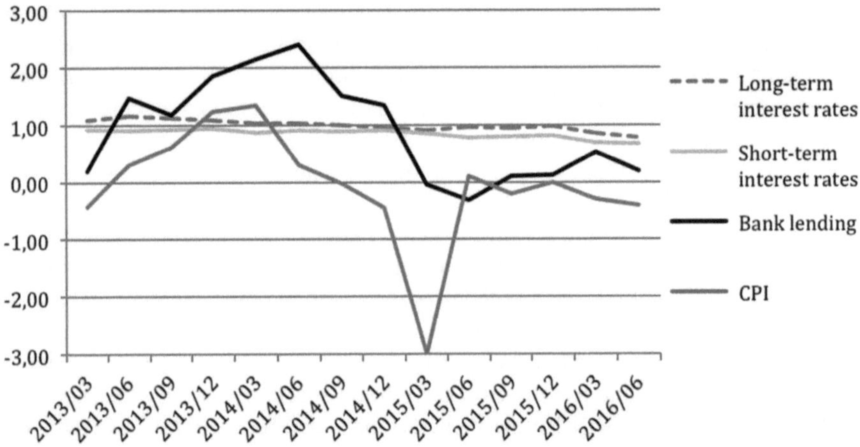

Fig. 6.9 Inflation, interest rates and growth in bank lending, 03/2013–06/2016. Source: Bank of Japan, Deposits and Loan Markets, www.stat-search.boj.or.jp; Statistics Bureau, www.stat.go.jp/english/data/cpi/index.htm. CPI and bank lending depict annual changes. CPI data from 2014/06 to 2015/03 are divided by (1.08/1.05) to account for VAT increase from 5 to 8% in April 2014

Table 6.2 Financial transactions of non-financial private corporations, FY 2013–2016

Additional financial investments		Additional funding	
Assets	trill. Yen	Source	trill. Yen
Currency and deposits	34.7	Loans by private financial inst.	10.4
Loans	10.7	Other loans	4.7
Debt securities	−0.7	Debt securities	−7.2
Equity	9.7	Pensions, guarantees	−6.1
Foreign direct investment	34.4	Equity	11.4
Other overseas investment	16.1	Other funding	29.0
Other financial investments	3.9	Total external funding	42.2
Total	108.8	Financial surplus	66.6

Source: Bank of Japan, Fow of Funds, www.stat-search.boj.or.jp

Although monetary expansion has continued for more than 20 years, the measures undertaken by the Bank of Japan are, in principle, temporary. They are supposed to be stopped—and even reversed—once the inflation goal has been reached. The vital questions that will have to be addressed then are: How can an exit from the present pace and level of monetary easing be accomplished? What effects will an exit or the continuation of monetary easing have on the economy? How will policy choices impact upon the sustainability of Japan's government debt?

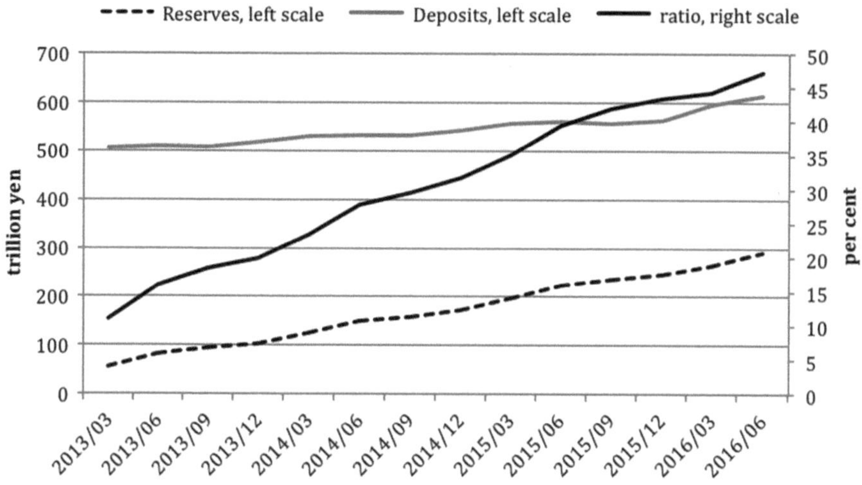

Fig. 6.10 Commercial bank reserves and demand deposits, FY 2013–2016. Data for reserves and transferable deposits refer to depository corporations. Ratio = 100 × deposits/reserves. Source: Bank of Japan, Flow of Funds, www.stat-search.boj.or.jp; own calculations

6.2.3 Fundamental Uncertainties Surrounding Fiscal and Monetary Policy

The sustainability of government debt depends on whether future financing needs can be funded. Annual financing needs are the sum of the primary balance,[6] interest-rate payments and the amount of outstanding debt reaching maturity and having to be repaid. The availability and the cost of funds are determined by the surplus conditions of the other sectors of the economy including the rest of the world, the level of trust investors have in the sustainability of public debt, and the monetary policy stance. It is not possible, and, for the argument put forward here, also not necessary to explore these demand and supply conditions fully. The following analysis mainly aims to highlight the uncertainties surrounding the various factors.

Future primary balances depend on the consolidation efforts of future governments, i.e., the willingness to cut expenditure and/or to raise taxes. Although the intermediate target formulated by the government in 2010 to halve the primary balance deficit by 2015 was achieved, the final goal of a primary balance surplus by and beyond the year 2020 is very likely to be missed even under relatively favourable macro-economic conditions (OECD 2015, pp. 108–112). Given Japan's demographic challenges and the persistent reluctance of past and present governments to raise taxes, the chances for a smooth and timely consolidation seem very

[6]The primary balance describes the difference between revenues and expenditures net of debt services.

unlikely. Reforms in the budget planning and monitoring process, as, for example, proposed by a recent IMF working paper, will be necessary to ensure political commitment to debt consolidation (Kopits 2016).

Interest-rate payments and re-financing needs are influenced by the maturity of outstanding debt. The increased issuance of JGBs with up to 40 years maturity allows the Japanese government to take advantage of the extremely low interest rate environment for many years to come, to delay the impact of future interest rate increases, and to move re-financing needs further into the future. These measures alone, however, will only buy time and not resolve the fundamental task of having to repay debt at some time in the future. A more radical approach would be the issuance of perpetual bonds with no maturity date, as suggested by some experts (Buckland and Nozawa 2016; Pesek 2016). Given the present monetary policy stance, the placement of such bonds might be feasible. They could be issued at a higher interest rate or with flexible interest rates to mitigate the interest rate risk borne by investors. However, the issuance volume will have to be very substantial if perpetual bonds are to reduce future re-financing needs significantly.

Future financial surplus conditions constitute a fundamental uncertainty on the supply side. The fact that governments around the world have recently been able to issue new sovereign bonds at historically low interest rates indicates that private savings have been surpassing private investments. Put in technical terms, the interest rate that would have been required to balance private savings and private investments in the absence of public deficits would have been negative. Given these conditions, government deficit spending did not crowd out private investors. Instead, it contributed to the stabilisation of aggregate demand. The important question is whether these conditions represent a transitory state or a "new normal". Leading economists are deeply divided on this question (Blanchard and Portillo 2016). While some argue that private investment demand will pick up and the world economy will return to the "old normal" of positive interest rates and moderate inflation (Rogoff 2016a), others see private savings in excess of private investments as a long-term phenomenon (Weizsäcker 2011; Summers 2016).

The answer as to whether we do or do not confront a "new normal" is of fundamental importance for the assessment of public debt positions not only in Japan. If the oversupply of private savings is only transitory, governments need to be strongly concerned about consolidating their debt positions. If the situation, however, continues for a longer period, consolidation should not be pursued. It would, in fact, be highly detrimental, as it would reduce aggregate demand.

Even if funds are available, investors will refuse to lend or require higher interest rates if they perceive a high risk of default. JGBs have been downgraded by international rating agencies and now range in the upper medium grade.[7] This, however, has not yet had an impact on the trust of domestic investors in Japan. They still consider JGBs as a safe asset. JGBs are still trading at historically low yield rates and the

[7]For an up-to-date comparison of four major ratings, see http://www.tradingeconomics.com/country-list/rating.

Japanese government continues to be able to place new bonds at equally low rates. The situation may nevertheless drastically change if domestic investors lose trust or if the government has to rely on foreign funds. The conditions for the first scenario can theoretically be formulated, but we do not know when or how they will be triggered (Yoshino and Vollmer 2014). Reliance on foreign investors will set in when Japan's current account turns negative. Again, it is not clear when this is to be expected or how quickly this would translate into higher funding costs.

The level of trust also depends on whether investors believe in the "new normal" interpretation of the global economic environment and on how they assess the future stance of monetary policy. Japan's expansionary monetary policy has helped the Japanese government to satisfy its financing needs at extremely low cost over the last 3 years, though, officially, this is only a side-effect. The legally-defined policy goals stipulated by the Bank of Japan Act of 1997 are price stability (Article 2), stability of the financial system (Article 1), and compatibility with the overall economic policy of the government (Article 4). Under the deflationary economic environment that has persisted over the last two decades, the measures taken by the BoJ have contributed simultaneously to all three goals (Waldenberger 2015). In the future, conflicts may well arise. For example, once the 2% inflation target is reached, it might be necessary to exit from the expansionary policy in order to preserve price stability. Such a policy shift implies the selling of JGBs by the BoJ. It will severely impact on Japan's fiscal situation, if no other sector is able or willing to buy. If the Bank refrains from selling bonds in order to support the government's fiscal condition, it will have to sacrifice price stability. Clearly, this dilemma only occurs if inflation actually picks up. Whether and, if so, when this will happen remains unclear.

Based upon the rudimentary analysis presented above, the major risks can be summarised with reference to the following scenarios:

- Under the most favourable scenario characterised by a "new normal" macro-setting and no inflationary pressures, no fiscal consolidation and no reversal in monetary policy is required. In fact, any reversal in fiscal and/or monetary policy would harm the economy. Fiscal consolidation would reduce aggregate demand, while monetary tightening would endanger fiscal stability with indirect negative effects on aggregate demand.
- If the financial surplus condition in the private sector disappears, as predicted by the proponents of the "old normal", interest rates will rise and inflationary pressures are likely to build up. In this case, fiscal consolidation and an exit from monetary easing will be required to avoid sovereign default and to contain inflation.
- Given the fundamental uncertainty with regard to the macro-setting, investor trust might vanish even if the favourable conditions of a "new normal" do, in fact, prevail. In this case, there is a high probability of the government neither being able to service its outstanding debt nor to raise new debt. The options then are to default, to increase taxes sharply or to cut expenditure or to put pressure on the BoJ to provide the funds needed.

From a policy perspective, the risks created by the fundamental uncertainties about the macro-setting, investor sentiments and political constraints are that:

- Policy-makers might not be able or willing to take preventive measures, i.e., fiscal consolidation or monetary tightening, when needed;
- They might mistakenly consolidate and/or reverse monetary policy when it is not needed;
- They may confront a severe trade-off between sovereign default and price stability.

The root of the problem is that the outstanding government debt and the monetary base are at extremely high levels. Their potentials as fiscal and monetary policy instruments have already been exhausted, implying that their levels are no longer affordable if the economy returns to the "old normal" and/or investors lose confidence. The proposed new monetary regime of fully reserve-backed money will—independent of the prevailing macro setting—enable the economic system to accommodate a monetary base higher than the one already realised thereby allowing the BoJ to absorb government debt permanently even in excess of what it has already purchased. In the new regime, the present level of outstanding government debt will not make consolidation a pressing issue, and the government can instead focus on other social and economic challenges. The BoJ, too, will not face the dilemma of choosing between fiscal stability and price stability. It can concentrate on the latter.

6.3 Fully Reserve-Backed Money

6.3.1 Basic Outline

The proposal of a 100% or fully reserve-backed money (FRBM) has a long history (Benes and Kumhof 2012; Phillips 2015). It has been formulated and supported by leading economic thinkers, including a group of economics professors from the University of Chicago, who proposed what became known as the "Chicago Plan for Banking Reform", by Irwin Fisher (1936) and later Milton Friedman (Friedman 1960). The ideas tend to gain momentum and attention after the burst of bubbles, as was the case in the 1930s and again after the recent world financial crisis in 2008. This is not surprising given that the main concern of FRBM is the stabilisation of the financial system. The huge build-up and subsequent implosion of credit and debt during the boom and bust of asset bubbles is seen to be largely the result of the banking sector's ability to create liquidity beyond what is needed for the accumulation of productive assets (Minsky 1992).

Banks create money by using demand deposits to finance new loans. This is possible for two reasons. First, although demand deposits give the holder the right to withdraw all the money deposited at any time, the proportion of cash needed is, under normal conditions, only a fraction of the amount deposited. Most of the money held in demand deposits is used for cashless transfers and thus stays within the system. Second, banks are only required to keep a marginal portion of the deposits as reserves with the central bank. The cash holding habits and the minimum reserve requirement ratios define the "money multiplier", the potential multiple of credit money that banks are able to create from one unit of central bank money (Samuelson and Nordhaus 1998, pp. 475–482). Proponents of FRBM emphasise that the textbook causality running from additionally provided central bank money to credit money is, in practice, reversed (McLeay et al. 2014). Banks can lend and create the respective demand deposits for the lender first, with the central bank afterwards providing the fractional reserves needed to back the deposits.

FRBM envisages a strict separation between: (a) money deposited in transactional, demand or current accounts used for cashless payments or immediate cash withdrawals; and (b) money paid into savings, time or investment accounts,[8] where the depositor agrees not to withdraw the money for a contractually specified period of time. Demand deposits do not earn interest and are perfectly secure as they are fully backed by central bank money. Savings, time or investment accounts bear an interest rate that also reflects the risk of the investment that they finance. Under the new system, banks are merely administrating the demand accounts.[9] They can no longer dispose of these accounts for the financing of loans, and the costs for their administrative services will have to be covered by fees (Jackson and Dyson 2012).[10] The financing of bank loans and other bank assets can only be done through risk bearing deposits or other funding instruments such a bonds or equity.

The proponents of FRBM argue that the separation of payment settlement and credit functions will smoothen credit and debt cycles and reduce the likelihood of asset bubbles. The financial system will be stabilised also for other reasons. Bank runs will no longer occur as the full amount of money is always in the account and not lent out, as in the present system. For the same reason, insurance for demand deposits is no longer needed. Banks that badly select and monitor lenders or otherwise take on too much risk can fail without endangering the payment settlement system. Public bailouts of banks are thus no longer necessary. All the distortions associated with deposit insurance and the public bailouts of banks can, therefore, be avoided.

The risk associated with savings deposits and other bank liabilities reflects the risk of the investments financed by these sources. Such risk can be dealt with by using the standard methods, such as credit ratings and monitoring of borrowers, the diversification of bank assets, bank equity, and, last, but not least, bankruptcy regulations.

---

[8]The terms are used interchangeably.

[9]It is not necessary for the accounts to be directly administered by the central bank as proposed by Huber and Robertson (2000, pp. 24–25).

[10]Friedman (1960) actually argues in favour of interest rates on bank reserves. If such rates are high enough and if competition among banks functions demand deposits will be free of charge and even earn some interest.

6.3.2 Critical Issues

The main institutional provisions of FRBM are the 100% reserve requirements for demand deposits. They imply the separation of payment settlements from lending functions within the system, and make the central bank the sole provider of liquidity in the form of money. Clearly, many details need to be decided when implementing these provisions, and many different regulatory designs can be thought of and have been proposed, also reflecting the advancement of electronic means of payments over time (Friedman 1960; Huber and Robertson 2000; Benes and Kumhof 2012; Jackson and Dyson 2012). For the purpose of the present argument, however, it suffices briefly to discuss the following three major critical aspects:

(a) The relationship between fiscal and monetary policy;
(b) Money and credit supply;
(c) The suppression of "near money" or *quasi*-money as means of payment.

Ad (a) The transition to FRBM requires the expansion of the central bank's balance sheet. This implies the acquisition of assets. Theoretically, different kinds of assets might be thought of. For example, the central bank might give out loans to commercial banks to finance the additional reserves that they need for the 100% backup of demand deposits (Fisher 1936, p. 19, Friedman 1960, p. 86). In practice, one will want to minimise the economic frictions and distortions caused by the transition. The Chicago Plan, Fisher (1936) and also the present chapter all argue in favour of government bonds because of the massive amount of outstanding public debt. Nevertheless, the focus on JGBs raises fundamental questions as to the future relationship between government debt and money supply. In principle, the transition to FRBM is a "once and for all" measure. It does not pre-condition the future relationship between monetary and fiscal policy. All proponents of FRBM stress that money supply can and should be decided independent of fiscal policy. The BoJ can adjust the asset side of its balance sheet by buying or selling JGBs and other assets that it deems suited. For the same reason, the government can decide to reduce or increase its outstanding debt independent of money supply conditions. The mutual independence of fiscal and monetary policy must be ensured by the respective governance structures and policy processes. The shift to FRBM could, in fact, provide a window of opportunity to improve Japan's budgetary process with regard to transparency and fiscal discipline, as, for example, proposed by Kopits (2016), and to safeguard the independence of the BoJ better against political pressures, as seen under the second Abe administration (Waldenberger 2015).

Ad (b) In the present system, banks can give out new credit by creating new demand deposits for lenders (Jackson and Dyson 2012). This is, of course, at the very root of the fragility of the financial system that the proponents of FRBM both criticise and aim to eliminate. On the other hand, the strict separation of money and credit supply, and the transfer of the money-supply function to a sole public authority might not allow for the flexible creation of liquidity as needed.[11]

Under FRBM, the central bank is able to adjust the amount of money in the same way as under the present system. It can use the same transmission channels, which means that it can delegate the allocation of additional money to financial intermediaries.[12] The only, albeit fundamental, difference under FRBM is that its decisions now fully determine the variations in the total amount of money, as commercial banks would be deprived of the ability to create demand deposits. For Friedman and others, who consider the stock of money to be the most appropriate monetary policy variable, and argue for simple money growth rules, this would enable a better, i.e., a more stable and predictable, money supply than the present system (Friedman 1960, Chap. 4).

FRBM allows for the financing of additional credit out of the existing stock of money, but also through the central bank providing new money to financial intermediaries, as under the present monetary regime. The financing of credit out of the existing stock of money requires an entity A to be willing to transfer some of its cash or demand deposits to its savings account from which the money will then be transferred to entity B.[13] Clearly, lending does not only occur through bank accounts. For example, A can directly conclude a loan contract with B and simply provide the money in cash. Also, if A delivers a good or service to B, agreeing to be paid later, it provides credit without having transferred cash or demand deposits to its savings account. However, in all these cases, the total amount of money, i.e., the sum of cash and demand deposits, remains constant. The typical mechanism regulating the supply of money to satisfy new credit demand without increasing the stock of money would be the variation in the rate of interest. Higher rates paid on savings deposits increase the opportunity cost of holding cash and demand deposits, thus increasing the willingness to shift money to savings accounts, thereby allowing for the re-allocation of purchasing power both among economic entities and across time. The early proponents foresaw no specific difficulties in accommodating credit demand under FRBM. They even envisaged a more efficient lending system, since banks and other lending institutions could be freed from regulations necessitated by the fact that, under a fractional reserve system, credit defaults can

[11]It is interesting to note that economists of the University of Chicago that proposed the "Chicago Plan" in 1933 advocating a state monopoly otherwise strongly believed in the efficiency of markets (Phillips 2015, pos 1066-1068).

[12]Some proponents of FRBM suggest money supply to become a new source of government revenue (Huber and Robertson 2000, pp. 8–9; Jackson and Dyson 2012, Chap. 7). However, at the same time, they stress that monetary policy must be free from government intervention. It is questionable whether independence can be achieved with a fiscal transmission channel (Friedman 1960, p. 106).

[13]Of course, A and B could be identical. For example, if a firm directly purchases capital goods out of its cash or demand deposits. In that case, no additional credit or debt relation would be established.

cause bank runs and endanger the functioning of the payment settlement system (Fisher 1936, p. 15; Friedman 1960, p. 80).

Ad (c) FRBM requires that cash and demand deposits be the only means of payment. Economic agents might accept other relatively safe assets with a high liquidity as means of payment especially if they can earn interest on them. Quite drastic measure have been proposed to suppress near-money assets from being used as means of payment, such as the full replacement of banks by investment trusts or the implementation of a financial system without private non-equity liabilities (Benes and Kumhof 2012, pp. 18–19). Friedman's idea of paying a (to be defined) risk free interest-rate on bank reserves offers a far more elegant and less radical solution (Friedman 1960, pp. 86–91). He argues that competition among banks will pass the interest earned on reserves to the holders of demand deposits thereby reducing the social cost of holding money and reducing the attractiveness of interest earning near-money as means of payment. Interest payments on bank reserves would also allow the seigniorage earned in the process of creating money to be distributed to money holders.

6.3.3 A "Chicago Plan" for Japan

The primary concern of the present chapter is Japan's fiscal and monetary policy challenges. FRBM provides a possible solution to these challenges. The transition from the present to the new monetary system implies the persistent expansion of central bank money, because commercial bank reserves held at the central bank need to match fully the amount of money in demand deposits. It is this "side-effect" of FRBM that makes it attractive for Japan and, possibly, other countries facing similar policy deadlocks. In fact, Irwin Fisher stressed the same positive side-effect when arguing for FRBM back in the mid-1930s, as already evidenced by the title of his publication "100% Money and the Public Debt" (Fisher 1936). He saw a window of opportunity for the introduction of FRBM and the consolidation of government debt:

> One way would be to provide the banks with the needed 100% reserve, not by lending it to them as suggested by Professor Angell, but by buying back the Government bonds they hold in exchange for the new reserve money. [...] In that way most of the Government debt could be paid almost over night. This would be one of the main immediate advantages of the 100% system. (Fisher 1936, p. 19).

> There are several reasons today beckoning us toward the 100% plan. One is the huge excess reserves. Unless these are absorbed by raising the reserve requirements, they will continue to threaten us with an inflation ten times their size. These reserves were created in a vain attempt by the Federal Reserve to increase business loans. [. . .] Another important fact is the provision now in the law for increasing reserve requirements. Why not take advantage of this provision and then keep going until 100% reserve is reached? (Fisher 1936, p. 21).

The same arguments can be made in the case of Japan today. The following calculations based upon data taken from the BoJ's flow of funds statistics for end of June 2016 show how far Japan has already de facto moved towards FRBM, what more

Table 6.3 BoJ and depository corporations' accounts before and after the transition to FRMB

Depository institutions				Bank of Japan			
Assets		Liabilities		Assets		Liabilities	
Before							
Reserves	290	Transfer. deposits	614	JGBs	345	Banknotes	101
JGBs	227					Reserves	290
Loans	726	Other	1276	Other	78	Other	72
Other	647						
Total	1890	Total	1890	Total	463	Total	463
After step 1: transferable deposits fully reserve backed							
Reserves	614	Transfer. deposits	614	JGBs	572	Banknotes	101
JGBs	0					Reserves	614
Loans	726	Other	1276	Other	215	Other	72
Other	550						
Total	1890	Total	1890	Total	787	Total	787
After step 2: shifting all BoJ assets to JGBs							
Reserves	614	Transfer. deposits	614	JGBs	787	Banknotes	101
JGBs	0					Reserves	614
Loans	726	Other	1276	Other	0	Other	72
Other	550						
Total	1890	Total	1890	Total	787	Total	787

Source: Based upon end of June 2016 figures from BoJ Flow of Funds Statistics

would be needed to complete the transition, and how much of the outstanding government debt could then be settled as a result (Table 6.3). Transaction accounts at depository corporations amounted to 614 trillion Yen. This corresponded to 70% of the total amount of outstanding JGBs, including FILP bonds. BoJ reserves of depository corporations were at 290 trillion Yen resulting in a de facto reserve ratio of 47%. Moving to a 100% regime would require an additional 324 trillion Yen in reserves. This could be achieved with the BoJ buying up the remaining 227 trillion JGBs on the balance sheets of depository corporations plus 97 of the 647 trillion of their other assets. The BoJ would expand its balance sheet by adding 324 trillion reserves on the liability side and the same amount on the asset side. At the present level of banknotes, transferable deposits and other BoJ liabilities, it could accommodate 787 trillion JGBs if it held no other assets, equivalent to 89% of outstanding JGBs. The balance sheet changes of the transition to FRBM are illustrated in Table 6.3.[14]

The size relations suggest that a shift to FRBM would allow Japan to consolidate a large portion of outstanding government debt and, for the time being, avoid the tough and risky fiscal and monetary policy choices described above. Although the transition

[14]Table 6.3 underlines the size relations of the relevant assets and liabilities and the balance sheet effects of the transition. It does not depict the institutional implications, i.e., the fact that transferable deposits and reserves no longer represent assets and liabilities in the strict legal sense, but are only administered by banks.

would not need to affect the amount of bank loans, it implies that banks would have to exchange interest-bearing assets for interest-free reserves. The fact that part of money deposited in transaction accounts was financing interest-bearing assets reflects the seigniorage earned by banks from the production of money. Such benefits would be lost under FRBM. It will be necessary to compensate banks for this loss in seigniorage. However, this could be avoided if Friedman's proposal of paying interest on bank reserves was implemented. This compensation effect in the transition process constitutes an additional argument in favour of interest-bearing reserves.

The balance sheet changes can be easily and quickly affected. However, various other adaptations will have to be made to adjust to the new system. One fundamental issue relates to the banks' liabilities. They will need to be re-structured to account for the fact that non-demand deposits will be fully exposed to the risks borne on the banks' asset side. Higher equity ratios would be a natural response. Here, again, interest rates paid on reserves could help banks to cope with the higher costs of securing finance.

6.4 Concluding Remarks

The fiscal and monetary policy constellations in Japan provide the ideal conditions required for a shift to FRBM:

- High reserves of depository corporations with a de facto reserve ratio for transferable deposits of already nearly 50%;
- A sufficiently high amount of government debt outstanding to serve as the asset to be purchased during the further expansion of the BoJ's balance sheet when moving towards a 100% reserve ratio.

The fiscal and monetary policy constellations represent not only a window of opportunity for introducing FRBM, they also constitute the strongest argument in favour of such a regime shift. The extreme levels of government debt and bank reserves constitute serious macro-economic challenges. Should the economy return to the "old normal" regime, government debt will no longer be sustainable and the continuation of monetary easing will end in high inflation. On the other hand, the attempt to consolidate government debt in a "new normal" setting would harm the economy by reducing aggregate demand. A shift to FRBM would considerably lower such uncertainties and risks, because a high level of deposit reserves financing a high level of government debt on the BoJ's balance sheet no longer constitutes a threat, but a system requirement. Under FRBM, neither the Central Government of Japan nor the BoJ would be pressured into taking drastic measures or risks. They could, instead, focus on other social, economic and monetary policy goals.

The situation is, in many respects, similar to the one that the US faced in the 1930s and which other leading economies are confronting today. But why have the respective reforms not been implemented to date? The history of the Chicago Plan, written by Phillips, offers various possible explanations. First, there was opposition from the financial, especially the banking, industry, as seen by public statements made against the proposal (Phillips 2015: pos 2336, 2358, 3189). Understandably, bankers would not want to see their traditional business model based upon the ability to create money become obsolete. Second, opposition was fueled by arguments that oversimplified and distorted, if not deliberately misinterpreted, the claims of the proposal by stating it would (a) give the government the power to create money at will and inevitably lead to inflation; and (b) mean the end of private lending institutions. The first issue clearly depends on the rules and governance of the public authority in charge of money supply, as briefly discussed above. The second argument neglects the explicit separation of the money supply and the lending functions made in the proposal. Only the former would be monopolised, while the latter would remain the business of private banks.[15] Other reasons for the failure of the plan included the blunders in the handling of the political and legislative process, and last, but not least, the onset of the Second World War (Phillips 2015: pos 2783 to 2800).

As pointed out above, the implementation of Friedman's idea of interest-bearing reserves could greatly increase the acceptance of FRBM by the banking sector, as seigniorage would not be retained by the state monopoly, but shared with the money holders. Interest payments on bank reserves runs, of course, counter to the present negative interest rate policy by the BoJ. The policy shows, in fact, that Japan's monetary authority is far from considering the implementation of a 100% reserve regime.

For sure, there are uncertainties surrounding both the transition to FRBM and the actual design. The theoretical soundness seems warranted by the reputation of the numerous economists in favour of FRBM. The theoretical claims have recently been validated in a dynamic stochastic equilibrium model for the US economy (Benes and Kumhof 2012). In the case of Japan, legislators will have to weigh the fiscal and monetary policy risks encountered when staying with the present regime, against the risk of moving to a new regime, which has historically been used, but, to date, not yet been tested, in a modern economy. The macro-economic risks are certainly high enough to consider FRBM for Japan seriously.

FRBM is likely to affect the demand for cash. Japan is known for its high ratio of cash relative to GDP. It is about double the ratios in the US and the Eurozone (Rogoff 2016b: pos 659). One reason for holding cash is lack of trust in the safety of bank deposits. However, under FRBM, such deposits will be as safe as cash. The introduction of FRBM can therefore be expected to reduce the demand for cash resulting from safety considerations. An additional shift from cash to demand deposits will probably occur if the latter should bear interest rates, as envisaged by Friedman's (1960) design proposal referred to above.

---

[15]Proponents of FRBM explicitly stressed that the separation of payment and lending function would reduce the need for government regulation and intervention in the lending business of banks (Fisher 1936, pp. 19–21; Friedman 1960, pp. 96–97).

References

Benes J, Kumhof M (2012) The Chicago plan revisited. IMF (IMF Working paper WP/12/202), Washington

Blanchard O, Portillo R (2016) A road map to "progress and confusion". In: Blanchard O, Rajan R, Rogoff K, Summers LH (eds) Progress and confusion. The state of macroeconomic policy. The MIT Press, Cambridge (e-book edition, no pagination)

Buckland K, Nozawa S (2016) Yen collapse seen by Kuroda Critic pitching perpetual bond plan, Bloomberg, July 21

Fisher I (1936) 100% Money and the Public Debt, Economic Forum, Spring Number 1936, 406–420 (reprint by Michael Schemmann, Thai Sunset Publications 2009)

Friedman M (1960) A program for monetary stability. Fordham University Press, New York

Huber J, Robertson J (2000) Creating new money. A monetary reform for the information age. New Economics Foundation, London

Jackson A, Dyson B (2012) Modernising money. Why our monetary system is broken and how it can be fixed. Positive Money, London

Koo RC (2003) Balance sheet recession. Japan's struggle with uncharted economics and its global implications. Wiley, Singapore

Kopits G (2016) The case for an independent fiscal institution in Japan. IMF (IMF Working Paper WP 16/156), Washington

McLeay M, Radia A, Thomas R (2014) Money creation in the modern economy. Q Bull 2014 (Q1):14–27

Minsky HP (1992) The financial instability hypothesis. Levy Economics Institute of Bard College, Working Paper no 74

OECD (2015) Economic surveys – Japan 2015. OECD, Paris

Pesek W (2016) BOJ's perpetual QE quandary. Japan Times, July 19

Phillips RJ (2015) The Chicago plan and new deal banking reform. Routledge, New York (e-book edition; first published 1995 by M.E. Sharpe)

Rogoff K (2016a) Debt supercycle, not secular stagnation. In: Blanchard O, Rajan R, Rogoff K, Summers LH (eds) Progress and confusion. The state of macroeconomic policy. The MIT Press, Cambridge (e-book edition, no pagination)

Rogoff KS (2016b) The curse of cash. Princeton University Press, Princeton (e-book edition, no pagination)

Samuelson PA, Nordhaus WD (1998) Economics, 16th edn. Irwin McGraw-Hill, New York

Summers LH (2016) Rethinking secular stagnation after seventeen months. In: Blanchard O, Rajan R, Rogoff K, Summers LH (eds) Progress and confusion. The state of macroeconomic policy. The MIT Press, Cambridge (e-book edition, no pagination)

Waldenberger F (2014) Japan's new monetary policy. In: Rövekamp F, Hilpert HG (eds) Currency cooperation in East Asia. Springer, Heidelberg, pp 43–55

Waldenberger, F. (2015): Central bank independence in times of high fiscal risk: the case of Japan. In: Rövekamp F, Bälz M, Hilpert H G (eds) Central banking and financial stability in East Asia. Springer, Heidelberg, pp 87–100

von Weizsäcker CC (2011) Public debt requirements in a regime of price stability. Reprints of the Max Planck Institute for the Research on Collective Goods, 2011/20. http://www.coll.mpg.de

Yoshino N, Vollmer U (2014) The sovereign debt crisis. Why greece, but not Japan? Asia Eur J 12:325–344

Part III
On the Way to Cashless Societies?

Chapter 7
A Coinless Society as a Bridge to a Cashless Society: A Korean Experiment

Woosik Moon

Abstract The Bank of Korea (BoK) is planning to create a coinless society by the year 2020. This initiative was initially motivated by the need to reduce the inconvenience associated with the use of coins, to save the cost of minting coins and to help the smooth change-over in the event of a possible redenomination of the Korean Won (KRW). But as Korea is well equipped with cashless payments such as credit cards and FinTech payments, this initiative was further expanded to test the possibility of a cashless society before ultimately shifting to it. Eliminating coins from circulation means that the BoK is developing an alternative payment instrument to coins for the giving and receiving of small change in commercial transactions. This study evaluates the merits of different possible electronic payment methods and services such as credits cards, public transportation cards, electronic cash receipts and digital wallets, and shows that Korea has a high potential to realise not only a coinless society but also a cashless society. If realised, a coinless society will mark a new era that will herald the end of the age of commodity money and eventually paper money.

7.1 Introduction

The Bank of Korea (hereinafter, the BoK) is planning to create a coinless society by the year 2020. In its 2016 edition of the Payment and Settlements System Report, it says:

> As the retail payment networks are well organised in Korea, and nearly every person has a current-account with a financial institution, the implementation of a 'coinless' infrastructure would serve to reduce the use of coins greatly. To this end, the BoK will form a joint research group together with financial institutions and specialised IT companies, and based upon the group's recommendations, work to devise the most effective measures for achieving a coinless society (Payment and Settlement System Report 2016a, pp. 65–6).

W. Moon (✉)
Seoul National University, Seoul, Korea
e-mail: mwoosik@snu.ac.kr

F. Rövekamp et al. (eds.), *Cash in East Asia*, Financial and Monetary Policy Studies 44, DOI 10.1007/978-3-319-59846-8_7

This initiative should receive special attention because, unlike the idea of the cashless society which was mainly motivated exclusively by the special monetary policy environment of some advanced countries characterised by zero and negative interest rates, the interest in the coinless society could be universal, and not be limited to Korea. There are indeed three main reasons why the BoK came to launch this project. No doubt, the first important reason will be related to the reduction of the social costs and inconvenience associated with the use of coins in diverse economic transactions, not to mention the direct cost of minting coins incurred by central banks. As pointed out, given Korea's well-developed non-cash payment instruments and methods such as credit cards and FinTech settlements and payments, these gains will be obtained with relatively small implementation costs. The second reason behind the initiative would be to take advantage of the experiment of a coinless society in order to test the *possibility* of a cashless society before ultimately shifting to it. Eliminating coins from circulation has smaller security risks and information protection costs than eliminating all cash, making the shift to a cashless society easier. A coinless society will mean that Korea is equipped with an electronic payment infrastructure which will allow it to dispense with coins for the giving and receiving of change in commercial transactions. For instance, if an individual buys an item worth Korean Won (KRW) 9500 and pays with a banknote of KRW 10,000, he or she should own credit cards or other electronic payment instruments to be credited with KRW 500 "change" or *virtual* change, instead of receiving a KRW 500 coin in *real*, physical, change.[1] In this process, diverse alternative instruments can be used such as credit cards, public transportation cards, electronic cash receipts or digital wallets. This infrastructure could be extended in order to realise a completely cashless society. The final reason that pushed forward this plan was the increasing public calls for the re-denomination of the Korean currency. The move towards a cashless society *via* the coinless project would help the smooth change-over in the event of a possible re-denomination of the Korean Won.

To explore the best way to move towards a coinless society in Korea, this study tries to evaluate the merits of different possible electronic payment methods and services in order to substitute coins in the giving and receiving of small change.

This study shows that, against the backdrop of Korea's highly developed IT and mobile phone infrastructure, there are already many private on-line and off-line payment instruments and services that will allow for coinless as well as cashless transactions. If these new payment services which, to date, have emerged rather spontaneously could be successfully harmonised and promoted with a clear target and direction set by the government and the BoK, it might not just be a simple dream to realise a coinless society in Korea by the year 2020. This will clearly be a historic event that officially announces the end of the age of commodity money, which might even be followed by the end of the age of paper money.

The organisation of this chapter is as follows. In Sect. 2, an evaluation of the current status of non-cash payment instruments in Korea is made. In Sects. 3 and 4, the

---

[1]The exchange rate of the Korean *won* (KRW) *vis-à-vis* US dollar is fluctuating between 1000 and 1200 KRW. But for the sake of simplicity, one can suppose that 1000 KRW = 1 US dollar.

cost and benefits of a coinless society is attempted, and, on these grounds, the best method for realising a coinless society is explored. In Sect. 5, different non-cash payment instruments and ways for creating a coinless society are reviewed, together with the current projects of the private sector. Finally, in Sect. 6, the time plan of this project pursued by the BoK is presented together with some of the possible challenges.

7.2 The Current Status of Non-cash Payments in Korea

The widespread use of Internet and mobile phones together with the development of financial technology are bringing about new digital payment instruments and services that are rapidly replacing the use of cash in payments. For instance, according to a survey on the use of payment instruments conducted by the BoK, the proportion of cash used in the transactions of individual Koreans dropped to 26% in volume and 13.6% in value in 2016 from 37% in volume and 17% in value in 2014. Underlying this trend is the fact that Korea is well equipped with high speed IT and mobile phone infrastructure, allowing it to operate highly effective retail payment systems and thus to avoid the use of cash in ordinary transactions. In particular, credit, debit, and prepaid cards are widely available and new mobile phone payment technology, combined with these, provide diverse new ways of paying in many circumstances. For instance, the proportion of credit-card use in 2016 was 50.6% in terms of the transaction payment volume and 54.8% in terms of payment value, surpassing that of cash (26% in volume and 13.6% in value respectively) by a wide margin (Figs. 7.1 and 7.2).

As a result, Korea is currently one of the countries with the lowest use of cash in the world (See Table 7.1).

Nevertheless, many Koreans still continue to use cash in their retail transactions. In 2015, ordinary Koreans were estimated to carry an average of KRW 74,000 in cash in their pockets, though it had declined slightly by KRW 3000 from KRW 77,000 in 2014 (BoK 2016a).

Currently, the BoK issues banknotes in four denominations KRW 1000, 5000, 10,000 and 50,000, and coins in six denominations KRW 1, 5, 10, 50, 100 and 500. Of the total amount of banknotes and coins issued, banknotes account for 97.14% and coins only 2.6%. Their unit issue costs are KRW 123 and 87 respectively. Among the banknotes, the KRW 50,000 and 10,000 banknotes make up most of the banknotes in circulation, accounting for 76.2% and 20.4% respectively. Among the coins, coins denominated below KRW 100 account for 90% of the coins in circulation while the KRW 500 coin, the largest coin in circulation, represents about 10%. At the end of 2015, the amount of banknotes and coins in circulation issued by the BoK stood at KRW 86.6 trillion.

Disregarding the risk for loss and damage, the use of cash, in particular, coins, is increasingly cumbersome, and the growing on-line banking and shopping makes it even more costly. For example, banks are incurring large administrative costs for the handling and withdrawal of coins. Merchants in shops such as pharmacies, convenience stores (small local shops with extended opening hours) and

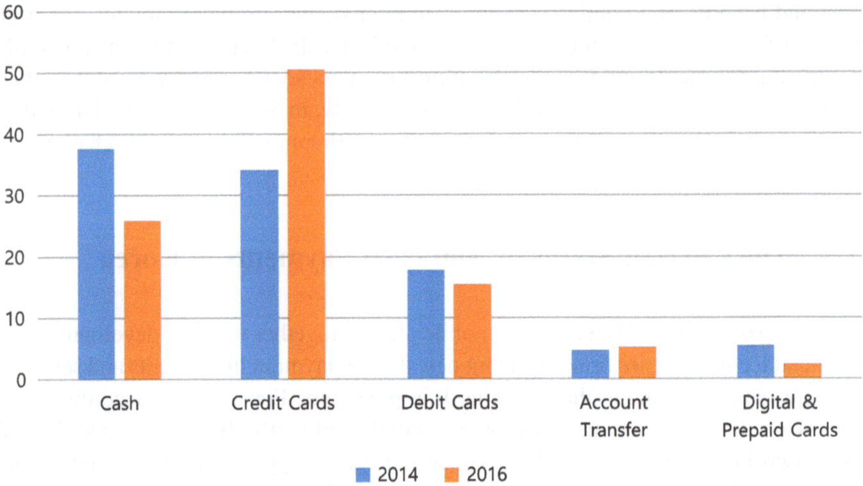

Fig. 7.1 Use of payment instruments by proportion (in transaction volume). Source: BoK

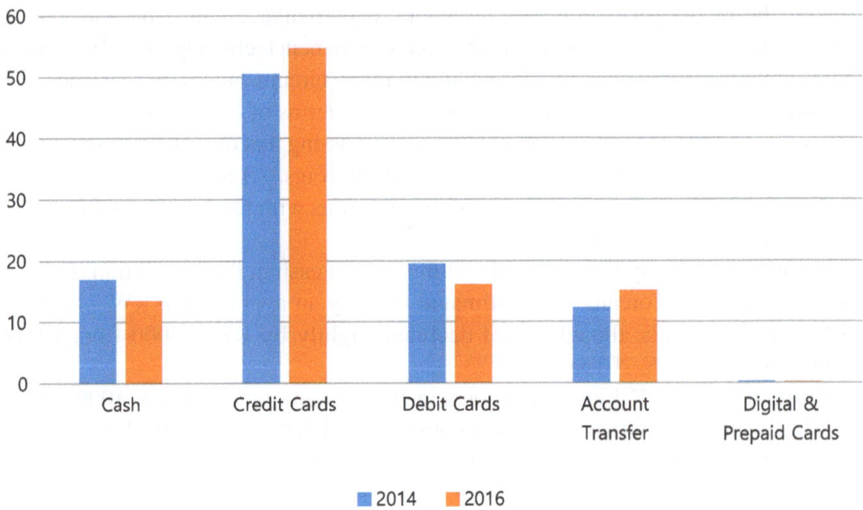

Fig. 7.2 Use of payment instruments by proportion (in transaction value). Source: BoK

supermarkets, have to have small coins, count them and pay them out in change in their business transactions, which requires them to spend extra time, effort and money. The use of coins is extremely costly. Concerning consumers, they have to accept the inconvenience of carrying coins, which are rapidly increasing as the volume and weight of the coins becomes larger. For example, when 20 pieces of the 100 Won coin can be replaced with one prepaid traffic card, the weight is reduced from 110 to 5 g and a separate coin wallet or purse is no longer needed.

Needless to say, the costs that the central bank incurs for the issuing and withdrawing of coins are substantial. As of the end of 2015, for example, there

Table 7.1 International comparison on the use of payment instruments (% in transaction volume)

	Korea (2016)	Germany (2014)	Netherlands (2014)	US (2014)	Canada (2013)	Australia (2013)
Cash	26.0	79.1	57.0	25.6	43.9	47.0
Credit Cards	50.6	1.3	1.0	23.3	30.8	19.0
Debit Cards	15.8	15.3	40.0	30.8	21.1	24.0
Others	7.6	4.3	2.0	20.3	4.2	10.0
Total	100.0	100.0	100.0	100.0	100.0	100.0

Source: BOK, Survey on the use of payment instruments (2016b)

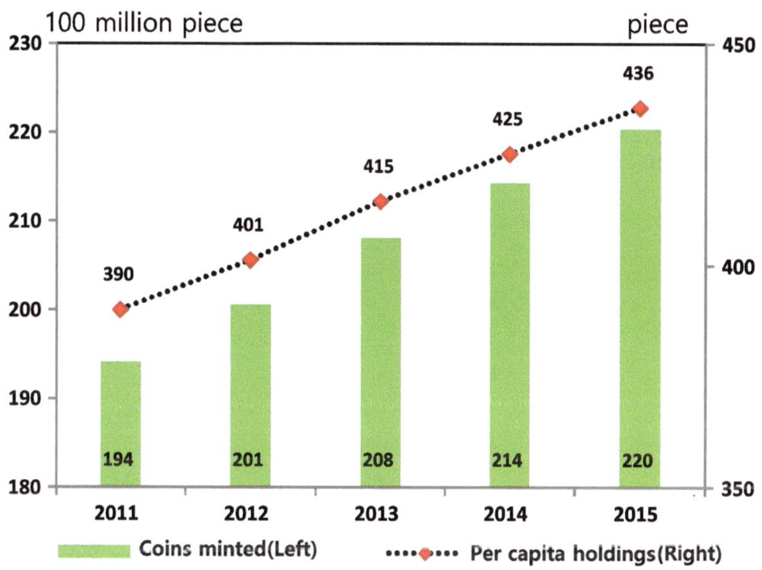

Fig. 7.3 Coins in circulation and per capita coin holdings. Source: BoK

were 22 billion coins in circulation in Korea and an individual Korean is estimated to hold 436 coins on average (See Fig. 7.3).

As the cost of minting the coins is approaching the face value of the actual coins issued, the benefit of seigniorage for the central bank, although slightly positive until now, is declining or likely to become negative. For instance, as of 2015, the BoK spent around KRW 53.9 billion issuing 620 million coins amounting to KRW 70 billion. This may be due to the increase in the issue of the KRW 500 coin, the largest coin in circulation. In 2014, when mainly small denomination coins were issued, the benefit of issuing coins was even inferior to the mint cost (See Fig. 7.4).

Moreover, compared to banknotes, coins rarely return to banks (See, for instance, Fig. 7.5). Many coins are hoarded and abandoned out of circulation. As of 2015, the value of coins damaged and abandoned reaches 1.6 billion KRW with 17.5 million coins (See Fig. 7.6).

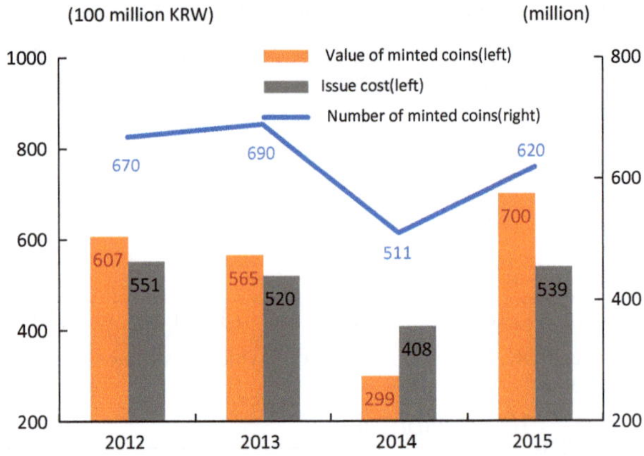

Fig. 7.4 Coins minted and their production costs. Source: BoK (2016c)

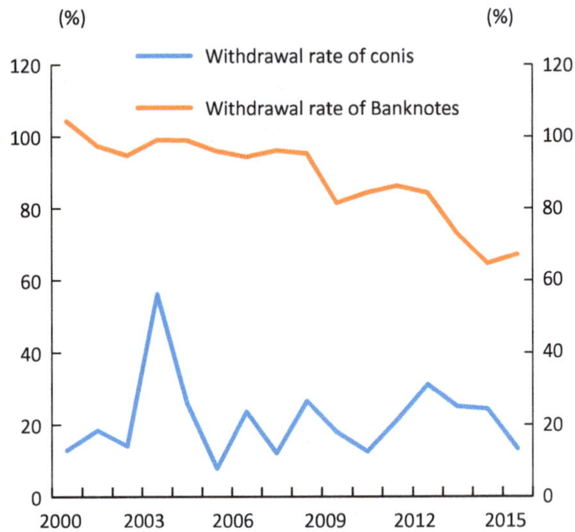

Fig. 7.5 Withdrawal rates of banknotes and coins. Source: BoK (2016c)

7.3 Expected Benefits and Costs

7.3.1 Benefits

As pointed out, the benefits for removing coins from circulation are threefold. First of all, the removal of coins allows the transactions costs to be reduced and efficiency increased. While the BoK saves on the cost of minting and administrating coins, banks and merchants can reduce their administration costs for handling coins and increase their business efficiency. In addition, consumers and households benefit from no longer having the inconvenience of carrying coins. Furthermore, the initiative to remove coins and eventually banknotes helps to contribute to the development of FinTech industries by strengthening the use of different digital instruments and promoting new settlement and payment technologies.

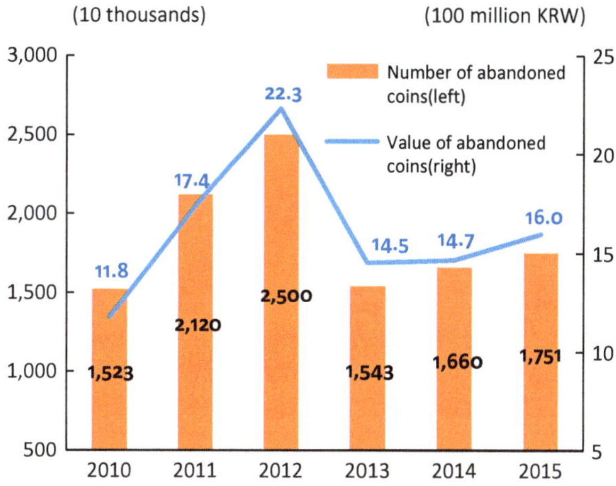

Fig. 7.6 Coins abandoned. Source: BoK (2016c)

The second advantage is associated with the fact that the initiative can be used to test the eventual feasibility of a completely cashless society. Indeed, there is a strong call to substitute cash with non-cash digital instruments in some European countries, thus paving the way for cashless societies. The cashless society, as described by Kenneth Rogoff (2014), is to phase out cash, beginning with large denomination banknotes and later extending to small bills and eventually coins as well. One of the main reasons behind this idea is to prevent anonymous transactions in cash, tax evasion and other illegal activities. Korea's coinless initiative is taking an inverse approach, and starting with the elimination of small denomination coins from circulation with the intention of then extending this to banknotes. Indeed, the anonymity of cash is a source of tax evasion and illegal activity, as Rogoff pointed out, but, at the same time, it is an important element that allows cash to be superior to other payment instruments, albeit not necessarily related to these illegal activities. So, the opposition to such an idea may well remain strong. Nevertheless, Korea's coinless initiative can overcome such opposition. Furthermore, it is important to note that all the existing cash, coins and banknotes, cannot be removed in one step. Before a complete switch-over to a completely cashless society, the experience of a coinless society could trigger a shift in consumer behaviour away from cash and towards digital payment instruments, thereby breaking the lock-in effect of cash use.

The third advantage can be found in the smooth transition to the eventual re-denomination of Korean Won. Compared to the size of Korean economy, the value of its unit of account, the "Won", is too low with USD 1 equaling KRW 1000. Thus, many Koreans think that it is the right time to start re-denomination, not only to fight deflation, but also to bring the underground economy into the open.[2] In Korea, some restaurants already write KRW 5000 (USD 5.00 roughly) as KRW 5.0

[2]Let alone its rounding effect, the denomination is expected to increase the expenditures on real goods by the people who hoarded the cashes, especially large denomination cashes, through illegal transactions or tax evasions because the latter will avoid reporting their cash hoardings to the banks which could be subject to the examination and investigation of tax authority.

on their menus. The number of zeroes should be dropped in line with the growth of the economy. Eliminating coins from circulation will help to familiarise Koreans with such practices and will support the smooth transition to the newly re-denominated unit of currency.

7.3.2 Costs

Just as a *cashless* society presents huge challenges, the transition to a *coinless* society faces more or less the same challenges. For example, coin using industries (such as vending machine companies) may be hit negatively, and certain sections of the population such as old people will not be familiar with the electronic payment instruments and services, which will make the idea of a coinless society unpopular to them. It should furthermore be noted that *any* technological advancement comes with risks and security threats. The importance of a very high degree of security to protect personal information from hackers cannot be over-emphasised. But, in so far as only a small sum of money is at stake, these hurdles are not serious and are likely to be overcome easily. Consequently, the realisation of a *coinless* society looks more probable than that of a cashless society.[3]

7.4 Methods

There are four types of initiatives to be envisaged, depending both on whether the target goal is to remove all cash or just coins, and on which sector is leading the project, the monetary authorities or the private sector, as follows (Table 7.2).

Regarding the withdrawal of cash, two approaches can be considered. The first immediate approach, called the top-down approach, is for central banks to stop issuing cash in the form of banknotes and coins, and to substitute it with non-cash payment instruments. This will automatically ensure the removal of coins and the transition to a cashless society, not to mention a coinless society. However, stopping the issuance of cash completely would not—neither economically nor politically—be a very realistic idea, except for some advanced central banks desperately seeking to enhance the effectiveness of negative interest-rate policies. The second approach, called the bottom-up approach, is to let private agents economise on their use of cash in their transactions. For instance, as some telecom or mobile payment companies offer bonus points and discount benefits, consumers

[3]It is worth noting that the goal of coinless society is not to ban the use of coins but rather to allow consumers to substitute coins with more convenient electronic or digital instruments. Just as the development of credit or debit cards has substituted for cheques, new digital instruments can compete with coins for wider use of consumers.

Table 7.2 Classification of removing cashes and coins

	Removing cash	Removing coins
Top-down approach (Central Bank's Initiative)	A Cashless Society	Issue of Digital Coin by Central Bank (or Mint)
Bottom-up approach (Private sectors' initiative)	Reduce the use of cash in transactions	A Coinless Society

are increasingly attracted to use mobile payment instruments rather than cash. As consumers become familiar with the use of diverse electronic or mobile payment instruments such as credit cards, public transportation cards and digital wallets, they will find the use of cash to be more and more inconvenient, but the complete transition to a cashless society will remain inconceivable for the near foreseeable future. One interesting idea in this regard might be to restrict cashless transactions to some parts of the population or to specific groups of people. For example, foreign tourists could receive cash cards, instead of exchanging their currencies directly into cash, and return them when they leave Korea.

Compared to the withdrawal of banknotes, the removal of coins would be politically and economically easy and the opposition of coin users would be very small. The major hurdle will, instead, be technical, because, as pointed out, there is an urgent need to develop an electronic payment system or service that could substitute for the use of coins in the giving and receiving of small change in everyday commercial transactions. That is, if, as already stated, an individual buys an item which costs KRW 9500 and pays with a KRW 10,000 banknote, he or she should own credit cards or other electronic payments which will be credited with KRW 500, instead of physically receiving a KRW 500 coin in change. Or, an individual should be equipped at least with a loyalty point card, like the airplane mileage system. In this case, small change can be converted into points and, independently of the cash transferred, the points can be debited from or credited to the individual's account. Since the points will not have any physical existence, they will also be safer against theft or loss. At any rate, the key point is to see how the cost of the transfer of information and of maintaining the related network could be sufficiently lowered.

Again, both the top-down and the bottom-up approaches can be considered. Concerning the top-down approach, the central bank (or the national mint) could be the issuer of digital coins, allowing users to store their transaction information on integrated circuit (IC) chips installed inside the digital coins, and to make payments with these. In theory, digital coins work in the same way as private credit cards do. The only difference is that they are created by the central bank. Given that every Korean has his or her own unique national identification card and number, it can be conceived even to add this type of digital coin function onto the identification card or number. This is because each account which stores transaction information that can be credited or debited corresponds to the individual's identification number.

Concerning the bottom-up approach, we can think of different electronic instruments, which correspond to the BoK's current coinless project for the replacement

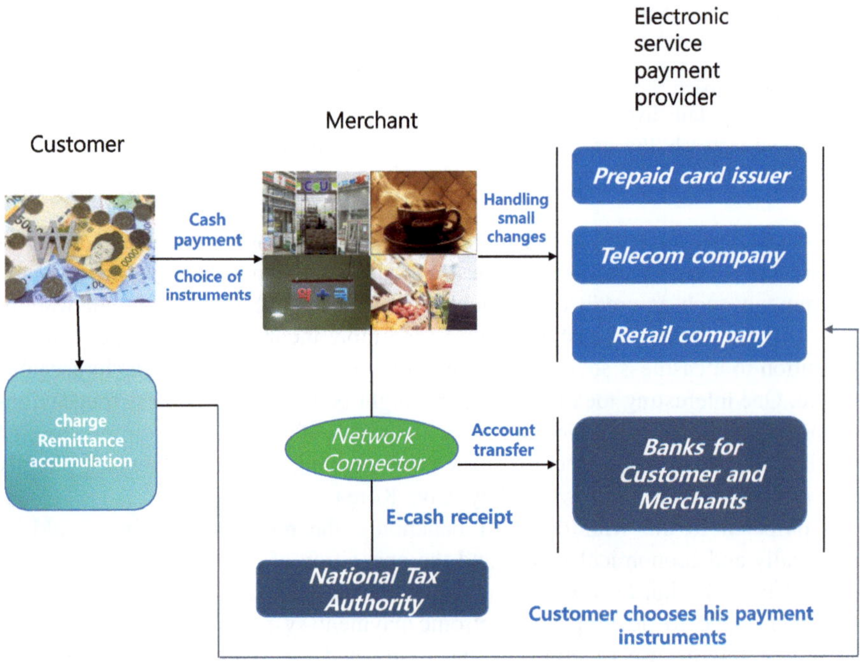

Fig. 7.7 Hypothetical coinless transaction flow chart in Korea. Source: BoK (2016c)

of coins that can be conceived in terms of technical conveniences, institutional environments and economic costs. It is especially worthwhile noting that retail businesses have a strong interest in the withdrawal of coins (but not banknotes) in their transactions because of the high transaction costs (for example, retail companies have to make coins readily available before the opening of their shops). There are already many private companies, retail or otherwise, developing penny change charge services at their own expense in Korea. To give and receive small change both to and from consumers, all different types of instruments are mobilised: prepaid cards, credit/debit cards, bank account transfers and/or digital wallets, etc. As stated, even systems in which consumers can receive their small change in loyalty points, instead of cash, are actively envisaged. Figure 7.7 shows the hypothetical coinless transaction flows under the BoK's coinless plan.

7.5 Exploring Coinless Payment Instruments and Services

Currently, the BoK is considering the following payment instruments or services in order to encourage coinless transactions.

7.5.1 Prepaid Cards

Prepaid cards were first introduced in September 1994 in Korea. They were used mainly at petrol/gas stations, department stores, convenience stores, etc. Currently, one of the most popular cards is for the payment for public transportation fares called *T-money*. T-money is a card and device for paying all public transportation services including buses, subways and also taxies, and is, in some cases, used even for transactions at convenience stores. The T-money function is often added onto various payment (credit/debit) and discount travel cards. When using T-money, the public transportation fare is KRW 100 cheaper than when paying with cash. Moreover, T-money can be charged both on-line and off-line.

Currently, the T-money provider is operating an on-line and off-line coin charging system which consists of using coins to charge for the T-money,[4] but it is faced with increasing operating costs in order to extend this system.

7.5.2 Electronic Cash Receipts

The electronic cash receipt system in Korea is a very unique system which was introduced in 2005 to increase the transparency of transactions and correct tax reporting. This system was initially conceived to thwart the rampant cash transactions that many self-employed business people, especially medical doctors and lawyers, were using in order to evade tax. According to the law, all retail and service sector businesses which earn above KRW 24 million annually are obliged to join this system. In the event that they do not join it, they have to pay 1% of their income as a penalty. In order for merchants to issue cash receipts through their issuing terminals, the customers simply give them either their credit card numbers or their mobile phone numbers together with their cash payments. Then the transaction details are transferred electronically to the National Tax Authority. Currently, the minimum value for an electronic cash receipt issuance is KRW 1 (Initially, it was KRW 5000). Also, in order to stimulate the demand for cash receipts, consumers can receive a tax refund depending on the accumulated value of the cash receipts issued. By the end of 2014, the total number of member shops was 2.8 million, and 1.43 million shops out of the total number of compulsory members, which is currently 1.45 million, had joined the system (98.8%). Currently, the issued receipts number 5.19 billion and the issued value is KRW 9.2 trillion.

The small change that is often required for every cash transaction could be accumulated in the system and returned to consumers via tax refunding. The advantage of this system is that, without any significant additional costs, it allows a network of coinless transactions to be set up.

[4]For instance, consumers can charge the T-money at subway stations and convenience stores directly or through bank ATM, Internet and mobile applications.

7.5.3 Credit/Check Cards

Credit cards were introduced as early as 1969 to increase the transparency of transactions for many self-employed merchants and to charge them the appropriate taxes as well. Credit cards are now the most widely used non-cash payment instrument in Korea, although in popularity, after credit cards, debit cards are also widely used. Consumers can use them in any place where credit cards are also accepted, since the service is provided through the credit card network. According to the specialised credit financial business law, a credit card member shop cannot refuse payment by credit cards or demand any supplementary charges for it, no matter how small the payment is. For example, a payment of 1 Won, the lowest possible amount, can be made through credit cards, despite the complaints of credit card companies about small payment transactions. However, anyone who violates this law will face up to one year in prison or a fine of 10 million Won. So, credit cards are widely used even for very small transactions. In contrast, in the USA, member shops can refuse payment by credit card for transactions of less than 10 dollars. Since May 2016, no signature has been required for transactions of less than KRW 50,000 in Korea.

Different methods and services for charging credit and check/cheque cards in return for small change or for transforming the small change into loyalty bonuses are currently under consideration. Very recently, one Korean credit card company called "*Shinhan Card*" has released the "Simple Plus Card", which offers its users a "penny off" discount benefit that dispenses with change for less than KRW 1000. A wide range of shops including restaurants, convenience stores, supermarkets, hospitals, pharmacies, coffee and bakery shops, etc., provide these benefits for transactions over KRW 20,000 and below KRW 100,000, with a monthly limit on the number of transactions to 10 times. As a result, KRW 100 unit transactions can be removed from the settlement account-balance of customers.

7.5.4 Digital Wallets

With the widespread use of mobile phones, new payment instruments and methods of payment have emerged. Although the use of mobile payments is still limited, it entered Korea in full swing and the proportion of people holding mobile payment instruments has increased dramatically. This provided the grounds for the expansion of digital wallet services. One of the most successful digital wallets is, for example, *Apple Pay*, which combines mobile phone payment with different payment functions and additional services. Currently, many banks and non-bank companies are competing with each other to provide such services and to dominate the market. Table 7.3 shows the list of major Korean companies that provide such digital wallet services along with their service features.

Table 7.3 List of digital wallet service providers in Korea

Sector	Company name	Service name	Remittance	Other functions
Telecom	KT	Moca Wallet	X	Loyalty points/coupons
	LG	Smart Wallet	X	Loyalty points/coupons
	SKT	Syrup	X	Loyalty points/coupons
Internet Platform	Kacao	Bank-wallet/Kacao-pay	O	Prepaid
	Naver	Naver-pay	O	Prepaid
Manufacturing	Samsung	Samsung-wallet/Samsung-pay	X	Coupons
Retail	Shinsege	S-Wallet	X	Gift cards/coupons
	Mobiliance	M-tic	O	Debit
Cards	Shinhan	Smart Wallet	X	Coupons
	Kookmin	Wise Wallet	X	Coupons
Banks	Hana	N-Wallet	O	Prepaid/Coupons
	Shinhan	ZOOMONEY	O	Prepaid/Coupons

Source: based upon Kim (2015)

Against this backdrop, an increasing number of companies that decided to provide coinless transaction services have emerged. For example, *Naver*, the largest Internet platform company in Korea, in collaboration with *Seven-Eleven*, a convenience store chain, has started a "penny charge" service that allows the consumers, after buying items at the convenience store, to convert the remaining pennies into *Naver* loyalty points. In the event that customers buy from *Seven-Eleven* stores with *Naver*-pay points, they can just show the clerk/cashier the barcode of the *Naver*-pay application downloaded from the *Naver* home page. Payment in *Naver* points is available in more than 8300 *Seven-Eleven* stores nationwide. *Naver*-pay can be charged up to 10,000 Won at a time, and up to a maximum of 100,000 Won. *Naver* pay points can also be utilised in more than 100,000 online stores, and in a variety of music, book and digital-content shops. *Shinsegae* (SSG), a retail company, is also implementing its own penny charge service that will allow its customers to earn SSG money, which replaces the pennies or coins that would need to be given in change after being paid with banknotes. SSG charged money can be used like cash at any of the affiliated shops of the retail company.

7.6 Task and Challenges

There are many "private sector"-led coinless initiatives and attempts under way in Korea. Thus, as consumers do not need to carry cash, given the widespread use of cards, it will be increasingly commonplace and interesting for them not to have to keep penny coins because of the use of penny charging services.

But the widespread use of these services and the full shift to a coinless society would not be possible without the active co-ordination and support of both the government and the central bank. In this regard, the key to the coinless society initiative is to provide the appropriate incentives to the disfavoured participants, in particular, to non-cash payment service providers and network providers for the time being, because they will have to bear the implementation costs of the project, such as the renewal and development of the terminal programmes. When coins are used for small change, the cost of minting the coins will be completely borne by the central bank (or the national mint). If the coins are to be removed by the efforts of private agents, then some of these agents will have to bear the costs, while the central bank will benefit unilaterally from the savings on the minting costs.

Thus, the central bank has a good rationale to support the private initiatives for a coinless society even financially in such a way as to compensate—in part or wholly—for their implementation costs within the limit of the saving in the minting costs. Concerning the financial support to the related participants, a two-tier support system may be needed.

First, to provide electronic payment service providers (such as value-added network (VAN) providers and Payment Gateway) fees for the service of transferring small change to the bank accounts of customers or for charging customers for digital payment instruments. The advantage of this support is that the replacement of coins can be achieved immediately without any additional considerations. As already pointed out with regard to electronic cash receipts, the National Tax Authority pays KRW 18.8 per transaction to the VAN providers, which will cost it KRW 60 billion annually. Similarly, the BoK could consider the provision of financial support, possibly KRW 10 per transaction and as a result KRW 30 billion annually, to these VAN providers.

Second, the BoK could extend its financial support to diverse digital payment service providers, especially if it may lead to a positive external economy. This will help to promote the use of diverse digital payment instruments and the growth of FinTech industries. But it will require time to devise the most appropriate method for the distribution of financial support to the different service providers. However, the BoK is planning to achieve a coinless society by the year 2020, and it is currently operating a working group in order to decide on the detailed procedure for implementing the coinless society initiative.

Once the problem of burden-sharing is fixed, it will not take long for coins to disappear from circulation. Indeed, the BoK hopes to stop minting coins from 2020, and, if it does so, it will also be the ideal moment to launch the re-denomination of the Korean currency.

Acknowledgements I would like to thank Lee, Jongryeol and Kim, Jung Hyeok, two members of staff at the Department of Payment and Settlements, Bank of Korea, as well as all the participants of the seminar, *Cash in East Asia*, for their helpful discussion and comments. I would also like to thank Chris Engert for his excellent language editing.

References

Bank of Korea (2016a) Payment and settlements system report 2015, August

Bank of Korea (2016b) Survey on the use of payment instruments 2016, December

Bank of Korea (2016c) Plan for a coinless society (In Korean). Department of Payment and Settlements

Beer C, Birchler UW, Gnan E (2015) Cash without future? Future without cash? A wider view. SUERF Policy Note Issue No 3

Kim C (2015) Mobile payment and settlements in Korea and abroad (In Korean). In: Paper presented at the digital banking seminar organized by the Bank of Korea

Rogoff K (2014) Costs and benefits to phasing out paper currency. Paper presented at NBER macroeconomics annual conference, April 2014

Chapter 8
The Ongoing Evolution of Payment Instruments in China: A Case Study in Financial Innovation, and on the Role of the Central Bank

Patrick Hess

Abstract Payment methods and habits are evolving over time, as a result of technological innovation and commercial development. China, where paper money was invented more than 1000 years ago, is no exception to this. This chapter looks into the ongoing evolution of payment instruments in mainland China, and the interest and role of the central bank. It finds that, in recent years, the use of non-cash payment instruments has been growing rapidly, driven by commercial, technological and regulatory developments, as well as by changing customer needs. In this dynamic environment, the People's Bank of China (PBoC) ensures an orderly development and the safety and efficiency of payment arrangements via regulations, the oversight of payment systems, instruments and service providers, as well as by providing payment infrastructure itself, such as the Internet Banking Payment System. With it, the PBoC responds not only to the rapid growth of Internet and mobile payments, but also to the increasing demand for instant payments, which is a global trend. The next technological shift might be a gradual one from electronic to digital money. In this area, the PBoC is also active, by overseeing and regulating Bitcoin and assessing digital currencies in general, including the potential issuance of a digital Yuan.

8.1 Introduction

Imagine a market in China today. You want to pay for a watermelon and the market-woman hands you a slip of paper with a Quick Response (QR) code printed on it. While you still look puzzled and ask yourself what to do with it, a user of

---

The views expressed in this chapter are solely those of the author and do not necessarily reflect those of the European Central Bank (ECB).

P. Hess (✉)
European Central Bank, Frankfurt am Main, Germany
e-mail: patrick.hess@ecb.int

F. Rövekamp et al. (eds.), *Cash in East Asia*, Financial and Monetary Policy Studies 44, DOI 10.1007/978-3-319-59846-8_8

"*Alipay*", the mobile payment arm of *Alibaba*, would do the following: he would open the scanner in his "*Alipay*" app, position his phone to read it, and, in about a second, the watermelon transaction would be settled. The QR code method is only one of the innovative ways that goods and services are paid for in China, and apps like "*Alipay*" or its competitor *WeChat wallet* allow people to transfer money, secure refunds for returned items, or receive "red envelopes", something very Chinese,[1] conveniently and swiftly. The payment apps have smart security features, and local businesses often provide discounts if you use them.[2]

Clearly, payment methods and habits are changing over time, as a result of technological innovation and commercial development. China, where paper money was invented more than 1000 years ago, is no exception to this trend. Cash, in the form of banknotes and coins, is facing increasing competition from non-cash payment instruments. The development of mobile payments in China seems to be particularly dynamic, which lends itself to a case study in financial innovation. Against this background, this chapter looks into the ongoing evolution of payment instruments in China by exploring the main drivers behind the growth of non-cash payments and discussing the respective role of the central bank.

The remainder of this chapter is organised as follows. Section 8.2 recalls the general drivers of payment methods and habits, and why central banks care about them. Section 8.3 looks at recent developments in the use of Chinese payment instruments and examines the drivers and the issues of the growth of non-cash payments, as well as the supporting payment infrastructure provided by the central bank. Section 8.4 briefly puts China's instant payments infrastructure into an international perspective, and Sect. 8.5 concludes with an outlook for the future.

8.2 The Drivers of Payment Methods and Habits, and Why Central Banks Care

Why are payment methods and habits changing? Generally speaking, there are three main factors that drive them: commercial development, technological innovation, and regulation.

Almost all commercial transactions involve some form of payment, and hence commercial development influences the way in which payments are made. More specifically, it leads to changing business and customer needs and expectations that payment instruments have to fulfil, for example, in terms of safety, convenience, speed and price. A good example of this is the development of e-commerce, or mobile commerce in its wireless form, over the last three decades, which has

[1]Red envelopes (*hongbao* 红包) are monetary gifts on occasions such as New Year, weddings or births.

[2]See, for example, Jessica Dolcourt, "China takes mobile payments to a whole new level", 22 April 2016 (available at http://www.cnet.com/news/china-takes-mobile-payments-to-a-whole-new-level).

created the need and expectation that payment instruments are no longer constrained by time and space, and has led to the emergence of Internet and mobile payments.

For these commercial and payment developments to happen, technological innovation is an important pre-requisite and facilitator. In the context of money as a medium of exchange and a store of value,[3] such innovation refers to the technologies underlying the secure transfer and durable storage of money. In this respect, three major innovations or technological shifts can be observed: the first was the paradigm shift from hard money to paper money, which started around 960 AD in Song Dynasty China and spread to the rest of the world a couple of centuries later. The second was the shift from paper money to electronic money, which started roughly half a century ago with the invention of the credit card[4] and electronic payments allowing direct debits and credits. The third is an ongoing trend, which could potentially result in a gradual shift from electronic money to digital money. It draws on technological advances from a range of areas including cryptography, game theory, and peer-to-peer networking. The key innovation of digital currencies is their typical use of a "distributed ledger", which no longer requires a central authority[5] as in the case of the issuer of the three previous types of monies. If the shift to digital money were actually to happen in the long run, it might, therefore, also impact upon the role of the central bank.

Regulation can also create conditions that induce change in payment methods and habits. An example of this can be found in the revised Payment Services Directive (PSD2) currently being implemented in Europe, which gives third-party payment providers access to payment accounts and may lead to an increased use of Internet payments.[6] Another example of regulation as a driver of payments behaviour is the plan of the Bank of Korea to create a coinless society in South Korea by the year 2020. (see chapter by Woosik Moon in this volume).

Why do changes in payment methods and habits matter for central banks? There are four main reasons why central banks care. First, central banks issue and provide

[3]For the definition and different roles of money see Michael McLeay, Amar Radia and Ryland Thomas, "Money in the Modern Economy: An Introduction", Bank of England, *Quarterly Bulletin*, 2014 Q1.

[4]The first credit card outside the US, where it was invented, was launched in 1966 in the UK. It took another 20 years before it arrived in China, where the first credit card was introduced in June 1986.

[5]For details, see Robleh Ali, John Barrdear, Roger Clews and James Southgate, "Innovations in Payment Technologies and the Emergence of Digital Currencies", Bank of England, *Quarterly Bulletin*, 2014 Q3.

[6]Directive (EU) 2015/2366 of the European Parliament and of the Council of 25 November 2015 on payment services in the internal market, Official Journal of 23.12.2015, L 337/35. For the original Payment Services Directive (PSD) and the larger regulatory initiative, of which it is part, *i.e.*, the Single Euro Payments Area (SEPA), see Ruth Wandhöfer, *EU Payments Integration: The Tale of SEPA, PSD and Other Milestones Along the Road*, (Basingstoke: Palgrave Macmillan, 2010); and European Central Bank, "The Integration of the Euro Retail Payments Market – SEPA and Beyond", *Financial Integration in Europe*, April 2013.

the economy with cash in the form of banknotes and coins, and earn seigniorage[7] revenue from this activity. Second, the smooth functioning of the payment system is a core task of central banks, which they ensure by overseeing payment, clearing, and settlement arrangements within their jurisdiction, and by providing own payment and settlement infrastructure in many cases.[8] Historically, the first two reasons have even been at the very origin of central banks, as Tommaso Padoa-Schioppa (former Executive Board member of the ECB) pointed out:

> Central banks originate from two fundamental changes in monetary systems over the past two hundred years. The first was, at the turn of the nineteenth century, the replacement of commodity currencies with paper currency. The second change was, about a century later, the development of commercial bank money (or bank deposits), which largely replaced notes and coins as a means of payment and store of value. To ensure the efficiency and safety of paper currency systems, most countries gradually entrusted one bank—which became the central bank—with the exclusive task of issuing banknotes. [. . .] These two changes were innovations in the *payment* practices. However, they have been decisive in shaping the other two central banking functions that gradually developed over the last century, namely the *supervision* of banks, and later, the conduct of *monetary policy*.[9]

Third, central banks have a keen interest in the safe and efficient use of the currency in payment transactions because it forms the basis of public confidence in the currency and is a pre-requisite for the transmission of monetary policy. Fourth, as a pre-condition for the smooth functioning of the economy, safe and efficient payment mechanisms are also crucial for economic growth, which is a public policy objective of many central banks.

8.3 Recent Developments in the Use of Chinese Payment Instruments

8.3.1 The Development of Cash and Non-cash Payment Instruments

How has the use of payment instruments in China developed in recent years? Figure 8.1 shows that, since 2011, cash usage has been in steady decline, while card payments, Internet payments and mobile payments (the latter albeit from a low base) have been growing rapidly. The chart is taken from a study conducted in 2014

---

[7] *Seigniorage* refers to the profit made by issuing currency, especially the difference between the face value of coins and notes and their production and distribution costs.

[8] See Tom Kokkola (ed), *The Payment System: Payments, Securities and Derivatives, and the Role of the Eurosystem*, (Frankfurt aM: European Central Bank, 2010), Chapter 7, for more details on the role of central banks as oversight authority, operator and catalyst in the field of payment, clearing and settlement.

[9] Tommaso Padoa-Schioppa, *The Euro and its Central Bank: Getting United after the Union*, (Cambridge MA: The MIT Press, 2004), p. 22.

Fig. 8.1 Growth of payment instruments in China. Source: Zhang (2014, p. 3). Note: The chart refers to payment "volume", but shows the value of transactions and not, as volume is normally defined and also used in this paper, the number of transactions

by the consultancy firm *Celent*. Comprehensive and reliable Chinese payment data are scarce, but the data published by the People's Bank of China (PBoC) broadly confirm the *Celent* estimate for 2014. According to the PBoC's *China Payment System Development Report 2014*, mobile and Internet payments grew in 2014 by 170% and 21% year-on-year respectively in terms of volume, and by 134% and 30% in terms of value.[10] In 2015 and 2016, however, the growth of mobile payments was even more dynamic than Fig. 8.1 suggests. Based upon quarterly statistics available on the Chinese website of the PBoC, mobile payments grew by 206% and 379% year-on-year in 2015 in terms of volume and value respectively, which is equivalent to a twofold and almost fourfold (!) increase in only 12 months.[11] In the first half of 2016, the volume growth of mobile payments continued further before slowing a bit, amounting to 308% and 168% quarter-on-quarter in Q1 and Q2 respectively.[12]

8.3.2 *Drivers Behind the Continued Growth of Non-cash Payments*

What has caused the rapid growth of non-cash payments in the form of card, Internet and, in particular, mobile payments? Ouyang Weimin, a former Director General of the Payment and Settlement Department of the PBoC, concluded as

[10]Zhongguo Renmin Yinhang Zhifu Jiesuan Si 中国人民银行支付结算司 – Payment and Settlement Department of the People's Bank of China, *Zhongguo zhifu tixi fazhan baogao 2014* 中国支付体系发 展报告 – China Payment System Development Report 2014, November 2015, p. 149.

[11]Zhongguo Renmin Yinhang Zhifu Jiesuan Si 中国人民银行支付结算司, "2015 nian zhifu tixi yunxing zongti qingkuang", 2015年支付体系运行总体情况, April 2016, p. 5.

[12]Zhongguo Renmin Yinhang Zhifu Jiesuan Si 中国人民银行支付结算司, "2016 nian diyi jidu zhifu tixi yunxing zongti qingkuang" 2016年第一季度支付体系运行总体情况, June 2016, p. 4, and "2016 nian di'er jidu zhifu tixi yunxing zongti qingkuang", 2016年第二季度支付体系运行总体情况, September 2016, p. 4.

Table 8.1 Comparison between Chinese cash and non-cash transactions (billion Yuan)

	1978	1988	1998	2008
Total value of cash transactions	175.25	734.28	2913.09	8223.37
Total value of non-cash transactions	4.01	321.05	2033.57	1,071,750.00
non-cash transactions/cash transactions	0.02	0.44	0.70	130.33

Source: Extract from Ouyang Weimin (2010, p. 36, Table 1) (own translation)

early as 2010 that "overall, the payment system of our country has already entered the age of non-cash payments". He compared cash with non-cash transactions over the last three decades and observed that "the total value of non-cash transactions amounted to 130.33 times that of cash transactions in 2008, while this ratio only stood at 0.02 in 1978" (see Table 8.1).[13] In other words, while 30 years ago, non-cash payments were just a tiny fraction of payments made by cash, they now dwarf cash transactions, and this trend continues. In 2014, the total value of non-cash transactions including bills,[14] bankcards and remittances[15] amounted to 1798.61 trillion Yuan (+11.88% y-o-y) according to the PBoC.[16]

There are several drivers behind the continued growth of non-cash payments in China, which are also, as discussed in Sect. 8.2, of a regulatory, technological, behavioural and commercial nature. First, the Chinese authorities have taken regulatory steps to accelerate the deployment of point-of-sale (PoS) equipment to merchants and to open the domestic bankcard market to competition, which have increased the volumes of bankcard payments.[17] The central bank also supports the settlement of non-cash payments by providing different payment systems (see Sect. 8.3.3). In addition, implementing guidance from the State Council and the Central Committee of the Chinese Communist Party (CCP), the PBoC has issued *Guiding Opinions* on improving rural payment services aiming at expanding financial inclusion, and taken concrete measures, such as carrying out mobile payment pilot projects, to promote the use of non-cash payment instruments in rural areas.[18]

Second, from a product and technological perspective, payments are no longer just money transfers, but are increasingly embedded into and combined with social media such as *Tencent*'s *WeChat* (*Weixin* 微信), e-malls such as *Taobao* or money market funds such as *Yu'e Bao* (both *Alibaba*). Payments are packaged with service

[13]Ouyang Weimin 欧阳卫民, *Xiandai zhifu lun* 现代支付论 (Study on Modern Payments), January 2010.

[14]The *bill* category includes bank drafts, commercial drafts, promissory notes, letters of credit and cheques (*zhipiao* 支票). The latter are the most widely used bills in China, making up more than 90% of all bill transactions in terms of volume and value. Cheque volumes are declining (−29.1% in 2015), while those of commercial drafts (*shangye huipiao* 商业汇票) are growing (+3.45% in 2015).

[15]*Remittances* refer to money transfers. They are predominantly initiated via Internet, as well as via fixed-line and mobile phones.

[16]Zhongguo Renmin Yinhang Zhifu Jiesuan Si (2015b, p. 210, Appendix 2).

[17]Capgemini and Royal Bank of Scotland, *World Payments Report 2015*, p. 9.

[18]Zhongguo Renmin Yinhang Zhifu Jiesuan Si (2015b, pp. 137, 154 and 156).

"scenarios" such as ordering a taxi or booking a train, and thus become "scenario-based financial services" (*changjinghua jinrong* 场景化金融), which the *Celent* analyst, Zhang Hua, sees as the future of financial services.[19] Examples include the payment capabilities of instant messaging tools such as *WeChat* and *Alibaba*'s *Laiwang* and *Aliwangwang*, or the automatic transfer of any "leftover" (*yu'e*) balance on an *Alibaba* e-commerce account to its money market funds "Leftover Treasure" (*Yu'e Bao* 余额宝), the name of which is derived from the mechanism to achieve investment returns for the client.[20]

Third, in terms of customer behaviour, on the one hand, online banking usage increases due to a wider Internet penetration, while, on the other, a rising penetration of mobile phones, especially in smaller towns and cities, results in increased mobile payments. As a result of low-cost smartphones created by manufacturers such as *Xiaomi* and *Meizu*, both the smartphone penetration and the willingness of consumers to pay by smartphone are considerably higher in China than, for example, in the US.

And fourth, the rapid growth of e-commerce and especially mobile e-commerce, fuelled by a fierce battle between the three Chinese Internet giants *Alibaba*, *Tencent* and *Baidu* for the end-customer, has brought about the fast growth of Internet and mobile payments and continues to do so. An infographic by the Berlin-based Mercator Institute for China Studies (MERICS) has compared the Internet rivals with the Three Kingdoms, the famous trio of warring Chinese states (220–280) after the demise of the Han Dynasty.[21] While this competition, together with the financial innovation that it spurs,[22] is the most important driver behind the growth of non-cash payments, additional volume is generated by banks and other service providers expanding into scenario-based financial services.

To understand the dynamics of the Chinese e-commerce market and the payments volume which it generates, it is worthwhile looking at *Alibaba* as an example. Founded in December 1998 by Jack Ma and others in Hangzhou, where the group is still headquartered today, *Alibaba* was the biggest US initial public offering in history, raising 21.8 billion USD, when it was listed on the New York Stock Exchange (NYSE) in September 2014. Starting as an online shopping platform, *Alibaba* expanded over the years into a plethora of other businesses and created many financial innovations along the way.

---

[19]See Zhang Hua, "Changjinghua jinrong: Xiayidai qudao" 场景化金融: 下一代渠道 (Scenario-based financial services: The next generation of channels), April 2016.

[20]See Usman W. Chohan, "Financial Innovation in China: Alibaba's Leftover Treasure", 20 March 2014.

[21]See the infographic under http://www.merics.org/merics-analysen/infografikchina-mapping/wie- chinas-internetgiganten-sich-bekriegen.html (only available in German).

[22]Examples include crowdfunding and peer-to-peer lending. For the latter, see Ferdinand Schaff, "Bringing Finance to the Masses: How Online Peer-To-Peer Lending is Transforming China's Financial Landscape", *Merics Web Special*, 26 March 2015.

Today, the *Alibaba* group comprises, among others, the following companies and associated entities, many of which are indeed "FinTechs" (innovative financial technology firms):

- The online retail platforms *Alibaba* 阿里巴巴, *Taobao* 淘宝 and *Tmall* (*Tianmao* 天猫);
- The above-mentioned payment platform "*Alipay*" (*Zhifu Bao* 支付宝), which charges no transaction fees;
- The money market funds *Yu'e Bao* (see above);
- The online pharmacy and medical services platform *Ali Health* (*Ali Jiankang* 阿里健康);
- The peer-to-peer (P2P) lending platform *Zhao Cai Bao* 招财宝;
- The online micro-loan provider *Ant Micro* (*Mayi Xiaodai* 蚂蚁小贷).
- The social media *Laiwang*[23] 来往 and *Aliwangwang* 阿里旺旺;
- The cloud computing service platform *Alibaba Cloud* (*Aliyun* 阿里云).

Taken together, the *Alibaba* universe generates a huge amount of non-cash payments traffic, especially, and increasingly, mobile payment traffic. On "*Alipay*" for example, payments through mobile phones accounted for 54% of all "*Alipay*" transactions in the first 10 months of 2014, compared to 22% in 2013.[24] This is not surprising if one considers that in October 2016 "*Alipay*" had 400 million registered users in China and its mobile application "*Alipay*" *9.0* (formerly "*Alipay*" *Wallet*) had 270 million active users, generating 175 million transactions per day.[25]

A typical online shopping scenario looks like this: You order goods on the Internet and they are delivered to you *via* an express service (*kuaidi* 快递), the use of which is recently also exploding. After checking the goods—in China, it is common to pay only after receipt—you scan the QR code provided by the deliverer with your smartphone, and pay for the goods *via* your payment app "*Alipay*" or Tencent's *Tenpay* (*Caifu Tong* 财付通).

8.3.3 Issues Connected with the Rapid Growth of Non-cash Payments

To maintain the public's confidence in the currency, the PBoC not only has to make sure that noteholders remain confident in the banknotes that it issues, i.e., their integrity, availability and resilience against the threat of counterfeiting, it also needs to ensure the safety, reliability and availability of non-cash payment instruments, schemes and systems. This is the role of the payment systems oversight

[23]Since October 2013, until then *Alibaba* had used *Tencent*'s instant messaging tool *WeChat*.

[24]Melanie Lee, "Alipay Report Shows Mobile Commerce Booming in China", 8 December 2014.

[25]See Alibaba statistics, October 2016 (available at: http://expandedramblings.com/index.php/alipay-statistics).

function of a central bank,[26] which, in the case of the PBoC, is performed by its Payment and Settlement Department. Payment and settlement rules are issued jointly by the central bank and the China Banking Regulatory Commission.[27] The overarching objective for the PBoC in overseeing payment arrangements is to ensure their safety and efficiency. This is done *via* regularly assessing the risks of the payment arrangements, in particular, credit, liquidity and operational risk, as well as systemic risk, and by taking corrective measures when necessary. The following extract from a publication on the webpages of the PBoC's Payment and Settlement Department well reflects its oversight considerations and the challenge of combining safety and efficiency in the digital age:

> In the internet era, everyone expects greater efficiency, but safety considerations are also increasing. How to manage the relation between the two is a difficult question that no payment service provider can avoid, and it is particularly important as far as internet payments are concerned. If you emphasize safety, you have to sacrifice on efficiency, and vice versa. While payment service providers have to do everything to find the right balance between the two, they must also pay special attention to setting up mechanisms for managing and mitigating risks. Emphasizing safety does not mean that no single loss can occur, or no single risk can be borne. But what is crucial is the ability to manage the involved risks, in particular the liquidity, IT and credit risk for the customer.[28]

Rapid developments often risk being disorderly, especially in China. The main issues arising for the PBoC from the recent rapid growth of non-cash payments and the corresponding proliferation of payment providers, the so-called "payment institutions" (PIs), are as follows:

- Applicable rules and procedures not observed by PIs, such as:
  - Settlement accounts opened or closed without PBoC approval;
  - Insufficient know-your-customer (KYC) procedures;
  - Risk management practices of PIs not sound enough.
- Transaction information reporting by PIs not complete and exact;
- Customer information not kept safe and confidential by PIs;
- Commercial banks refusing to honour bills presented by customers;
- Commercial banks booking incorrect value dates for customers to gain benefit;
- Fraud (for example, card fraud), money laundering and other criminal activities.

To address these issues, the PBoC is using a number of regulatory tools such as off-site and on-site supervision of PIs, penalties, public criticism and moral suasion.

---

[26]See Kokkola, note 8 above, pp. 160–164, for the central bank as oversight authority and for the distinction between prudential supervision and payment systems oversight.

[27]See Bank for International Settlements (BIS), Committee on Payment and Settlement Systems (CPSS), *Payment, Clearing and Settlement Systems in the CPSS Countries*, Vol. 2, November 2012, pp. 31-34, for the institutional framework in China, and Patrick Hess, "Securities Clearing and Settlement in China – Markets, Infrastructures and Policy-Making", *ECB Occasional Paper Series*, No. 116, July 2010, pp. 21-22 for the role of the PBoC as operator, overseer and catalyst.

[28]Zhongguo Renmin Yinhang Zhifu Jiesuan Si (2015a) 中国人民银行支付结算司 (Payment and Settlement Department of the People's Bank of China), Hulianwang shidai de zhifu biange 互联网时代的支付变革 (The evolution of payments in the internet era), 23 April 2015 (own translation).

In addition, in order to control the risks involved and to prevent illegal practices, it started, in 2011, to license all existing and new PIs, from big providers like "*Alipay*" to the small issuers of pre-paid cards. In February 2013, the PBoC also undertook a reform of the pricing policy for bankcard transactions with the aim of reducing merchant fees and of increasing the use of card payments, thereby fostering consumption.

8.3.4 Central Bank Infrastructure to Support Non-cash Payments

The PBoC ensures the smooth functioning of the payment system not only by acting as a regulator and overseer, but also by providing core financial market infrastructure. Taken together, it operates five domestic interbank payment systems for the settlement of different types of non-cash payments, which, in the following citation from the PBoC's *China Payment System Development Report 2014*, are large-value payments, retail payments, Internet payments, cheque payments and payments in foreign currency respectively:

> The High-Value Payment System (HVPS), the Bulk Electronic Payment System (BEPS), the Internet Banking Payment System (IBPS), the Cheque Image System (CIS) and the China Domestic Foreign Currency Payment System (CDFCPS) developed and operated by the PBoC played a key role in facilitating the circulation of financial resources and supporting the economic and financial development.[29]

If one compares these five payment systems, it is not surprising that HVPS, which processes large-value interbank payments, displays the highest transaction value, and IBPS, which handles interbank retail payments initiated from Internet banking, mobile banking and telephone banking, shows the highest transaction volume. In 2015, HVPS processed transactions worth 2952.06 trillion Yuan (+25.79% y-o-y), with a daily average value of 11.86 trillion Yuan, and IBPS processed 2.96 billion transactions (+80.48% compared with 1.64 billion transactions in 2014), with a daily average of 8.19 million transactions.[30] In the light of the above-mentioned rapid growth of Internet payments, it is not surprising, either, that IBPS is the fastest growing system of the five, both in terms of volume and value (Fig. 8.2).

IBPS, which went live in 2010 and was rolled out nationwide in 2011, is also relevant from a financial innovation perspective, as it operates on a 24/7/365 basis and is able to process so-called instant (or immediate) payments in real-time. The

---

[29]Zhongguo Renmin Yinhang Zhifu Jiesuan Si (2015b, p. 5). See BIS, CPSS, *Payment, Clearing and Settlement Systems in the CPSS Countries*, Volume 2, November 2012, pp. 42-50 for a detailed description of the systems mentioned in the quotation.

[30]Zhongguo Renmin Yinhang Zhifu Jiesuan Si (2016b, p. 6).

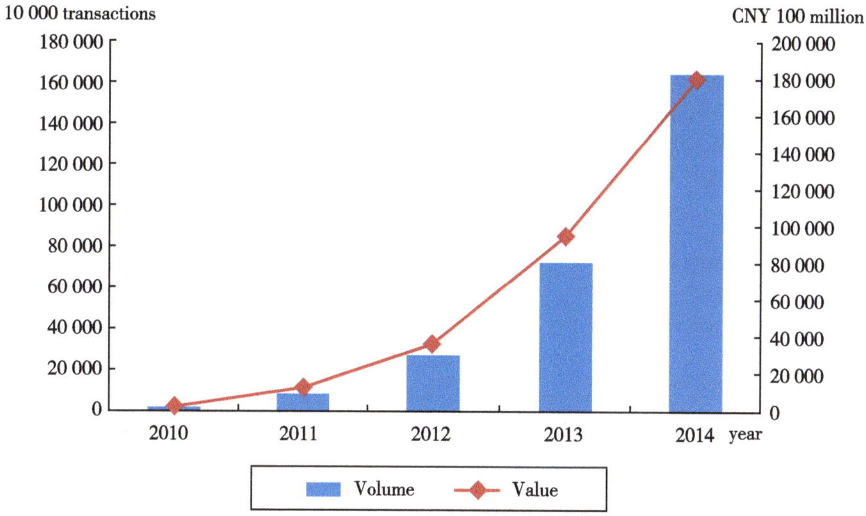

Fig. 8.2 Growth of Transaction Volume and Value of IBPS during 2010–2014. Source: Zhongguo Renmin Yinhang Zhifu Jiesuan Si (2015b, p. 167)

emergence of innovative solutions for instant payments is an increasingly global trend as the next section shows.

8.4 China's Instant Payments Infrastructure in International Comparison

IBPS is an "instant payments solution", which is commonly defined as an electronic retail payment solution, which is available 24/7/365 and results in the immediate crediting of the payee's account with confirmation to the payer (within seconds of payment initiation), irrespective of the underlying payment instrument used (credit transfer, direct debit or payment card).[31] Table 8.2 and Fig. 8.3 show how IBPS compares with other instant payments solutions in Asia and Europe and elsewhere on the globe. While China embarked relatively late on instant payments, it has rather quickly reached very high figures, at least in absolute terms. In 2015, the average daily turnover of IBPS was second only to South Korea.

And the PBoC is not alone in enabling instant payments. In many countries, such as Japan, Denmark, Poland and the UK, for example, the central bank payment system is supporting the instant payment service. In some mature economies such as Australia, the US and the Euro area, instant payment projects are under way or currently being initiated (Fig. 8.3).

[31] Heike Mai, "Instant Revolution of Payments? The Quest for Real-time Payments", *Current Issues – Global Financial Markets*, Deutsche Bank Research, 9 December 2015, p. 2.

Table 8.2 IBPS in comparison with other instant payments solutions

Instant payments solution	Country	Start of operation	Average daily number of transactions
Interbank Home/Firm Banking Network (HOFINET)	Korea	2001	10 million
Internet Banking Payment System (IBPS)	China	2010	8.2 million
Zengin System	Japan	1973	5.6 million
UK Faster Payments	UK	2008	2.9 million
Swiss Interbank Clearing (SIC)	Switzerland	1987	1.8 million
Intermediate Payment System (IMPS)	India	2010	160,000
Payments in Real Time (BIR)	Sweden	2012	8200
Express Elixir	Poland	2012	4100
Straksclearing	Denmark	2014	NA

Sources: FIS, "Flavours of fast: A trip around the world in immediate payments", May 2015, and KIR website for Express Elixir, https://www.kir.pl/en/about-us/o-firmie/about-kir-sa (accessed on 30 August 2016)

8.5 Conclusion and Outlook

The ongoing evolution of payment instruments in China, where state-issued banknotes were invented more than a millennium ago, illustrates that innovation in payment technologies is inevitable. Although Chinese consumers, like consumers elsewhere, tend to use cash for an increasingly smaller proportion of the payments they make, cash is nonetheless unlikely to disappear, and, like other central banks, the PBoC will continue to invest in banknote technology and supply. The use of non-cash payment instruments is, however, growing rapidly in China, driven by commercial, technological and regulatory developments as well as by changing customer expectations and needs. Customers expect the same level of availability, speed and reliability from payments as they are used to from other digital services, and they are no longer willing to pay high prices for payment transactions. Service providers such as *Alibaba* and *Tencent* have realised this and offer their clients a seamless universe with a maximum level of comfort, which includes payment services (often offered free of charge as in the case of "*Alipay*") and other financial services. In this dynamic environment, the PBoC tries to ensure an orderly and healthy development *via* regulations and the oversight of payment services and providers. And the central bank provides supporting non-cash payments infrastructure such as notably its Internet Banking Payment System. With it, the PBoC responds to the rapid growth of Internet and mobile payments, and to an increasing demand for instant payments, which is not specific to China, as the global comparison shows.

The last in a series of technological shifts with regard to money is the potential gradual shift from electronic to digital money, and, also in this field, the central bank is actively following the latest developments. The PBoC regulates and

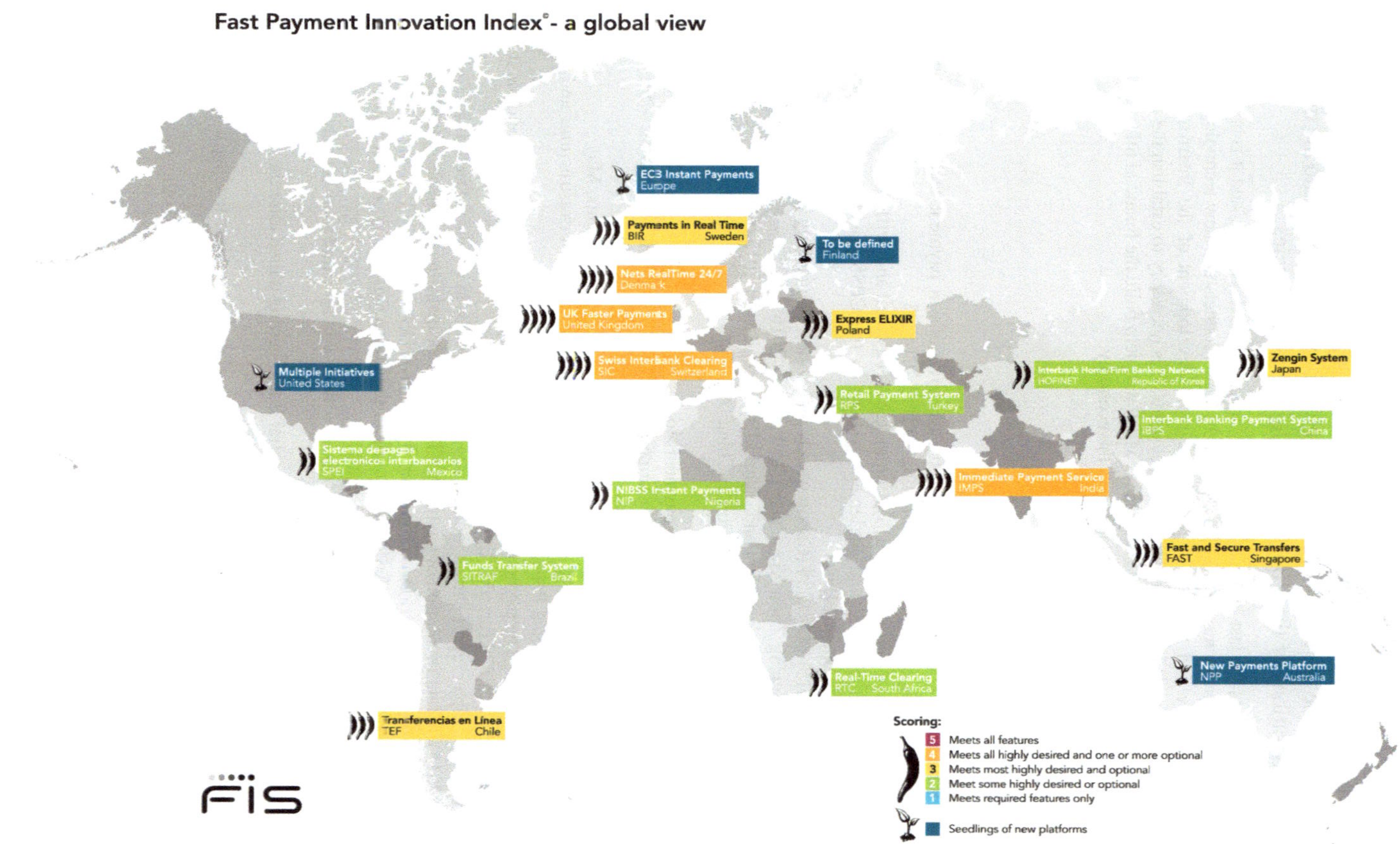

Fig. 8.3 Global trend towards enabling instant payments. Source: FIS, Flavours of Fast (2015, pp. 54–55)

oversees Bitcoin, which is quite popular in China, and has been assessing digital currencies in general for a long time, including the potential issuance of a digital Yuan. In an interview with the weekly *Caixin* in February 2016, Governor Zhou Xiaochuan made the following remark, which provides insights into the motivation and considerations of the PBoC in studying digital currencies:

> Paper money, as the last generation currency, lacks high-tech support, and it is an irresistible trend that paper money will be replaced by new products and new technologies with greater security and lower costs. With the rapid development of the Internet and the significant changes in the global payment systems, it is necessary to establish the issuance and circulation system of digital currency, which will help build the financial infrastructure and improve the quality and efficiency of the economy.[32]

References

Ali R, Barrdear J, Clews R, Southgate J (2014) Innovations in payment technologies and the emergence of digital currencies. Bank Engl Q Bull 2014:Q3

Bank for International Settlements (BIS), Committee on Payment and Settlement Systems (CPSS) (2012) Payment clearing and settlement systems in the CPSS countries, vol 2. Bank for International Settlements, Basel

Caixin Zhoukan (2016) 财新周刊 (Caixin weekly magazine), "Zhuanfang Zhou Xiaochuan" 专访周小川 (Interviewing Zhou Xiaochuan), 15 February 2016

Capgemini and Royal Bank of Scotland, World Payments Report 2015, p. 9

Chohan UW (2014) Financial innovation in China: Alibaba's leftover treasure – 余额宝, 20 Mar 2014

Dolcourt J (2016) China takes mobile payments to a whole new level, 22 Apr 2016

European Central Bank (2013) The integration of the euro retail payments market – SEPA and beyond. Financ Integr Eur, April 2013, 115–128

FIS (2015) Flavours of fast: a trip around the world in immediate payments, May

Hess P (2010) Securities clearing and settlement in China – markets, infrastructures and policy-making. ECB Occasional Paper Series, No 116, July 2010

Kokkola T (ed) (2010) The payment system: payments, securities and derivatives, and the role of the eurosystem. Frankfurt aM, European Central Bank

Lee M (2014) Alipay report shows mobile commerce booming in China, 8 Dec 2014

Mai H (2015) Instant revolution of payments? The quest for real-time payments. Current Issues – Global Financial Markets, Deutsche Bank Research, 9 Dec 2015

McLeay M, Radia A, Thomas R (2014) Money in the modern economy: an introduction. Bank Engl Q Bull

Ouyang W (2010) 欧阳卫民, *Xiandai zhifu lun* 现代支付论 (Study on modern payments). Zhongguo Chang'an chubanshe, Beijing

Padoa-Schioppa T (2004) The euro and its Central Bank: getting united after the Union. The MIT Press, Cambridge

Schaff F (2015) Bringing finance to the masses: how online peer-to-peer lending is transforming China's financial landscape, Merics Web Special, 26 Mar 2015

Wandhöfer R (2010) EU payments integration: the tale of SEPA, PSD and other milestones along the road. Palgrave Macmillan, Basingstoke

[32]Caixin Zhoukan, 财新周刊 (Caixin weekly magazine), "Zhuanfang Zhou Xiaochuan", 专访周小川 (Zhou Xiaochuan interview), 15 February 2016.

Zhang H (2014) China's retail payments market: mobile payments and a developing payments ecosystem, Celent research paper, May 2014
Zhang H (2016) Changjinghua jinrong: Xiayidai qudao" 场景化金融: 下一代渠道 (Scenario-based financial services: the next generation of channels), April 2016
Zhongguo Renmin Yinhang Zhifu Jiesuan Si (2015a) 中国人民银行支付结算司 (Payment and Settlement Department of the People's Bank of China), "Hulianwang shidai de zhifu biange", 互联网时代的支付变革 (The Evolution of Payments in the Internet era), 23 Apr 2015 (own translation)
Zhongguo Renmin Yinhang Zhifu Jiesuan Si (2015b) 中国人民银行支付结算司 – Payment and Settlement Department of the People's Bank of China, Zhongguo zhifu tixi fazhan baogao 2014 中国支付体系发展报告 – China Payment System Development Report 2014, November 2015, p. 149
Zhongguo Renmin Yinhang Zhifu Jiesuan Si (2016a) 中国人民银行支付结算司, "2015 nian zhifu tixi yunxing zongti qingkuang", 2015年支付体系运行总体情况 (Overall situation of payment system operations in 2015), April 2016, p 5
Zhongguo Renmin Yinhang Zhifu Jiesuan Si (2016b) 中国人民银行支付结算司, "2016 nian diyi jidu zhifu tixi yunxing zongti qingkuang", 2016年第一季度支付体系运行总体情况 (Overall situation of payment system operations in the first quarter of 2016), June 2016, p 4
Zhongguo Renmin Yinhang Zhifu Jiesuan Si (2016c) 中国人民银行支付结算司, "2016 nian di'er jidu zhifu tixi yunxing zongti qingkuang", 2016年第二季度支付体系运行总体情况 (Overall situation of payment system operations in the second quarter of 2016), September 2016, p 4

Chapter 9
The Use of Cash in Germany: Status and Outlook

Erwin Gladisch

Abstract Due to the rising reluctance towards cash because of its inferred connection to criminal activity, a thorough examination of why cash is still the preferred payment option in Germany becomes mandatory. As a result of financial and political uncertainty, cash is still highly demanded as a means of payment, as well as a store of value, although it only plays a minor role regarding transactions involving larger payment amounts.

However, external effects, such as the cohort effect, still need to be reviewed. It is not clear whether the younger generations will use cash as frequently as the older generations.

A substantial argument for abolishing cash seems to be its high costs, but there is no evidence that other payment options are significantly less expensive. Moreover, the high circulation of higher banknotes in other countries creates doubts that an issuance stop of the 500 € banknote will lead to a significant decline in illegal activities. In addition, cashless payment options are also used for tax evasion or the financing of terrorism. Cash allows for data protection and operates as a back-up solution if cashless systems fail.

Lastly, it is of huge importance to analyse the advantages of cash as performed in this chapter before making imprudent assumptions about the declining influence of cash.

9.1 Introduction

Representatives of politics, academia and the finance industry are currently engaged in a "War on Cash". This alliance argues that cash is technologically outdated, and that limiting its use would lead to more efficient payment transactions. Moreover, according to some cash sceptics, reducing the availability of

---

All views expressed are those of the author and do not necessarily reflect the position of the Deutsche Bundesbank.

E. Gladisch (✉)
Deutsche Bundesbank, Frankfurt am Main, Germany
e-mail: erwin.gladisch@bundesbank.de

F. Rövekamp et al. (eds.), *Cash in East Asia*, Financial and Monetary Policy Studies 44, DOI 10.1007/978-3-319-59846-8_9

cash would help to reduce tax evasion, crime and terrorism. Cash users, however, are unimpressed by these arguments against cash, and continue to use it as a means of payment and as a store of value. After all, in the eyes of its users, cash is easy, quick and safe to use—and it is safe central bank money that, by definition, is not subject to a default risk.

The following chapter expresses some views on this currently ongoing debate. It begins with some background information on the demand for cash in Germany, likewise covering selected studies on payment behaviour. Next, the costs of retail payment instruments, with a particular focus on cash, are discussed. The chapter continues by offering views on the current debate about the introduction of caps on cash payments, as well as the ECB decision to stop the issuance of the 500 € banknote around the end of 2018. At the end, an answer to the question of whether cash has a future in Germany is attempted.

9.2 Motives for the Demand for Cash

The number of euro banknotes and coins issued by the Eurosystem has been rising continuously since 2002 with positive, yet narrowing, annual growth rates above the rate of inflation. Cash demand has risen from 234 billion euro at the end of January 2002, to 1153 billion euro at the end of 2016. Of the total volume of euro banknotes in circulation, which amounts to 1126 billion euro, more than 592 billion euro, i.e., just over the half, was issued by the *Bundesbank*. Estimates suggest that around 70% of the banknotes issued by the *Bundesbank* have migrated abroad to other euro-area countries or to countries outside the euro-area. It is estimated that consumers in Germany hoard 25% of the issued banknotes and only use around 5–10% for transaction purposes. Hence, at most, 10% of the total value of the banknotes issued by the *Bundesbank* is related to the use of cash as a means of payment in Germany.[1]

Two specific shifts in the demand for euro banknotes are noticeable: first, the enormous increase in the demand for cash during the wake of the Lehman crisis at the end of 2008, and second, a significant rise in the demand for cash, particularly in Germany, since 2012. These developments are related to uncertainty about the stability of individual credit institutions, as occurred in 2008, and to concerns about the health of the banking system as a whole or to political uncertainties.

[1]These figures are derived from the extrapolation of estimates published in Nikolaus Bartzsch, Gerhard Rösl and Franz Seitz, Foreign demand for euro banknotes issued in Germany: estimation using direct approaches, *Deutsche Bundesbank* Discussion Paper, Series 1: Economic Studies, No 20/2011, and Nikolaus Bartzsch, Gerhard Rösl and and Franz Seitz, Foreign demand for euro banknotes issued in Germany: estimation using indirect approaches, *Deutsche Bundesbank* Discussion Paper, Series 1: Economic Studies, No 21/2011. See, also, the summary in *Deutsche Bundesbank*, Foreign demand for euro banknotes issued in Germany, Monthly Report, January 2011, pp. 29–41.

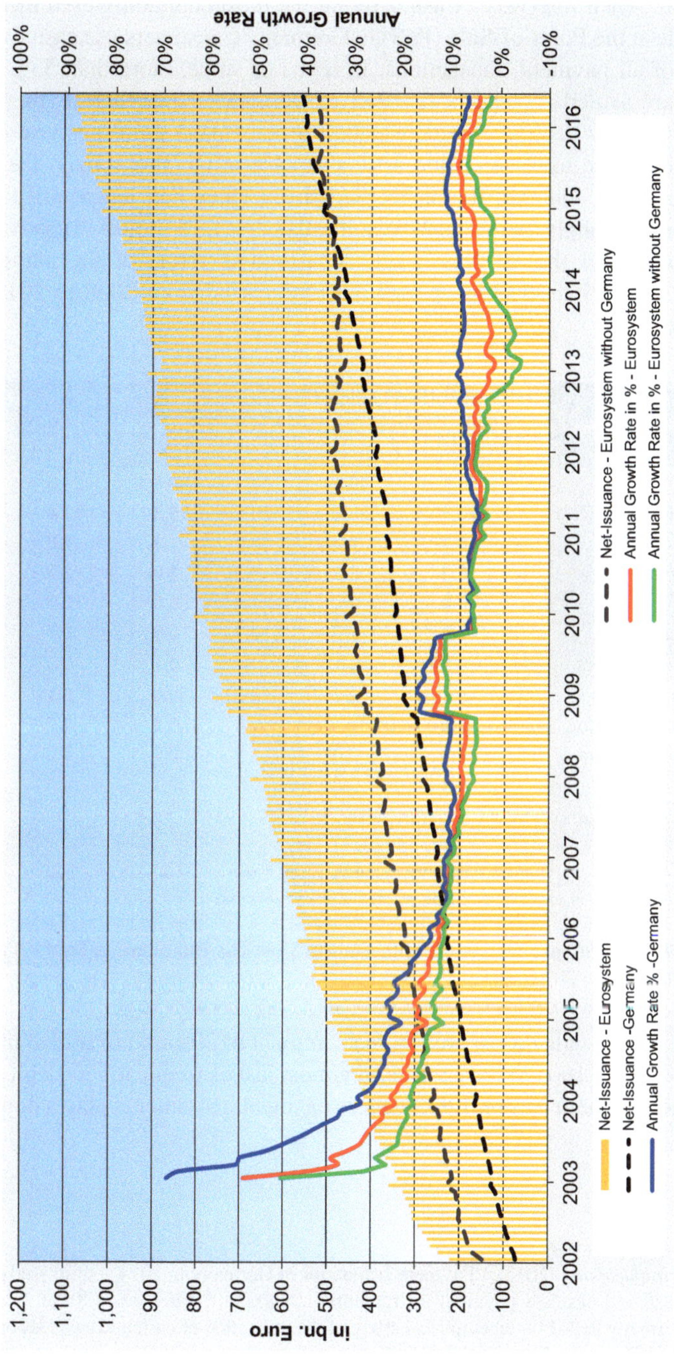

Banknotes in circulation in Germany and the Eurosystem. Source: Deutsche Bundesbank, own chart based upon information provided by ECB, Currency Information System (CIS2)

Since 2008, the *Bundesbank* has been carrying out studies on payment behaviour in Germany at 3-year intervals.[2] Cash is by far the most commonly used means of payment made at the Point-of-Sale (PoS) in Germany. Consumers use cash to settle almost 80% of all payment transactions. In terms of value, more than 53% of all transactions are settled in cash at the PoS in Germany. Nevertheless, there is a continuous and slow decline of just over half a percentage point per year in the share of payments in terms of value settled in cash at the PoS. Given the more intensive use of the Internet, the share of cash by value had temporarily fallen somewhat more strongly between 2008 and 2011 by 4.8% points. However, by 2014, it stabilised at the level of 2011. Measured in terms of the number of transactions, the decline by 3.4% points over the period from 2008 to 2014 was slightly weaker.

Payment instruments	Breakdown by turnover (in %)			Breakdown by number of transactions (in %)		
	2014	2011	2008	**2014**	2011	2008
Cash payment	**53.2**	53.1	57.9	**79.1**	82.0	82.5
Girocard (with PIN and ELV)	**29.4**	28.3	25.5	**15.3**	13.4	11.9
Credit card	**3.9**	7.4	3.6	**1.3**	1.8	1.4
Credit transfer	**5.3**	8.2	8.9	**1.0**	1.3	1.8
Direct debit	**3.0**	0.7	1.9	**0.5**	0.3	0.6
E-payment scheme	**2.8**	1.7	0.3	**0.9**	0.7	0.1
Contactless card payment	**0.1**	0.1	---	**0.1**	0.0	---
Store card	**0.1**	0.1	0.2	**0.0**	0.1	0.1
Prepaid payment card	**0.0**	0.1	0.6	**0.0**	0.2	0.7
Payment via mobile phone	**0.0**	0.0	---	**0.0**	0.0	---
Others	**0.1**	0.2	0.4	**0.1**	0.1	0.2
Cashless payment, instrument not stated	**2.3**	---	---	**1.7**	---	---
Total	**100**	**100**	**99**	**100**	**100**	**99**

Percentage share (2008): does not add up to 100% due to payment instrument not stated.

Transaction cash—use of payment instruments. Source: Deutsche Bundesbank, Study "Payment behaviour in Germany in 2014", p. 27

Over 90% of low-value payments up to an amount of 20 euro are settled in cash, and, up to a value of 100 euro, cash is used almost just as frequently as debit cards. Only for larger payment amounts do cashless payment instruments play a dominant role.

[2]See *Deutsche Bundesbank* (2015), "Payment behaviour in Germany in 2014 – third study of the utilisation of cash and cashless payment instruments", *Deutsche Bundesbank* (2012), "Payment behaviour in Germany in 2011 – an empirical study of the utilisation of cash and cashless payment instruments", and *Deutsche Bundesbank* (2009), "Payment behaviour in Germany—an empirical study of the selection and utilisation of payment instruments in the Federal Republic of Germany".

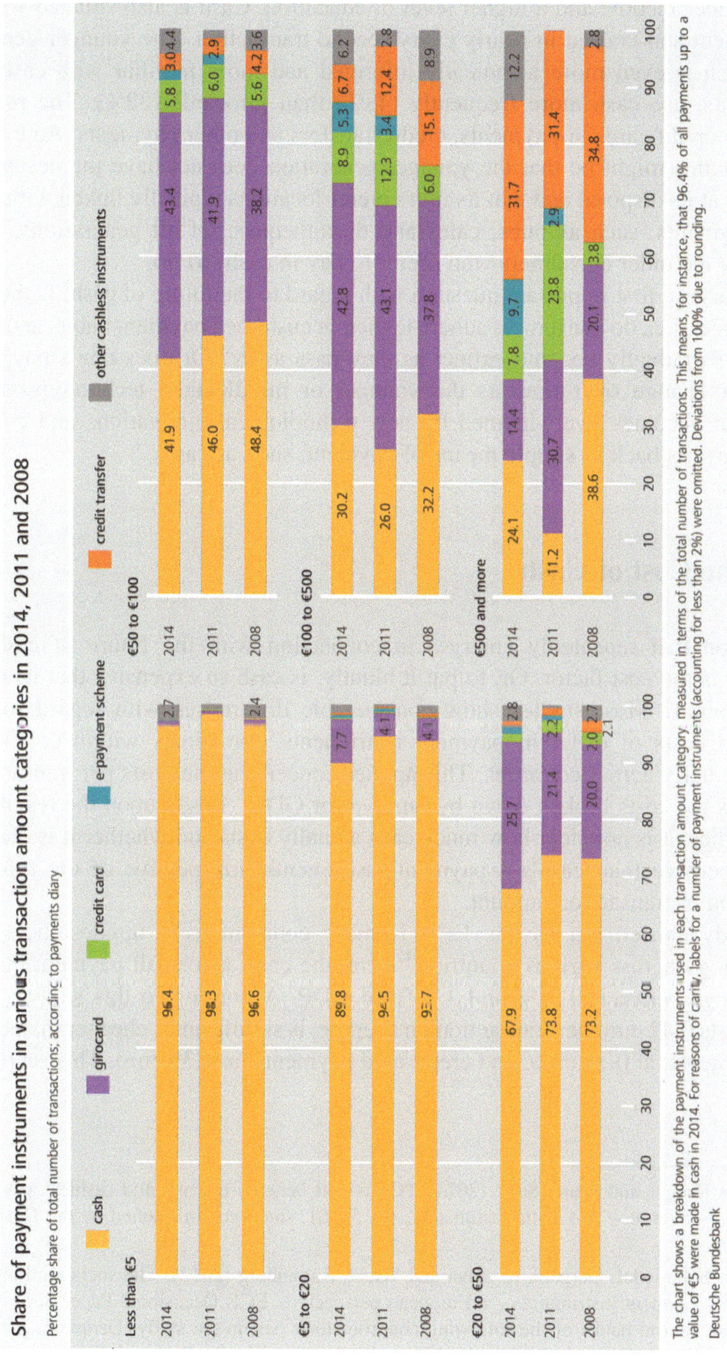

Payment behaviour recorded in payments diary. Source: Deutsche Bundesbank, Study "Payment behaviour in Germany in 2014", p. 31

Cashless payment instruments are primarily used by middle-aged consumers with a higher income and a higher level of education. Cash is also situated within this segment and is used in nearly every second transaction. The younger generation, which is even more technically informed and more familiar with cashless instruments, use cash more frequently (48%) than girocards (32%). The rest is shared by credit cards, e-payments, credit transfers and other payments. An explanation for this might be that the younger generation does not have the necessary resources at its disposal and that its users prefer locations typically linked with low value payments, such as pubs, cafes and discotheques. Of all generations, it is especially the older consumers who prefer to pay in cash (61%).

This raises a first important question with regard to the future of cash: Is there a cohort effect, i.e., do consumers adhere to their accustomed payment habits and will cash users gradually become extinct as they pass away? Or does one's payment behaviour change over time as the younger or middle-aged technology-savvy generation becomes overwhelmed by new technological innovations and consequently reverts back to simple means of payment, such as cash?

9.3 The Cost of Cash

A question that repeatedly emerges in connection with the future of cash in Germany is the cost factor. Or, to put it bluntly, is cash so expensive that its days are numbered? Most studies show considerable differences with regard to the quantified costs of different payment instruments, sometimes within countries, but particularly across countries. This applies concerning the costs per transaction as well as the costs broken down by turnover or GDP.[3] Based upon the results of these studies, it is not clear how much cash actually costs and whether it is always more expensive than cashless payment instruments, irrespective of the type of transaction or transaction amount.

A study carried out by the ECB is more coherent as it applies the same methodology across various countries.[4] Here, the costs across all payment instruments range between 0.42% and 1.35% of GDP. According to this study, cash, which costs 0.42 euro per transaction on average, is significantly cheaper than debit card payments, at 0.70 euro, and credit card payments, at 2.39 euro. This seems to

[3]See Malte Krüger and Franz Seitz (2014), "Costs and benefits of cash and cashless payment instruments – overview and initial estimates", pp. 57–61, study commissioned by the *Deutsche Bundesbank.*

[4]See Heiko Schmiedel, Gergana Kostova and Wiebe Ruttenberg (2012), The social and private cost of retail payment instruments – a European perspective, ECB Occasional Paper Series 137. The national central banks of the following countries took part in the study: Denmark, Estonia, Finland, Greece, Hungary, Ireland, Italy, Lithuania, the Netherlands, Portugal, Romania, Spain, and Sweden.

be plausible, as cash has relatively low fixed and relatively high variable costs, whereas the opposite applies for cashless payment instruments.

In 2003, the German banking industry estimated its costs of cash to be around 6.5 billion euro.[5] A study conducted by Wincor-Nixdorf in 2009 estimated the costs of cash for the banking sector to be less than 4 billion euro.[6] At the *Bundesbank* cash symposium in 2014, the President of the German Savings Banks and Giro Association, Ludger Gooßens, put the cost of cash for the institutions belonging to this association at about 1 billion euro.[7] Because the saving banks are responsible for around 50% of all cash transactions of all the credit institutions, the total amount of costs for this sector seems roughly estimated at around 2 billion euro. This means, if the estimations are correct, that the credit institutions reduced their internal costs during the last couple of years in a distinct way.

For the retail sector, EDEKA, one of the large supermarket chains in Germany, reports costs for the whole cash handling of 0.14% of its turnover and 0.47% for giro card payments.[8] With the exception of the Wincor-Nixdorf study cited above, which estimates the cost to be around 7 billion euro, there are no published empirical studies available for the retail trade sector. The European Commission has also tried to quantify the costs of the various payment instruments for retailers by a questionnaire. As a consequence, the interchange fees were caped, aiming on more competition between cash and cashless instruments. This suggests that cash is not the most expensive method of payment for the retail trade sector.

It is, in any case, unclear whether a cashless society would really lead to lower costs for consumers and retailers. After all, for a long time, technological progress had not resulted in a reduction of fees, i.e., for debit cards paid by retailers and therefore costs for consumers. Costs did not fall until the Federal Cartel Office became involved and large retail chains used their market pressure only to accept cards if the fees were reduced. Handing over the responsibility for payment completely to private institutions might well give some providers a dominant market position. Potentially, this could lead to higher costs for both consumers and retailers.

As an interim summary, the following conclusions can be drawn. Cash is expensive, but it is doubtful, to say the least, that other payment instruments are significantly cheaper. The factors that affect costs are primarily time-related components, meaning the total time required to carry out the actual payment transaction at the PoS, multiplied by the wage costs for cashiers and the number of transactions.

---

[5]See Zentraler Kreditausschuss (ZKA): Towards our Single European Cash Area (SECA), The National Cash Plan for Germany, 2004, p. 7.

[6]See http://www.wincor-nixdorf.com/static/finanzberichte/2008-2009/q4/de/dasunternehmen/cashcyclemanagement.html, last accessed 22 July 2016.

[7]See Ludger Gooßens (2014), "Optimal bezahlen – Wo steht das Bargeld?", pp. 55–64 in the proceedings of the *Deutsche Bundesbank* cash symposium 2014.

[8]See http://www.derhandel.de/news/finanzen/pages/shop.phd, last accessed 2 February 2012.

These cost factors are likely to be similar for both cash and cashless payment instruments.

Moreover, credit institutions have started to reduce their infrastructure costs in recent years. For example, the level of automation can be explained by the number of cash recycling machines and the number of processed banknotes. These machines check the lodgements of clients, separate unfit banknotes as well as counterfeit notes from circulation and offer other clients the checked cash for withdrawals. The number of cash recycling machines has significantly risen from less than 2000 in the beginning of 2008 to more than 16,000 at the end of 2015. In addition, the back office recycling with staff operated machines has also increased over the last couple of years, albeit not at the same speed as the cash recycler. This automisation reduces the number of transport and additional external processing steps in a central bank or a private cash centre. Round about 18% of banknotes or 3.6 billion banknotes were recycled in 2015 by these machines in credit institutions.

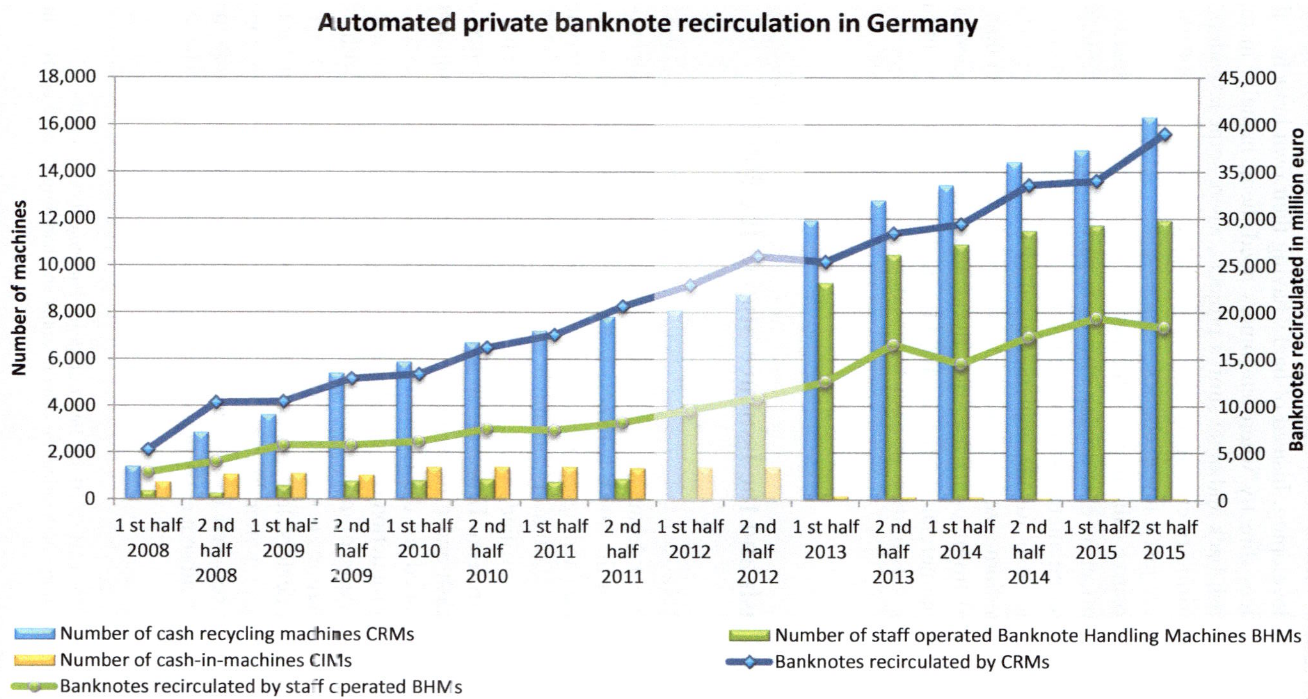

Source: CIS

Banknote re-circulation—private cash recycling. Source: Deutsche Bundesbank, own chart based upon information provided by the ECB, Currency Information System (CIS2)

Retailers are also increasingly automating their processes at the PoS and in the back office. Moreover, further co-operative agreements between the banking industry and retailers are developing. Instead of banks having their own branches, they offer their cash services directly where customers need them, namely, in retail outlets themselves. Cash-back and other similar projects, where some providers are even testing the depositing of customers' money in bank accounts in co-operation with a retail market, are just a few examples.

However, these positive initiatives on the part of the market participants are unfortunately partly offset by cost-driving effects, in particular, by the regulatory and administrative requirements surrounding cash. The banking industry, for instance, bemoans the costs for the implementation of the EU coins regulation[9] which, for a single, medium-sized, regional institution might well be higher than the financial loss incurred from counterfeit coins throughout the whole of Germany. The real losers are commercial enterprises and ultimately the consumers; in turn, this might result in a substitution of cash by cashless means of payment in the medium term.

9.4 Caps on Cash and the Issuance Stop of the 500 € Banknote

Unfortunately, the current debate about capping cash payments at some upper limit and the issuance stop of the 500 € banknote seems to be re-enforcing substitution effects. This is because capping cash payments and abolishing specific denominations probably unsettles cash users and might also lead to increasing cost.

Both measures are justified by claiming that they will help to combat tax evasion, crime and terrorism. However, up until now, there is little evidence of a direct link between cash and criminality. A new and important study on money laundering commissioned by the German Finance Ministry has been used as a justification for the introduction of a cash limit. The study compares the number of unreported suspected cases of money laundering in the banking industry with other areas.[10] It shows that reports of suspected cases by real estate and insurance agents, jewellers, car and art dealers, lawyers and notaries, for instance, account for only around 1% of the cases reported by the financial-sector. Starting from this conclusion, a dark figure of between 15,000 and 28,000 suspicious cases per year in the non-financial sector is subsequently derived using survey methodology. The study

[9]See Regulation (EU) No 1210/2010 of the European Parliament and of the Council of 15 December 2010 concerning authentication of euro coins and handling of euro coins unfit for circulation.

[10]See Kai Bussmann (2015), "Dark figure study on the prevalence of money laundering in Germany and the risks of money laundering in individual economic sectors", Summary, Martin-Luther-University Halle-Wittenberg.

then estimates a stunningly high volume of money laundering in Germany based upon this finding.[11] However, what the study disregards is that more than 90% of the reports made by the banking industry are not investigated, which essentially means that the study equalises information regarding suspicions with real cases of money laundering.[12] Moreover, in the study, these presumed crimes are exclusively related to cash transactions. The implied assumption that cashless instruments do not play a role in these kinds of undesired activities seems dubious.

Rather, cashless instruments are probably also important especially for tax evasion. Gabriel Zucman, a French economist, estimates that 6.9 trillion euro worth of private assets are held in tax havens around the world, the vast proportion of which is undeclared.[13] And Thomas Piketty targets individual countries' tax dumping strategies, referring to corporate tax rates as an example.[14]

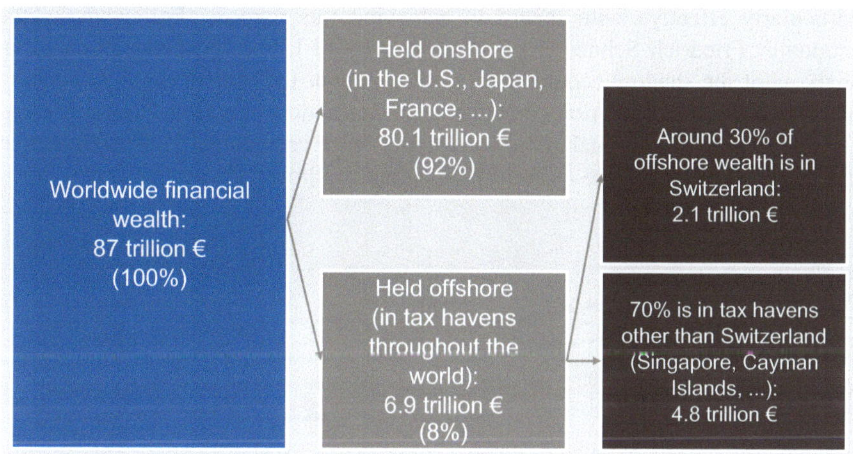

Financial assets in tax havens (Status 2014). Source: Deutsche Bundesbank, own chart based upon information provided by Fig. 3 in "Tables and figures included in the book" available at: http://gabriel-zucman.eu/hidden-wealth

[11]For a detailed critical analyse to the Bussmann study, see Friedrich Schneider (2016), "Der Umfang der Geldwäsche in Deutschland und weltweit, Einige Fakten und eine kritische Auseinandersetzung mit der Dunkelfeldstudie von Kai Bussmann", in: Friedrich Naumann Stiftung, FÜR DIE FREIHEIT.

[12]See Friedrich Schneider, in Norbert Häring, Handelsblatt, 2 May 2016, available at: http://www.handelsblatt.com/my/politik/deutschland/geldwaesche-in-deutschland-die-spur-des-geldes/13528054.html

[13]See Gabriel Zucman (2015), *The Hidden Wealth of Nations*, Chicago, September 2015, see http://gabriel-zucman.eu/hidden-wealth, Figure 3 last accessed on 30 January 2017.

[14]Thomas Piketty, "Die Schlacht um den Euro", *Libération*, 7 December 2010, Munich 2015, p. 85 *et seq.*

The current discussions about tax havens, government tax dumping in the EU, numbered accounts and letterbox companies is nothing new. But it seems as though it is only journalists, and not the responsible government agencies, who are capable of doing the necessary research. An interesting anecdote in this connection is that the Chinese authorities are fearful of the abolition of cash because, as they say, cash is the simplest way to uncover illegal activities in China, since it leaves traces and is easy to find. By using cashless instruments, such as vouchers, anonymous prepaid cards and goods sold well below the market price, bribery and corruption are supposedly possible without leaving any traces, and can therefore hardly be discovered.[15]

There is no doubt that cash is also used to finance both transactions in the shadow economy and criminal activities, and that every avenue should be pursued to restrict illegal activity. However, the policy measures currently debated do not seem to be particularly effective with regard to achieving this purpose. For example, the economist Friedrich Schneider of the University of Linz, who conducts in-depth analyses of the shadow economy, is sceptical about the effectiveness of banning high banknote denominations or large cash transactions, arguing that these measures would have a minimal impact on illicit work or criminality.[16] He believes that the proposed measures are more like "apparent solutions".[17]

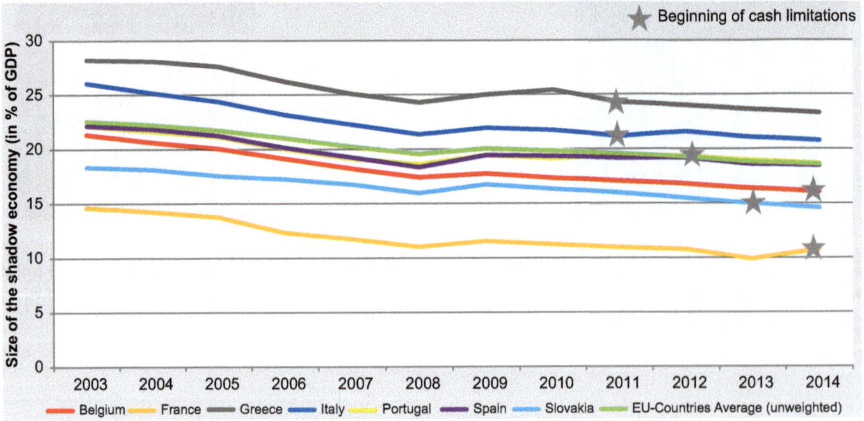

Cash limitations in different euro-area countries. Source: Deutsche Bundesbank, own chart based upon information provided in Schneider et al. (2015, p. 45)

[15]See http://www.faz.net/aktuell/wirtschaft/korruption-in-china-bestechung-ohne-bargeld-14088830.html, last accessed 22 July 2016.

[16]See, also, a detailed analysis about the impact of the shadow economy by Friedrich Schneider in Chap. 3.

[17]See http://www.faz.net/aktuell/wirtschaft/plan-der-bundesregierung-die-bargeld-bremse-sorgt-fuer-streit-14054545.html, last accessed 22 July 2016.

Michel Sapin, the French minister of finance, argued in favour of a cap on cash payment by saying that, "Limits would also make terrorist financing more difficult",[18] only to note subsequently that "Attacks such as the recent ones in Paris can be financed with relatively small sums as low as 10,000 euro–30,000 euro".[19] So, even if terrorists observed the caps on cash payments, which is doubtful, it is only necessary to split the payment among a few people in order to meet the required limits. Furthermore, doubts about the efficacy of these measures are justified because a large number of attackers in the past have come from countries which already had caps on cash payments in place.

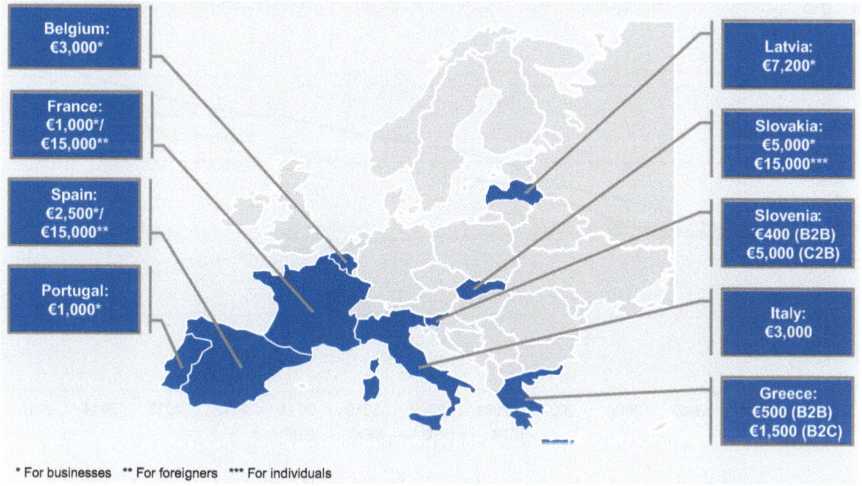

Limitations of cash in Europe. Source: Deutsche Bundesbank, own chart based upon information provided by the ECB, 2016

Here again, the question of cashless payment instruments arises. A German television network asked why credit institutions in the Islamic State (IS) territory were not disconnected from the SWIFT system, pointing out that this would significantly limit opportunities to launder money electronically via sham companies. But this suggestion seems, in the opinion of the reporter of the news broadcast, to be scuppered by more far-reaching political interests than clearing transactions, such as oil deliveries from the IS-held territory.[20]

Not only in Germany and the Eurosystem, but also in other countries, the total amount of cash has risen strongly over the past few years, with the notable

[18]See Michel Sapin in: *Handelsblatt*, 26 January 2016, p. 17.

[19]See http://www.reuters.com/article/us-mideast-crisis-financing-france-idUSKBN0U02MZ20151217, last accessed 25 July 2016.

[20]See http://www.rbb-online.de/kontraste/ueber_den_tag_hinaus/terrorismus/die-geldquellen-des-is.html, last accessed 19 January 2017.

exception of Sweden. And this development seems to be independent of the level of the highest banknote offered by the central bank. So, despite the highest denomination in the US being the 100 USD bill and in the UK being the 50 sterling banknote, and the fact that both are lower than the 500 € banknote, the demand for cash is similar. The increase in the demand for the euro has been a little bit stronger than those of the USD during the last years. This seems to be logical, because of the function of the euro as an international reserve currency is a new one and offers market participants the possibility of diversification.

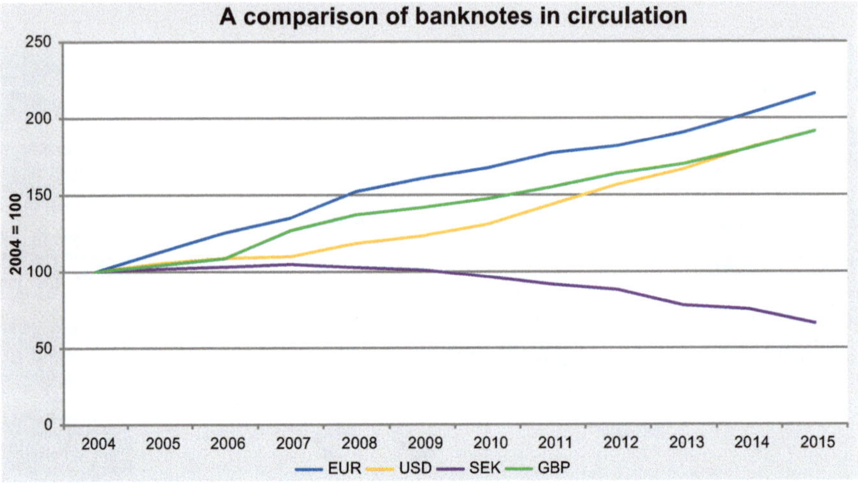

Comparison of banknotes in circulation. Source: Deutsche Bundesbank, own chart based upon information provided by ECB, Federal Reserve, Sveriges Riksbank and the Bank of England, 2016

Turning now to the stop of the issuance of the 500 € banknote, a frequently voiced argument in favour of such a move is the share of high-denomination banknotes in the overall volume of currency in circulation. The most issued banknote in terms of value in Germany as well as in the Eurosystem is the 50 € note followed by the 500 € banknote. Even though the share of the 500 € banknote in the total volume of currency in circulation is around 30%, it is not actively used by the majority of Germans. In a representative population survey conducted on behalf of the ECB, approximately 56% of respondents replied they had never seen or used a 500 € banknote.[21] These numbers are quite often interpreted as evidence of the illegal use of the 500 € banknote.

[21]See *European Central Bank*, The use of euro banknotes – Results of two surveys among households and firms, Monthly Bulletin, April, 2011, p. 85 & 89.

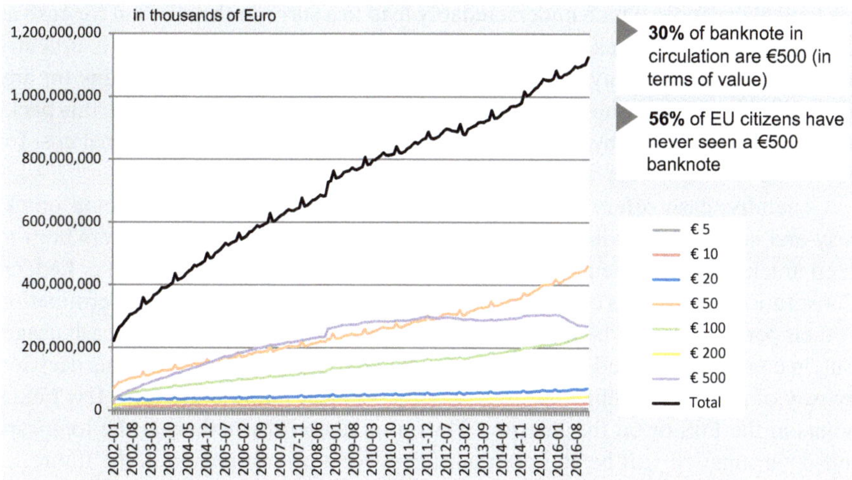

Development of banknote demand in terms of value. Source: Deutsche Bundesbank, own chart based on information provided at https://www.ecb.europa.eu/stats/money/euro/circulation/html/index.en.html and ECB, Monthly Bulletin, April 2011, p. 85

However, a high concentration of currency in circulation in high-denomination banknotes is quite common across different currencies. The share of high-denomination banknotes (CHF 100 to 1000) issued by the Swiss National Bank in overall currency in circulation is 92%, with the CHF 1000 banknote alone accounting for around 62 percentage points of this figure (November 2016). The 100 USD banknote constitutes around 78% of the volume of US dollars in circulation (end 2015). Against this background, the market share of the 100 €, 200 € and 500 € banknotes of 52% at the end of 2015 is relatively low compared with other currencies. Hence, it is doubtful that the 500 € banknote, in particular, should play a dominate role in crime activities, calling into question one of the leading arguments in support of the stop of the issuance of the 500 € banknote. The idea that more cash equals more crime therefore makes as little sense as the notion that less cash equals less crime.

9.5 Does Cash Have a Future?

Taken together, there are many reasons to keep cash. When Japanese women were asked after the nuclear accident in Fukushima in 2011 what they needed most urgently in the days following the catastrophe, they replied: flat shoes, a toothbrush and cash.[22] Regardless of the nature of a crisis, people almost always increase their demand for cash. Mistrust in the banking industry or an uncertain political situation

[22]See http://www.xifanyang.com/wp-content/uploads/2011/05/NEON_Japan_Tagebuch.pdf

are typical instances which understandably lead to a surge in the demand for cash as a store of value. In the case of natural disasters or of a power cut, cash is urgently needed as a means of payment. Clearly, a society needs back-up solutions for any event in which their cashless systems should cease to function. Currently, this back-up solution is provided by cash, but, in a world without cash, the additional cost for providing such a system would arise.

Generally, cash offers many advantages.[23] It is seen by users as being quick, easy and secure, and it is also valued as an instrument that enables users both to keep track of their spending and to facilitate budgeting. Finally, the Federal Constitutional Court has emphasised the individual's right to the self-determination of their personal data, which is often brought up in the discussion about cash usage. But, in contrast to the Federal Constitutional Court, the people weaken this decision by way of their daily behaviour and provide personal information for a few bonus points at the PoS or on the Internet. Thus, it is doubtful whether, in the long-run, self-determination will be an important factor for a private person in the future.

Far more crucial are the problems faced by enterprises in connection with these "glass consumers". Naturally, every business wants to have information about the purchasing habits of its customers, but what it is even more interested in is the purchasing profile of its competitors' customers. But each company wants to save the personal data of its own clientele, which seems sometimes to be more efficient than the self-protection of the client itself. Nevertheless, cash seems to be the best form of protection in all possible scenarios against the unauthorised use of personal data.

Clearly, innovations in cashless payment instruments represent a threat to cash. But also new, innovative payment instruments often substitute other cashless payment instruments. An example here can be found in the introduction of the debit card, which contributed to the disappearance of the EC cheque. Overall, a sizeable part of the market share that the debit card now possesses has been gained at the cost of other cashless instruments. It is also important to note that the increasingly large number of different cashless payment instruments might confuse consumers, makes it more difficult to realise economics of scale, and also increases the infrastructure costs for cashless instruments. This further questions whether a cashless society would really lead to more efficient payment transactions. And when coins—heavy, cumbersome, hard to differentiate—are rejected as obsolete, there is no obituary for the sleek, modern, alternative prepaid e-money card, which was designed to replace coins.

To summarise, consumers want a generally accepted, simple means of payment that can be used without any technical set-up. In the eyes of many users, these requirements are best fulfilled by cash.

Alongside minimum reserves, cash constitutes the central bank money, which cannot be created by private credit institutions. If the private sector withdraws cash

[23]For a more extensive discussion of these advantages, see *Deutsche Bundesbank*, Cash as a means of payment and a store of value, Annual report 2015, pp. 25–45.

from credit intuitions, they have to obtain credit in central bank money. This limits the possibility of credit institutions creating book money and influencing the interest level. Cash is a factor for a functioning monetary economy, the banking industry, and gives the central banks the opportunity to pursue monetary policy. Although other mechanisms are also conceivable, banknotes represent an autonomous factor in the liquidity policy framework. Today, with the discussion about the efficiency of negative interest rates, which seems only possible for private persons and with cash losing its storage function, the question is whether cash shields the general public from monetary policy.[24] Without cash, private persons have no possibility of withdrawing themselves from negative interest rates on their savings and protecting themselves against the bankruptcies of credit institutions. So, in the absence of cash, it is predominantly savers who bear the brunt of the negative repercussions of a monetary policy that has been failing to achieve its targets for quite some time now.[25]

9.6 Conclusion

This chapter has addressed the question of whether cash has a future (in Germany). John Cryan, chief executive of the *Deutsche Bank*, has a clear answer. During a panel discussion at the World Economic Forum in Davos, John Cryan predicted the demise of cash within the next 10 years.[26] This chapter, in contrast, expresses a more differentiated view on the future of cash. For a variety of reasons, the demand for cash is rising and will most likely stay at a high level for years to come.

However, cash users have to face powerful vested interests. By attacking cash, governments and government-run agencies around the world hope to curtail tax evasion, crime and terrorism. By forcing consumers to use cashless means of payment, the financial industries want both to earn fees and to collect valuable data on the behaviour of consumers. Abolishing cash would certainly strengthen the financial sector's position by forcing savers into the banking sector. Ultimately, it is an open question of whether the interest of cash users can stand up against this powerful alliance.

[24]See Kenneth S. Rogoff, "Den Zehner würde ich behalten", *Welt Am Sonntag*, 18 September 2016.

[25]See Norbert Häring, "Die Abschaffung des Bargeldes und die Folgen. Der Weg in die totale Kontrolle", Cologne, 2016.

[26]See John Cryan, available at: https://www.weforum.org/events/world-economic-forum-annual-meeting-2016/sessions/the-transformation-of-finance-8824a51b-91e1-4f29-88a2-abbfabb5fa8f, last accessed 22 July 2016.

References

Bartzsch N, Rösl G, Seitz F (2011a) Foreign demand for euro banknotes issued in Germany: estimation using direct approaches, Deutsche Bundesbank Discussion Paper, Series 1: Economic Studies, No 20/2011

Bartzsch N, Rösl G, Seitz F (2011b) Foreign demand for euro banknotes issued in Germany: estimation using indirect approaches. Deutsche Bundesbank Discussion Paper, Series 1: Economic Studies, No 21/2011

Bussmann K (2015) Dark figure study on the prevalence of money laundering in Germany and the risks of money laundering in individual economic sectors. Summary, Martin-Luther-University Halle-Wittenberg

Cryan J (2016) Available at: https://www.weforum.org/events/world-economic-forum-annual-meeting-2016/sessions/the-transformation-of-finance-8824a51b-91e1-4f29-88a2-abbfabb5fa8f. Last accessed 22 July 2016

Deutsche Bundesbank (2015a) Annual Report 2015. Cash as a means of payment and a store of value, pp 25–45

Deutsche Bundesbank (2015b) Payment behaviour in Germany in 2014 – third study of the utilisation of cash and cashless payment instruments

Deutsche Bundesbank (2012) Payment behaviour in Germany in 2011 – an empirical study of the utilisation of cash and cashless payment instruments

Deutsche Bundesbank (2011) Foreign demand for euro banknotes issued in Germany. Monthly Report, January 2011, 29–41

Deutsche Bundesbank (2009) Payment behaviour in Germany – an empirical study of the selection and utilisation of payment instruments in the Federal Republic of Germany

European Central Bank (2011) Monthly Bulletin April 2011, The use of euro banknotes – results of two surveys among households and firms, April 2011, 75–90

Gooßens L (2014) Optimal bezahlen – Wo steht das Bargeld? 55–64 in the proceedings of the *Deutsche Bundesbank* cash symposium 2014

Häring N (2016) Die Abschaffung des Bargeldes und die Folgen. Der Weg in die totale Kontrolle, Cologne, 2016

http://www.rbb-online.de/kontraste/ueber_den_tag_hinaus/terrorismus/die-geldquellen-des-is.html. Last accessed 19 Jan 2017

http://www.wincor-nixdorf.com/static/finanzberichte/2008-2009/q4/de/dasunternehmen/cashcyclemanagement.html. Last accessed 22 July 2016

http://www.derhandel.de/news/finanzen/pages/shop.phd. Last accessed 2 Feb 2012

http://www.faz.net/aktuell/wirtschaft/korruption-in-china-bestechung-ohne-bargeld-14088830.html. Last accessed 22 July 2016

http://www.faz.net/aktuell/wirtschaft/plan-der-bundesregierung-die-bargeld-bremse-sorgt-fuer-streit-14054545.html. Last accessed 22 July 2016

http://www.reuters.com/article/us-mideast-crisis-financing-france-idUSKBN0U02MZ20151217. Last accessed 25 July 2016

http://www.xifanyang.com/wp-content/uploads/2011/05/NEON_Japan_Tagebuch.pdf.html. Last accessed 1 Feb 2017

Krüger M, Seitz F (2014) Costs and benefits of cash and cashless payment instruments – overview and initial estimates, study commissioned by the *Deutsche Bundesbank*

Piketty T (2010) Die Schlacht um den Euro *Libération*, 7 December 2010, Munich 2015, p. 85 *et seq*

Regulation (EU) No 1210/2010 of the European Parliament and of the Council of 15 December 2010 concerning authentication of euro coins and handling of euro coins unfit for circulation

Rogoff K (2016) Den Zehner würde ich behalten. Welt Am Sonntag, 18 Sept 2016

Sapin M (2016) Handelsblatt, 26 Jan, 17

Schmiedel H, Kostova G, Ruttenberg W (2012) The social and private cost of retail payment instruments – a European perspective, ECB Occasional Paper Series 137. The national central banks of the following countries took part in the study: Denmark, Estonia, Finland, Greece, Hungary, Ireland, Italy, Lithuania, the Netherlands, Portugal, Romania, Spain, and Sweden

Schneider et al (2015) Shadow economy and tax evasion in the EU. p 45

Schneider F (2016a) Norbert Häring, Handelsblatt, 2 May 2016, http://www.handelsblatt.com/my/politik/deutschland/geldwaesche-in-deutschland-die-spur-des-geldes/13528054.html

Schneider F (2016b) Der Umfang der Geldwäsche in Deutschland und weltweit, Einige Fakten und eine kritische Auseinandersetzung mit der Dunkelfeldstudie von Kai Bussmann, in: Friedrich Naumann Stiftung, FÜR DIE FREIHEIT

Zentraler Kreditausschuss (ZKA) (2004) Towards our single European cash area (SECA), The National Cash Plan for Germany

Zucman G (2015) The hidden wealth of nations, Chicago, September 2015, see http://gabriel-zucman.eu/hidden-wealth, Figure 3. Last accessed 30 Jan 2017

Chapter 10
Restricting the Use of Cash in the European Monetary Union: Legal Aspects

Helmut Siekmann

Abstract Clear signs are visible that the use of cash is being increasingly restricted inside the European Monetary Union (EMU). The main argument for this drive was cost-effectiveness. The handling of cash was declared expensive and risky, mainly by economists. Empirical evidence is, however, scarce, and in fact tends to show the opposite; at least for small amounts of money to be paid. More recently, the pressure has been augmented considerably. Part of it is the phasing out of the 500 € banknote. This time, the argument is fighting criminal activities and, in particular, terrorism. More likely, the true reason is to make the "unconventional" measures of the European System of Central Banks (ESCB) more effective: negative nominal interest rates and inflation targeting.

Several legal concerns exist in this context. The total abolition of cash would neither be compatible with EU law nor with German constitutional law. Although the wording of Article 128 TFEU only empowers ("may") the European Central Bank (ECB) to issue euro-banknotes, it presumes the existence of cash. The ECB does not have the power to abolish it. The same result may be derived from Article 20 paragraph 1 Federal Constitution of Germany ("social state").

Restricting the use of issued banknotes and coins denominated in euro would be incompatible with their property of being legal tender following Article 128 TFEU. It is highly questionable whether such measures would be in conformity with the principle of proportionality enshrined in Article 1 paragraph 1 and 4 TEU and protocol no 2 of the primary law of the EU.

The obligation to accept cash denominated in euro follows already from its virtue as legal tender; also for government entities. In addition, this result also follows from the secondary law of the EU: Commission decision 2010/191/EU of 22 March 2010; notwithstanding recital 19 of Regulation (EC) 975/98 that is legally not part of the norm.

H. Siekmann (✉)
Goethe University, Frankfurt am Main, Germany
e-mail: siekmann@imfs-frankfurt.de

F. Rövekamp et al. (eds.), *Cash in East Asia*, Financial and Monetary Policy Studies 44, DOI 10.1007/978-3-319-59846-8_10

10.1 Introduction

There are clear signs that the use of cash is being increasingly restricted inside the European Monetary Union (EMU). For quite some time, not only financial institutions, but also authorities, have being exerting pressure on both businesses and consumers to refrain from using cash. Even statutory rules have been passed to prohibit the use of cash exceeding a certain, albeit rather low, limit. The following examples may illustrate the rich host of obstacles that can be observed:

- Financial institutions impose fees or charges for withdrawing cash from a bank account or depositing cash into it.
- Businesses refuse to accept cash, especially, higher denomination banknotes.
- Government entities require permission to charge taxes, fees or other dues from a bank account,[1] and do not accept cash.[2]
- Tax administrations refuse to disburse refunds other than to bank accounts.[3]
- Limits for using cash in business transactions have been introduced in several Member States by law; sometimes with partial exemptions for visitors, or private persons in general.[4]
- At least one case is known in which German law enforcement authorities considered the mere possession of 9000 € to be sufficiently suspicious to trigger intense criminal investigations, although the possession of such a sum of money is entirely legal in Germany.[5]

[1]For example, Section 13 paragraph 1 sentence 1 n. 1 German vehicle tax act (*Kraftfahrzeugsteuergesetz*).

[2]Most notorious are the quarrels over the use of cash for paying the special contributions to finance the public law broadcasting system in Germany (*Rundfunkanstalten*) regardless of its actual use; based upon Section 9 para 2 sentence 2 RBStV (*Rundfunkgebührenstaatsvertrag*) in conjunction with Section 10 para 2 of the by-laws of the respective public law broadcasting institution; critically, see Norbert Häring, "Beitragsservice reagiert auf Handelsblatt-Experiment", *Handelsblatt*, 16 June 2015. The conduct of the system was recently justified by an unpublished decision of the Administrative Court of Munich of 1 June 2016, docket no M 6 K 15.5638 (*VG München, Urteil vom 1. Juni 2016, Az. M 6 K 15.5638*). A decision of a superior court is, however, lacking.

[3]Section 224 para. 3 phrase 1 of the German tax code (*Abgabenordnung*).

[4]See, for example, Benjamin Angel and Aliénor Margerit, "Quelle est la portée du cours légal de l'euro?", (2009) 532 *Revue du Marché commun et de l'Union européenne*, p. 587, at 588; Norbert Häring, "Bargeld auf dem Rückzug", *Handelsblatt* 26 January 2016, p. 29. A detailed overview of the various limits and restrictions for using cash, enacted by several Member States of the EU is given in a paper by the research service of the German federal parliament (Wissenschaftliche Dienste, Deutscher Bundestag Ausarbeitung WD 4 – 3000 – 043/16, p. 8 et seq.). The thresholds range from 1500 to 15,000 euros or its equivalent for the non-euro states; preparation to introduce such a limit in Germany was disclosed by the Federal Ministry of Finance, *Börsen-Zeitung*, 4 February 2016, p. 6, but later denied (Deutscher Budestag, printed matter 18/7794 of 04/03/2019, p. 23) and postponed for a legislative act of the EU (Deutscher Bundestag, Committe of petitions, 26/04/2017, hib 269/2017).

[5]Hans Theile, "Der Sündenbock", *Frankfurter Allgemeine Zeitung*, 16 November 2014.

- On 5 May 2016, the Governing Council of the ECB decided to end the production and issuance of 500 € banknotes.[6]

These measures have been successful to varying degrees in the Member States of the EU whose currency is the euro. In some countries, they have led to the replacement of cash as a means of payment or storage of value, on a large scale. In other Member States, such as Austria and Germany, cash is still widely used.[7] Here, the extent to which this is due to a difference in the intrinsic preferences of the acting persons has to be left open.

The next, and considerably more incriminating, step would be the total abolition of cash. Macro-economists, such as Lawrence Summers,[8] Kenneth Rogoff, and Peter Bofinger, have explicitly demanded such an interdiction.[9] In a purely theoretical world of macro-economics, this might be an advisable step, especially from a predominantly Keynesian perspective. The existence of cash is seen as an effective zero lower bound on nominal interest rates. This lower bound might even be a few

---

[6]"Press release of 4 May 2016:

- The ECB has decided to discontinue production and issuance of 500 € banknote;
- Europa series of euro banknotes will not include the 500 €;
- 500 € banknote remains legal tender and will always retain its value.

Today the Governing Council of the European Central Bank (ECB) concluded a review of the denominational structure of the Europa series. It has decided to permanently stop producing the 500 € banknote and to exclude it from the Europa series, taking into account concerns that this banknote could facilitate illicit activities. The issuance of the 500 € will be stopped around the end of 2018, when the 100 € and 200 € banknotes of the Europa series are planned to be introduced. The other denominations—from 5 € to 200 €—will remain in place." This decision was criticised by: the President of the German Bundesbank, Jens Weidmann, *Handelsblatt*, 25 February 2016, p. 30; Daniel Stelter, "Mit der Abschaffung der 500er Note ist ein Tabu gefallen", *Börsen-Zeitung*, 7 May 2016, p. 4; the member of the German Council of Economic advisers, Volker Wieland, cited in: "Große Bedenken gegen Bargeldobergrenzen", *Frankfurter Allgemeine Zeitung*, 14 June 2016; idem, cited in: *Frankfurter Neue Presse*, 14 June 2016, p. 4; anonymous, *Börsen-Zeitung*, 6 May 2016, p. 6; "decidedly in favour of retaining the €500 banknote", Sebastian Jost, *Die Welt*, 13 February 2016: "It protects the currency."

[7]See Malte Krüger and Franz Seitz, Costs and Benefits of Cash and Cashless Payment Instruments, (2014), p. 20–52; Christof Freimuth, "Article 128 AEUV", in: Helmut Siekmann (ed), *Kommentar zur Europäischen Währungsunion*, (Tübingen: Mohr Siebeck, 2013), at margin no 6. There are also signs that the use of digital money is no longer growing to the extent that some governments and financial institutions would like. At the moment, the growth rates of the Digital Money Index calculated by Imperial College, London University and Citigroup has come down to 1.3 per cent; see Andreas Hippin, "'Zivilisationsaufbau' durch digitales Bezahlen", *Börsen-Zeitung*, 27 January 2016, p. 2.

[8]Lawrence Summers, "It's time to kill the $100 bill", *Washington Post*, 16 February 2016; anonymous, "Peter Bofinger, Wirtschaftsweiser für Abschaffung des Bargelds", *Frankfurter Allgemeine Zeitung*, 16 May 2015; dissenting Carl-Ludwig Thiele, Diskussion um das Bargeld: Hätte eine Abschaffung von Banknoten und Münzen wirklich Vorteile? *Ifo-Schnelldienst* 13/2015 of 16 July 2015, p. 3.

[9]Kenneth Rogoff, "Costs and Benefits of Phasing out Paper Currency", NBER Macroeconomics Annual Conference, 11 April 2014; most recently, idem, *Handelsblatt Nr. 185*, weekend edition 23/24/25 September 2016, p. 28 *et seq*., declaring the risk of insolvency of a bank with an ensuing "bail-in" a "hysteria".

basis points to the negative, as there are costs of holding cash. In the real world, staggering impediments and detrimental downsides of such a decision are visible.[10]

In addition, experience shows that this would probably not be the last step. In some countries at least, the chances are high that the population would try to protect itself and use other commodities as a means of payment or as a store of value: seashells, paintings, cigarettes, liquor, precious metals, jewels, vouchers, special drawing rights, foreign currency, just to name a few. In essence, any tangible object which is relatively rare and cannot be produced without an input of resources may serve. As a consequence, the possession and the use of precious metals as bullion or coins was also interdicted, often in combination with the threat of draconian measures in cases of disobedience. The same was true for the possession or use of foreign currency. Two well-known examples from the twentieth century may be given:

- The possession of gold coins, gold bullion, and gold certificates within the continental United States exceeding five troy ounces was made a criminal offence for all private persons from 1 May 1933 onwards by Executive Order 6102, signed by President Roosevelt on 5 April 1933.[11] Immediately thereafter, the U.S. dollar substantially depreciated against the price of gold. In effect, this was an (indirect) expropriation of savings.
- In Germany, all foreign currency (and all financial instruments denominated in foreign currency) were confiscated in the course of the hyperinflation of 1923. The regulation of 25 August 1923 was based upon Article 48 of the constitution,[12] which allowed emergency legislation by the president (*Notverordnungsrecht*). Earlier, the *Reichsbank* had been granted the power to require, under certain circumstances, the exchange of foreign currencies or precious metals into—by that time already almost worthless—domestic currency, as *per* Section 9 of the regulation of 8 May 1923.[13]

At a first glance, the sketched barriers can be divided into three groups:

- Factual or indirect impediments;
- Restrictions based upon statutory rules closing channels for the use of cash or making them less viable;
- Outright interdictions by law.

[10]See for example: Claudio Borio, "Comment", in: Charles Bean, Christian Broda, Takatoshi Ito, and Randall Kroszner, *Low for Long? Causes and Consequences of Low Interest Rates*, (Geneva: International Center for Monetary and Banking Studies - ICMB, London: Center for Economic Policy Research – CEPR-Press, 2015), Geneva Reports on the World Economy 17, p. 93 et seq.; Fritz Zurbruegg, ibid, p. 94 et seq.

[11]Franklin D. Roosevelt, *The Public Papers and Addresses of Franklin D. Roosevelt. Volume Two, The Year of Crisis, 1933: With a Special Introduction and Explanatory Notes by President Roosevelt*, (New York: Random House, 1938), p. 111.

[12]*Official Journal* part I, p. 833 (Verordnung des Reichspräsidenten über die Ablieferung ausländischer Vermögensgegenstände of 25 August 1923, Reichsgesetzblatt I, 833).

[13]*Official Journal* part I, p. 275 (Verordnung des Reichspräsidenten aufgrund des Notgesetzes (Maßnahmen gegen die Valutaspekulation) of 8 Mai 1923, RGBl I, 275); not judged as tax or contribution by the German supreme civil court, RGZ 110, 344 at 346.

In the present situation, some economists readily acknowledge the abolition of cash as useful and—as experts in constitutional law—quickly come to the conclusion that constitutional concerns are unfounded as a fundamental right for cash does not exist. This is not really surprising. In any case, the restrictions would serve, in the opinion of the supporters, a good purpose: they would grant to the "unconventional" monetary policy, which has been established by central banks on a large scale, finally the—so far not clearly visible—effectiveness.[14] Lawyers, on the other hand, are more in favour of the argument that the restrictions for using cash would hinder money laundering.[15] The former president of the German Federal Constitutional Court, Hans-Jürgen Papier, judges restrictions on the use of cash as non-justified intrusions into civil rights and lacking the undispensable proportionality.[16]

It is definitely worthwhile taking a closer look at some of the puzzling questions of:

1. The nature of cash;
2. The conformity of an abolition with EU law;
3. The conformity of restrictions with EU law;
4. The requirements of German constitutional law;
5. The legal consequences of not accepting cash.

10.2 The Nature of Cash

According to the State Theory of Money, only those signs (chattels) which serve the monetary functions that are created by a state are money, and all such signs created by a state are money. Friedrich Georg Knapp, professor of economics at the University of Strasbourg, is almost unanimously credited for this theory[17] since he commenced his famous treatise on the "State Theory of Money" in 1905 with these words:

---

[14]Christian Odendahl, "Es gibt kein Grundrecht auf Bargeld.", *Zeit online*, 20 February 2016.

[15]Joachim Kaetzler, *Börsen-Zeitung*, 3 March 2016, p. 7; dissenting: Jost, note 6 above; Bernd Wittkowski, *Börsen-Zeitung*, 6 May 2016, p. 1; also sceptical, see Weidmann, note 6 above.

[16]See research service of the German Federal Parliament [Deutscher Bundestag, Wissenschaftliche Dienste], note 4 above, p. 7; also cited for his critical view in: "Große Bedenken gegen Bargeldobergrenzen", *Frankfurter Allgemeine Zeitung*, 14 June 2016; "Verfassungswidrig?", *Frankfurter Neue Presse*, 14 June 2016, p. 4.

[17]Recent examples: Karsten Schmidt, "Die 'Staatliche Theorie des Geldes': Jahrhundertwerk oder Makulatur?", in: Albrecht Weber (ed), *Währung und Wirtschaft, Festschrift für Prof. Dr. Hugo J. Hahn zum 70. Geburtstag*, (Baden-Baden: Nomos Verlag, 1997), p. 81; David Fox, François R. Velde and Wolfgang Ernst, "Monetary History between Law and Economics", in: David Fox and Wolfgang Ernst (eds), *Money in the Western Legal Tradition*, (Oxford: Oxford University Press, 2016), p. 3, at 13 *et seq*; L. Randall Wray, "From the State Theory of Money to Modern Money: An Alternative to Economic Orthodoxy", ibid., p. 631, at 632–636.

> Money is a creation of the legal system; it has appeared in history in various forms: a theory of money can therefore only be a work of legal history.[18]

From this starting-point, it was well justified and consistent for him to re-iterate:

> Money is a creation of the state. Only legal tender is money and all legal tender is money.[19]

Following this definition, the term "money" is equivalent to that of legal tender—for all practical purposes.[20] It was, however, a now almost forgotten German law professor—at that time in Basel—who had made the same discovery using partially the same wording decades before Knapp. For the sake of academic and historical truth, it is Gustav Hartmann who should be credited with the "State Theory of Money".[21]

The majority of economists has criticised this view as being too narrow[22] and instead favours a functional understanding of money: anything that is generally accepted as a medium of exchange, a unit of account, and a store of value has to be treated as money.[23] Good reasons exist to follow this path in economic analysis, but

[18]Friedrich Georg Knapp, *Staatliche Theorie des Geldes*, (Leipzig: Duncker & Humblot, 1905), p. 1: "Das Geld ist ein Geschöpf der Rechtsordnung; es ist im Laufe der Geschichte in den verschiedensten Formen aufgetreten: eine Theorie des Geldes kann daher nur rechtsgeschichtlich sein." [Money is a creation of the legal system; in the course of history, it has emerged in most different forms: that is why a theory of money can only be a phenomenon of legal history.]

[19]Knapp, note 18 above, p. 123, in specific for banknotes.

[20]In essence agreeing, Frederic A. Mann, *The Legal Aspects of Money*, fifth edn., (Oxford: Clarendon Press, 1992), p. 16 *et seq.*; Olaf R. Dahlmann, *Das Recht des Geldes*, (Berlin: Metzner, 1960), p. 400; Hermann Fögen, *Geld- und Währungsrecht*, (Munich: Beck, 1969), p. 7; Karsten Schmidt, "Vorbem. zu §§ 244 ff.", in: J. von Staudingers, *Kommentar zum Bürgerlichen Gesetzbuch mit Einführungsgesetz und Nebengesetzen, Zweites Buch, 13. Bearbeitung*, (Berlin: Sellier and Walter de Gruyter, 1997/8), A 3, A 12, for money signs (tokens) as consequence of the two-pronged definition (A. 11); idem, note 17 above, p. 88 & 90 with reservations.

[21]Gustav Hartmann, *Über den rechtlichen Begriff des Geldes und den Inhalt von Geldschulden*, (Braunschweig: Leibrock, 1868), pp. 4, 7, 12, 48; (critical) review by Otto Karlowa, Kritische Vierteljahresschrift für Gesetzgebung und Rechtswissenschaft vol. 11 n. 4 (1869), p. 526, but agreeing that the recognition by the legal system is essential for the virtue of being money (at 536 et seq.); see already before him: Johann Christian Ravit, *Beiträge zur Lehre vom Gelde*, (Lübeck: Aschenfeldt, 1862), p. 12, but less clear.

[22]See, for example, Joseph A. Schumpeter, *Das Wesen des Geldes*, ed. F.A. Mann, (Göttingen: Vandenhoeck & Ruprecht, 1970), p. 56; from a legal perspective, see Frank Vischer, *Geld- und Währungsrecht im nationalen und internationalen Kontext*, (Basel: Helbing Lichtenhahn, 2010), p. 4, 17 *et seq.*; for clearly a different view, see Carl Menger, *Untersuchungen über die Methode der Sozialwissenschaften, und der politischen Oekonomie*, (Leipzig: Duncker & Humblot, 1883), p. 176, with comprehensive citations from (ancient) history (p. 172-174); discussion at: Helmut Siekmann, "Deposit Banking and the Use of Monetary Instruments", in: David Fox and Wolfgang Ernst (eds), *Money in the Western Legal Tradition*, (Oxford: Oxford University Press, 2016), p. 489, at 510 *et seq*; Wray, note 17 above, pp. 631–652 with in-depth analysis of various authors and emphasizing the "government budget constraint" in view of creating money.

[23]See, for example, Alan J. Auerbach and Laurence J. Kotlikoff, *Macroeconomics*, second edition, (Cambridge MA, London: The MIT Press, 1998), p. 172 *et seq*; Frederic S. Mishkin, *The Economics of Money, Banking, and Financial Markets*, eleventh edition, (Harlow: Pearson, 2016), pp. 96-98; Rudolf Richter, *Geldtheorie*, second edition, (Berlin-Heidelberg: Springer Verlag, 1990), p. 103 *et seq.*, & 108; already discussed in nineteenth century by Ravit, note 21 above, p. 527 *et seq.*

they do not justify the monopolisation of the term "money".[24] From the legal perspective, money is widely acknowledged as a creation of law, as Knapp assumed.[25] Its "existence has to be understood within a legal framework".[26] Sometimes, it is even contended that the "state theory of money" has been accepted by "modern constitutions" "as a necessary consequence of the sovereign power over currency", "entrenched in modern constitutions".[27] It may be left undecided whether this reasoning is entirely in conformity with the content of this "theory". At its core, it is, however, true that a close conjunction of the definition of money and the legal system exists. Even if the cited constitutions do not use the term, money, in the legal sense of the word, it can be identified as a creation of the sovereign and as "legal tender".

It can be discussed whether deposits in an account at the central bank should be included in the definition of money in the legal sense, as, for all practical purposes, cash and such claims against the central bank may be interchanged at will. An insolvency risk does not exist, as a central bank is the only institution which may legally produce cash (legal tender) in any amount, and cannot become insolvent. Then, the legal definition of money would get close to the economic category of base money, with the exception of legal tender held by credit institutions.

Within the European Union (EU), only the banknotes issued by the European Central Bank (ECB) or the national central banks with the permission of the ECB "have the status of legal tender", Article 128 paragraph 1 sentence 3 Treaty on the

[24]Also, among economists, it is consented that this functional view is a definition of economists for economic purposes; Mishkin, note 23 above, p. 95.

[25]See, for example, Ravit, note 21 above; Hartmann, note 21 above, p. 7 & 12-17; Mann (1992), note 20 above, p. 16; Schmidt, note 20 above, Vorbem. Zu §§ 244 ff., A 11; in principle, also Charles Proctor, *Mann on the Legal Aspects of Money*, seventh edition, (Oxford: Oxford University Press, 2012), note 1.67, 1.68 (p. 40 *et seq.*) with some adjustments; Martin Selmayr, *Das Recht der Wirtschafts- und Währungsunion*, (Baden-Baden: Nomos Verlag, 2002, p. 32 & 37; Rosa Lastra, *International Financial and Monetary Law*, second edition, (Oxford: Oxford University Press, 2015), margin n. 1.29; Siekmann, note 22 above, p. 511; disagreeing, Vischer, note 22 above; partially merely descriptive and advocating a "relative" term of money, see Hugo J. Hahn and Ulrich Häde, *Währungsrecht*, second edtition, (Munich: C.H. Beck, 2010), § 3 *Der juristische Begriff des Geldes*, but eventually also demanding state authorisation (p. 19).

[26]Lastra, note 25 above, margin n. 1.29; drawing substantially from Mann (1992), note 20 above, p. 461.

[27]Carl-Theodor Samm, "'Geld' und 'Währung' – begrifflich und mit Blick auf den Vertrag von Maastricht", in: Weber, note 17 above, p. 227, at 233 ["*Der gegenständliche Begriff des Geldes (...) ergibt sich aus der staatlichen Theorie des Geldes* (in footnote 22 reference to Knapp), *die zwinged aus der in den modernen Verfassungen verankerten Geldhoheit des Staates folgt;*"]; Lastra, note 25 above, margin n. 1.42, uses almost the same words, however, without reference to Samm: "The State theory of money—recognized in modern constitutions (in footnote 55 reference to some constitutions)—has been typically construed as a necessary consequence of the sovereign power over currency"; for more details with references on the link between sovereign rights and the creation of money, see Helmut Siekmann, "The Legal Frameworks for the European System of Central Banks", in: Frank Rövekamp, Moritz Bälz and Hanns Günter Hilpert (eds), *Central Banking and Financial Stability in East Asia*, (Cham-Heidelberg-New York-Dordrecht-London: Springer International Publishing, 2015), p. 43 at 46.

Functioning of the European Union (TFEU).[28] For coins issued by the Member States whose currency is the euro, the status of legal tender follows from Article 11 Regulation 974/98.[29]

As a result, the term "cash", i.e., banknotes and coins denominated in euro, is identical with legal tender and the term "money" in the legal sense of the word.[30] It is the only money which has to be accepted as fulfilment of a monetary claim.[31] Recent developments, especially the creation and diffusion of electronic instruments of exchange such as Bitcoins, do not yet require a modification of this delineation. Aside from other downsides, for example their extreme volatility,[32] they do not have the property of legal tender, at least not in Germany.[33] In general, nobody is obliged to accept Bitcoins.[34] Another question is whether specific statutes

---

[28]Consolidated versions of the Treaty on European Union and the Treaty on the Functioning of the European Union, Official Journal of 26.10.2012, C 326/01, addition by Council Decision of 25 March 2011 amending Article 136 of the Treaty on the Functioning of the European Union with regard to a stability mechanism for Member States whose currency is the euro, Official Journal of 6.4.2011, L 91/1.

[29]Council Regulation (EC) No 974/98 of 3 May 1998 on the introduction of the euro, Official Journal of 11.5.1998, L 139/1.

[30]Freimuth, note 7 above, at margin n. 4; disagreeing, see Bernd Krauskopf, "How Euro Banknotes Acquire the Properties of Money", in: European Central Bank (ed), *Legal Aspects of the European System of Central Banks, Liber Amicorum Paolo Zamboni Garavelli, European Central Bank*, (Frankfurt am Main: ECB, 2005), p. 243, at 248: "consistent with tradition" but "does not appear to be absolutely essential"; earlier in favour of a wider understanding of the term "money", see Samm, note 27 above, p. 234 *et seq.*

[31]See, for example, RGZ 134, 73 at 76; BGH, (1953), *Neue Juristische Wochenschrift*, 897 at 108; BGHZ 58, 108 at 109; OLG Hamm, (1988), *Neue Juristische Wochenschrift*, p. 2115; OLG Frankfurt, (1986), *Juristen Zeitung*, p. 1072; Joachim v. Spindler, Willy Becker & O.-Ernst Starke, *Die Deutsche Bundesbank*, 4th edition, (Stuttgart-Berlin-Cologne-Mainz: Kohlhammer, 1973), § 14 annotation 3 (p. 285); Fögen, note 20 above, p. 7; Schmidt, note 20 above, Vorbem. Zu §§ 244 ff., A 19, 24, 30; Jan Endler, *Europäische Zentralbank und Preisstabilität*, (Stuttgart-Munich-Hannover-Berlin-Weimar-Dresden: Boorberg, 1998), p. 119; Selmayr, note 25 above, p. 31 *et seq.*, 425; Patrice de Lapasse, "The Legal Status of the Euro" in: European Central Bank (ed), note 30 above, p. 235, at 237; Angel and Margerit, note 4 above, p. 588 & 592; Freimuth, note 7 above, at margin n. 81 with minor reservations; Benjamin Beck, "Bitcoins als Geld im Rechtssinne", (2015) *Neue Juristische Wochenschrift* – NJW, p. 580, at 581; disagreeing, see Christoph Herrmann, *Währungshoheit, Währungsverfassung und subjektive Rechte*, (Tübingen: Mohr Siebeck, 2010), p. 315; for the historic evolution, see Krauskopf, note 30 above, pp. 246–248); Siekmann, note 22 above, p. 507.

[32]Rogoff, above n. 8, p. 1. For the extent of their useage see note 7 above.

[33]On its website, the Bank of England dissolves, to some extent, the content of the term legal tender, as it declares the "acceptability as a means of payment a matter of agreement between the parties", but gives the debtor "a good defence in law" if he is sued for non-payment when he has offered to pay the due amount of money in legal tender", cited from Proctor, note 25 above, para. 2.24, footnote 49. The status and function of legal tender in the UK is anyhow awkward as the banknotes issued by the Bank of England have the status of legal tender only in England and Wales, but not in Scotland; see Proctor, note 25 above, para 2.30.

[34]Beck, note 31 above, at 581.

may be enacted to force certain providers of (public) services to accept bank-issued instruments of payments, such as credit cards.[35]

10.3 The Conformity of an Abolition with EU Law

The legality of an abolition of cash will essentially depend on whether the EU or the European Central Bank are obliged to create cash denominated in euro. The answer to this question is crucial, since cash has been identified in the preceding section as legal tender, and legal tender may be essential. An in-depth analysis of the problem has not been undertaken to date.

10.3.1 Foundations

In applying EU law, a clear distinction between the "primary" and the "secondary" law of the Union has to be made. The primary law has been created directly by the parties adopting the European Treaties; initially, the Treaties forming the European Communities, especially the European Economic Community (EEC), and finally the European Union (EU). As this body of law is comprehensive and specifically entrenched,[36] it is functionally equivalent to the constitutional law of modern constitutions. The provisions of the Treaties should be regarded as the constitutional law of the EU taking precedence over the law of the Member States.[37] It is the supreme law of the land. At present, it is enshrined in the Treaty on European Union (TEU) and the Treaty on the Functioning of the European Union (TFEU)[38] including the protocols and the annexes to the Treaties which form an integral part thereof (Article 50 TEU).

The secondary law is created by the organs and institutions of the Union. As these bodies "have to act within the powers conferred upon them by the Treaties", it is "subordinate to those primary norms".[39] This hierarchy of norms may be derived

[35]The Administrative Court of Berlin upheld, in a preliminary judgment of 24 June 2015 (docket n. 11 L 213.15), a regulation obliging the providers of taxi services to accept credit cards and to have the necessary hardware in working condition (*Verwaltungsgericht Berlin, Beschluss vom 24. Juni 2015 – Az. 11 L 213.15)*, confirmed by the Superior Adminsitrative Court of Berlin in a judgment of 18 December 2015 (docket n. OVG 1 S 76.15) (*Oberverwaltungsgericht Berlin-Brandenburg, Beschluss vom 18.12.2015 – OVG 1 S 76.15)*, BeckRS 2016, 40395 – beck-online.

[36]Amending the primary law is, in principle, only possible unanimously, Article 48 TEU, even when using the "simplified" revision procedures following Article 49 paragraphs 6-7 TEU.

[37]Koen Lenaerts and Piet van Nuffels, *European Union Law*, third edition, (London: Sweet & Maxwell, Thomson Reuters, 2011), margin-n. 22-007, with further references especially from the rich jurisprudence of the Court of the EU (ECJ/CJEU).

[38]Reference in footnote 28 above.

[39]Lenaerts and van Nuffel, note 37 above, margin-n. 22-003.

from Article 262 TFEU. Primary and secondary EU law also take precedence over all national law. Although this concept is not self-evident to lawyers in all jurisdictions, it is acknowledged by the Court of the EU[40] and has been familiar to other decentralised systems, such as the U.S., since its inception.[41] Only for the extreme cases of a severe (or evident) transgression of competences (*ultra vires*), or a violation of the core content of the constitutional identity (*Verfassungsidentität*) of Germany, has the Federal Constitutional Court of this country reserved the right to review the conformity of acts of institutions of the EU with EU law and a possibly resulting infringement of the Federal Constitution of Germany, the Basic Law.[42] Only in such cases may EU law not have precedence.[43]

10.3.2 Safeguarding the Existence of Legal Tender

At first sight, it is not clear whether the primary law requires the existence of cash in the sense of banknotes and coins denominated in euro. Article 128 paragraph 1 sentence 2 TFEU only states that the "European Central Bank and the national central banks *may* [emphasis added] issue such notes" (i.e., euro banknotes). For coins issued by the Member States, subject to approval by the European Central Bank (ECB), the wording is similar in paragraph 2 of this article; but not identical. In addition, this language is re-iterated in Article 282 paragraph 3 sentence 2 TFEU which states: "It [the ECB] alone may authorise the issue of the euro."

Moreover, Article 128 paragraph 1 sentence 3 TFEU decrees that "the banknotes issued by the European Central Bank and the national central banks shall be the only such notes to have the status of legal tender within the Union". From this, it might follow that the primary law pre-supposes the existence of legal tender, banknotes and of coins denominated in euro. But this reasoning might not be

[40]Judgment of 15 July 1964, Case 6/64 *Costa/E.N.E.L.*, Reports of Cases 1964, 587 (594); judgment of 9 September 1978, Case 106/77 *Simmenthal*, Reports of Cases 1978, 630 margin n. 17: "automatically inapplicable"; BVerfGE 31, 145 (173f.); 37, 271 (277 *et seq.*); 73, 339 (375 *et seq.*); 89, 155 (175); see, for example, for more details, Hermann-Josef Blanke, *Föderalismus und Integrationsgewalt - Die Bundesrepublik Deutschland, Spanien, Italien und Belgien als dezentralisierte Staaten in der EG*, (Berlin: Duncker & Humblot, 1991), p. 290; Hans D. Jarass and Saša Beljin, "Die Bedeutung von Vorrang und Durchführung des EG-Rechts für die nationale Rechtsetzung und Rechtsanwendung", (2004) 23 *Neue Zeitschrift für Verwaltungsrecht*, p. 1; Burkhard Schöbener, "Das Verhältnis des EU-Rechts zum nationalen Recht der Bundesrepublik Deutschland", (2011) 43 *Juristische Arbeitsblätter*, p. 885, at 889 *et seq.*

[41]Seminal U.S. Supreme Court, *Marbury* vs. *Madison*, 5 U.S. (1 Cranch) 137 at 176 (1803); earlier already Pennsylvania District Court, (2 Dallas) 304 at 308 (1795); see, also, Article 31 of the Basic Law, the German federal constitution for the precedence of the law of the central state over the law of the decentralised entities (*Länder*); even their constitutional law.

[42]BVerfGE 58, 1 (30 and 31); 75, 223 (235, 242); 89, 155 (187 *et seq.*); 113, 273 (296); 123, 267 (354); 126, 286 (302 - 304); 133, 277 (316 at n. 91); 134, 366 (381-384).

[43]See specifically BVerfGE 134, 366 at margin n. 22 and 27.

considered as a stringent argument. More important is the fact that the legal systems of the Member States build on the existence of legal tender created by exercising the *lex monetae* of the EU. They would collapse if legal tender no longer existed.[44]

The following situation would be decisive: the ECB calls in all euro banknotes in circulation and stops issuing new banknotes. In addition, the Member States quit minting euro coins. The question would then be whether the EU or the Member States would be allowed to declare a substitute legal tender.

10.3.2.1 Banknotes

In this case, the Member States, or their central banks, would not be allowed to fill the gap by creating new legal tender in the form of notes, as the European Central Bank has the "exclusive right" to authorise the issue of euro banknotes and no other euro banknote may have the "status of legal tender", Article 128 paragraph 1 sentence 3 TFEU. This clause precludes at least the Member States and the other institutions of the EU from issuing any kind of paper sign (token) with the status of legal tender. The monopoly of the ECB to govern the creation of euros is re-confirmed by Article 282 paragraph 3 sentence 2 TFEU with the term "alone". In addition, it is widely accepted—but not beyond any doubt—that the competence of the ECB also includes the specification and design of the notes issued.[45] The

---

[44]Partially disagreeing in view of the situation in Switzerland between 1930 and 1936, see Krauskopf, note 30 above, p. 248.

[45]At least this is how it is handled in practice:

- Decision of the European Central Bank of 7 July 1998 on the denominations, specifications, reproduction, exchange and withdrawal of euro banknotes, ECB/1998/6, Official Journal of 14. 1. 1999, L 8/36; amended by: Decision of the European Central Bank of 26 August 1999 amending the Decision of the European Central Bank of 7 July 1999 on the denominations, specifications, reproduction, exchange and withdrawal of euro banknotes, ECB/1999/655, Official Journal of 5. 10. 1999, L 258/29;
- Replaced by: Decision of the European Central Bank of 30 August 2001 on the denominations, specifications, reproduction, exchange and withdrawal of euro banknotes, ECB/2001/7, Official Journal of 31. 8. 2001, L 233/55; amended by: Decision of the European Central Bank of 3 October 2001 amending the Decision of the European Central Bank of 3 December 2001 on the denominations, specifications, reproduction, exchange and withdrawal of euro banknotes, ECB/2001/14, Official Journal of 9. 1. 2002, L 5/26;
- Replaced by: Decision of the European Central Bank of 20 March 2003 on the denominations, specifications, reproduction, exchange and withdrawal of euro banknotes, ECB/2003/4, Official Journal of 25. 3. 2003, L 78/16;
- Replaced by: Decision of the European Central Bank of 19 April 2013 on the denominations, specifications, reproduction, exchange and withdrawal of euro banknotes, ECB/2033/10, Official Journal of 30. 4. 2013, L 118/37;

see, also, Krauskopf, note 30 above, p. 244; Panagiotis Papapaschalis, "Article 128 AEUV [*TFEU*]", in: Hans von der Groeben, Jürgen Schwarze & Armin Hatje (eds), *Europäisches Unionsrecht*, seventh edition, (Baden-Baden: Nomos, 2015), at margin n. 7.

division of responsibilities within the European System of Central Banks (ESCB) in view of the issue of banknote has been regulated by the ECB as well.[46]

10.3.2.2 Coins

When framing the Treaty of Maastricht, there was consensus that the competence to issue coins denominated in euro should remain with the Member States[47] following an old tradition in Europe that this power was not vested in central banks but was reserved to the sovereign. A closer analysis of the wording of Article 128 TFEU shows that this difference has been acknowledged by the primary law: "authorise" in para 1 for banknotes, and "approval" in para 2 for coins.[48] As the issue of coins falls within the competence of the Member States, they do not need an authorisation. This was decided despite the fact that no material reasons existed anymore to justify splitting the competences for this specific type of legal tender between two separate institutions,[49] aside from pure fiscal greed as profits from minting coins can be collected directly for the state budgets in this way.[50]

As only *one* monetary policy can rationally exist in a currency area, the EU and the ECB—notwithstanding—had to be given considerable powers in view of coins denominated in euro and issued by the Member States. They are part of the concept of creating a single currency. The volume of an issue needs the approval of the ECB, Article 128 paragraph 2 sentence 1 TFEU. The unitisation and technical specifications of the coins have been set by the EU Council.[51] The rules have to be

[46]Decision of the European Central Bank of 13 December 2010 on the issue of euro banknotes (recast), ECB/2010/29, Official Journal of 9. 2. 2011, L 35/26; amended by: Decision of the European Central Bank of 21 June 2013 amending Decision ECB/2010/29 on the issue of euro banknotes, ECB/2013/16, Official Journal of 6. 7. 2013, L 187/13; Decision of the European Central Bank of 29 August 2013 amending Decision ECB/2010/29 on the issue of euro banknotes, ECB/2013/27, Official Journal of 21.1.2014, L 16/51; Decision of the European Central Bank of 27 November 2014 amending Decision ECB/2010/29 on the issue of euro banknotes, ECB/2014/49, Official Journal of 21.2.2015, L 50/42.

[47]Article 16.3 of the Draft Statute; René Smits, *The European Central Bank*, (The Hague-London-Boston: Kluwer, 1997), p. 205; Freimuth, note 7 above, at margin n. 87; Papapaschalis, note 45 above, margin n. 24; consenting with the result: Hahn and Häde, note 25 above), § 1 margin n. 19, 62.

[48]This careful delineation is blurred by the—once more erroneous—official translation into German ("*genehmigen*" and "*Genehmigung*"); see, also, Papapaschalis, note 45 above, at footnote 60.

[49]Klaus Stern, *Das Staatsrecht der Bundesrepublik Deutschland*, Band II, (Munich: C.H. Beck, 1980), p. 477; Helmut Siekmann, "Article 88", in: Michael Sachs (ed), *Grundgesetz*, seventh edition, (Munich: C.H. Beck, 2014), at margin n. 21; Krauskopf, note 30 above, p. 248.

[50]Helmut Siekmann, "Einführung [introduction]" in: Siekmann (ed), note 7 above, margin n. 135, pointing out that this reservation in favour of the government had already been abolished by the allied powers in Germany after World War II and was re-introduced when establishing the *Bundesbank* in 1957.

[51]Council Regulation (EC) No 975/98 of 3 May 1998 on denominations and technical specifications of euro coins intended for circulation, Official Journal of 11.5.1998, L 139/6; amended by

based upon Article 128 paragraph 2 sentence 2 TFEU,[52] which has priority over Article 133 TFEU,[53] even if this provision has a wide enough scope since the Treaty of Lisbon.[54] From this, it follows that whether the Council has the competence to act as it did may be called into question.

Not only are the volume, unitisation, and technical specifications for euro coins set by institutions of the EU, but also the property of legal tender.[55] It would not legally be possible to pave the way for introducing other types of coins as legal tender by simply repealing or modifying these regulations, even though it is only secondary law in contrast to Article 128 paragraph 1 TFEU.[56]

10.3.2.3 Creation of Legal Tender other than Banknotes and Coins by Member States

From Articles 128, 133, 140 paragraph 3 and 282 paragraph 3 sentence 2 TFEU, it can at least be derived that the primary law assumes the existence of only one currency, the "single" currency named the "euro", within the Member States without a derogation.[57] Legal tender in other denominations should cease to exist after a transition period of six months.[58] From this, it follows that, if a sign (token)—other than notes—is declared legal tender, it must be denominated in euro. The regulations on the issue of coins as legal tender have respected this requirement of the primary law.[59] This, however, is not a final answer to the question of whether the primary law allows the Member States to define legal tender aside from notes whose issue is authorised by the ECB.

Council Regulation (EC) No 423/1999 of 22 February 1999 amending Regulation (EC) No 975/98 of 3 May 1998 on denominations and technical specifications of euro coins intended for circulation, Official Journal of 27. 2. 1999, L 52/2; amended by Council Regulation (EU) No 566/2012 of 18 June 2012 amending Regulation (EC) No 975/98 of 3 May 1998 on denominations and technical specifications of euro coins intended for circulation, Official Journal of 29.6.2012, L 169/8.

[52]Unclear Papapaschalis, note 45 above, at margin n. 27.

[53]Martin Selmayr, "Article 133 AEUV [*TFEU*]", in: von der Groeben, Schwarze and Hatje (eds), note 45 above, margin n. 8, 9, 26.

[54]See, for details, Selmayr, note 53 above, at margin n. 5, 7, who considers this article as a basis for a comprehensive "euro currency law" (margin n. 1, 5); less wide Florian Becker, "Article 133 AEUV [TFEU]", in: Siekmann (ed.), note 7 above, Article 133 AEUV [*TFEU*].

[55]Note 29 above.

[56]Papapaschalis, note 45 above, at margin n. 44, with the argument that the right of the ECB to authorise the issue of coins would otherwise be infringed; in effect, see, also, Selmayr, note 53 above, at margin n. 2.

[57]Even broader Article 3 paragraph 4 TEU: "The Union shall establish an economic and monetary union whose currency is the euro."

[58]Article 15 of Council Regulation (EC) No 974/98, note 29 above; Papapaschalis, note 45 above, at margin n. 1, 35.

[59]See the references in note 51.

The exclusion of Member States or their central banks from implementing and issuing any other kind of legal tender may be derived from Article 3 paragraph 1 lit. c TFEU, which confers the "exclusive competence" in the area of "monetary policy for the Member States whose currency is the euro", upon the Union. The term "monetary policy" covers the creation of legal tender in the form of banknotes, Article 128 paragraph 1 TFEU, and, indirectly, of euro coins by regulating the issue of coins in paragraph 2 of the same article. Further details have to be delineated by secondary law based upon Article 128 paragraph 2 sentence 2 TFEU and Article 133 TFEU. Article 128 and Article 133 TFEU are specific embodiments of "monetary policy" as they are systematically positioned in the chapter on monetary policy.[60] In addition, Article 128 paragraph 1 TFEU is the only clause which touches expressly within this chapter upon the topic of legal tender. The euro is the "key element" of the EU monetary policy.[61]

A reservation in view of the exclusive competence of the EU might, however, exist. In the older German literature, a distinction was made between sovereign acts in monetary law as part of the public law and the regulation of obligations denoted in money as part of the private law.[62] As a consequence, the power to define legal tender as the instrument which had to be accepted as a fulfilment of any monetary obligation might have been attributed to private law, which still belongs to the competences of the Member States. This distinction could not, however, be translated into the categories of the law of the Union. It was not, in its entirety, adopted by the law of the European Community and—later—of the European Union when creating the European Economic and Monetary Union. The public law of the Monetary Union supersedes the private law of the Member States.[63] All competences and powers to create a single currency and to safeguard its functioning were transferred in total to the European level,[64] irrespective of the wording of Articles 128, 133 and 140 paragraph 3 TFEU, which might be interpreted in a more narrow sense. This transfer includes the competence to define legal tender. The detailed and

---

[60]Part Three: Union Policies and Internal Actions, Title VIII: Economic and Monetary Policy, Chaper 2: Monetary Policy.

[61]Étienne de Lhoneux, "The Eurosystem", in: European Central Bank (ed), note 30 above, p. 161, at 165.

[62]For example, Otto Sandrock, "Der Euro und sein Einfluß auf nationale und internationale privatrechtliche Verträge", Betriebs Berater – BB, 1997, p. 1 at 11; Hahn and Häde, note 25 above, § 23 at margin n. 89 (p. 281 *et seq.*) but stipulating a broad competence for the Union; the differentiation is retained in Principle by Ulrich Häde, Article 133 AEUV [*TFEU*], in: Christian Calliess and Matthias Ruffert (eds), *EUV/AEUV*, fifth edition, (Munich: C.H. Beck, 2016), margin n. 2 but conceding a wide space of discretion to the Parliament and the Council; see, also, de Lapasse, note 31 above, at p. 236: "Monetary Law has never been supposed to govern everything."

[63]Dietrich Schefold, "Die Europäischen Verordnungen über die Einführung des Euro", WM Sonderbeilage 4/1996, p. 1, at 5; Michael Eberhartinger, "Ausgewählte Rechtsfragen zu den Euro-Verordnungen", (1998) *Zeitschrift für Verwaltung*, p. 771 at 772; consenting, see Selmayr, note 53 above, at margin n. 8; unclear, see Häde, note 62 above.

[64]In so far agreeing, see de Lapasse, note 31, p. 237; Selmayr, note 53 above, at margin n. 1.

nuanced provisions in Articles 128 and 133 TFEU for euro banknotes and coins including the power of the institutions of the EU[65] to control their volume, unitisation, technical specifications and safety would largely run at idle if Member States were allowed to create other types of legal tender.

As a result, Article 128 TFEU has to be understood as an exclusive and exhaustive regulation of the matter with a limited exemption from the general rule: to wit, the exclusive competence of the EU, for the issue of coins by the Member States, confirmed by Article 282 paragraph 3 sentence 2 TFEU.[66] The sovereign power to define what (tangible) good or (electronic) instrument has to be treated as legal tender now resides with the EU. Member States whose currency is the euro do not retain the competence to define "legal tender" or to prohibit the use of virtual currencies as endangering the single currency, the euro.[67]

Even upon the basis of this interpretation, the competence of the Member States to define legal tender might be derived from Article 2 paragraph 1 TFEU. Although this clause provides that the Union may "empower" Member States to act within the domain of exclusive competences, it may not be construed as opening the door for the transference of core competences back to the Member States.[68] The creation of legal tender in the form of banknotes over the years had become one of the main

[65]Whether the specification and unitisation of banknotes falls within the competence of the ECB, as it is handled at present supported by the majority of scholars or whether the Council would be allowed to act in this matter following Article 133 TFEU is a question in debate but not relevant for the question here, see for details of the debate Selmayr, note 53 above, at margin n. 16.

[66]Papapaschalis, note 45 above, at margin n. 1, assumes that both paragraphs regulate legal tender although the second paragraph does not use this term explicitly.

[67]Explicitly, Samm, note 27 above, at p. 241; Christoph Ohler, "Die hoheitlichen Grundlagen der Geldordnung", (2009) *Juristen Zeitung*, p. 317, at 318; Angel and Margerit, note 4 above, p. 587; Papapaschalis, note 45 above, at margin n. 45; Selmayr, note 53 above, at margin n. 27; dissenting Herrmann, note 31 above, p. 308 *et seq.*, however, not regarding the change in the wording of Article 133 TFEU and misunderstanding the function of section 14 paragraph 1 sentence 2 Bundesbank Act; see Freimuth, note 7 above, at margin n. 79 footnote 86, with a tendency to deny a competence of the Member States to define legal tender, probably also Jean-Victor Louis, *L'Union européenne et sa monnaie, Commentaire J. Maigret*, 3rd edition, (Brussels: Editions de l'Université de Bruxelles, Institut d'études Européennes, 2009), n. 370, p. 263.

[68]Christoph Schaefer, "Die Ermächtigung von Mitgliedstaaten bei ausschließlicher Gemeinschaftszuständigkeit: Regelwidrigkeit in der Kompetenzordnung?", EuR 2008, p. 721 at 735; Christian Calliess, "Article 2 AEUV [*TFEU*]", in: Calliess and Ruffert (eds), note 62 above, margin n. 10; Hans Diekmann and Carsten Bernauer, "Mögliche Rechtsfolgen für vertragliche Verhältnisse bei einer Währungsumstellung eines Mitgliedstaates der Europäischen Währungsunion", (2012) *Neue Zeitschrift für Gesellschaftsrecht*, p. 1172, at 1174; dissenting Martin Seidel, "Der Euro – Schutzschild oder Falle?", Zentrum für Europäische Integrationsforschung, – ZEI, *Working Paper* B 01/2010, p. 26, without proper reasoning; indirectly perhaps also Christoph Herrmann, "Griechische Tragödie – der währungsverfassungsrechtliche Rahmen für die Rettung, den Austritt oder den Ausschluss von überschuldeten Staaten aus der Eurozone", (2010) *Europäische Zeitschrift für Wirtschaftsrecht*, p. 413, at 415, in a brief comment without reasoning.

reasons for establishing central banks at all.[69] Vesting this power outside the central bank would remove one of the characteristic traits of a central bank.[70]

10.3.2.4 Creation of Legal Tender other than Banknotes and Coins by the EU

One possible backdoor still has to be examined: the EU could try to transform some kind of electronic construct into legal tender, following the due course of the legislative process. The EU—not the ECB—might have the necessary competence to do so, because of Article 3 paragraph 1 lit. c TFEU, but it would be highly questionable whether the EU has the power to create a type of legal tender which was unknown before.

Article 133 TFEU can hardly provide the necessary authority. This provision allows the European Parliament and the Council, "without prejudice to the powers of the European Central Bank", "to lay down the measures necessary for the use of the euro as the single currency". The referred powers of the ECB (as an institution of the EU[71]) mainly concern banknotes, the authorisation of their issue and the fixing of their volume. In addition, it is widely accepted that they also comprise the specification and design of the notes issued.[72] The powers of the ECB with regard to coins denominated in euro are considerably more restricted. They consist mainly in giving consent to the overall volume of their issue, Article 128 para 2 TFEU. Design and technical specifications are left to the EU as a whole. This is also the reason why the respective legal acts were enacted by regulations of the EU Council,[73] and not of the ECB, in contrast to banknotes.[74]

The EU may have the power to declare coins legal tender[75] even if this authority is not explicitly provided for in the primary law.[76] Article 133 TFEU is, however, not a suitable basis for declaring anything unknown to the primary law to be legal tender. Coins are a type of money which have been in use for several thousand years and—more importantly—coins are explicitly referred to in the primary law, Article

---

[69]See Charles Goodhard, *The Evolution of Central Banks*, (Boston MA: The MIT Press, 1988, pp. 20-23 & 123, however, with an underlying sympathy for "free" banking; Proctor, note 25 above, paras. 1.36-1.38; Siekmann, note 22 above, pp. 506-508.

[70]Smits, note 47 above, p. 203 *et seq*.

[71]Article 13 para. 1 recital 6 TEU, falsely translated into German as "organ".

[72]For the practical handling, see the references in footnote 29.

[73]See note 51 above.

[74]See note 45 above.

[75]Article 11 of Council Regulation (EC) No 974/98 of 3 May 1998 on the introduction of the euro, Official Journal of 11.5.1998, L 139/1.

[76]This result was not unanimously accepted because of an alleged lack of a suitable basis in the primary law. Article 109 l EC was interpreted only as a transitory provision for the introduction of the euro and Article 235 EC (now Article 352 TFEU) was considered as too unspecific which is still correct, even if the Commission used it. After Article 133 TFEU was enacted by the Treaty of Lisbon these doubts are now unfounded; see, for details, Selmayr, note 53 above, at margin n. 3.

128 paragraph 2 TFEU. Both arguments are, however, not valid for entirely new instruments, such as some electronic structure chosen at will.

Moreover, a completely new type of legal tender would almost certainly undermine or circumvent the elaborated safeguards to secure the stability of the euro, especially the extensively guaranteed independence of the ESCB and its organs. The safety and stability of this new type of legal tender would be unknown and wide open for undisclosed and almost impossible to detect manipulation by criminals and governments.[77] Article 128 TFEU might, however, cover the issuance of these types of instruments by the ECB parallel to traditional banknotes since the ECB would retain control over its volume, safety, and security overriding Article 133 TFEU as *lex specialis.*

Furthermore, it should be remembered that, despite the alleged decline of the relative importance of banknotes in several Member States, and despite the introduction and dissemination of payment cards and other electronic means of payment, the issuing of "paper money" was, from the beginning, considered one of the characteristic tasks of central banks,[78] including the newly created ECB. The development of these new instruments was already well known at the time of adopting the relevant clauses,[79] and an extension to include other means of payment could have been adopted, but was refrained from.

Finally, the fundamental principle of proportionality would be infringed in the event of an abolition of banknotes and coins as legal tender,[80] as it is enshrined in both the primary law of the EU[81] and the constitutional law of the Member States.[82]

To sum up, a legal obligation to issue banknotes as legal tender or to authorise their issuance has to be acknowledged. It may be called an "institutional guarantee" of legal tender.

10.3.2.5 Secondary Law

The Council Regulation introducing the euro[83] and the Council Regulation specifying euro coins[84] both clearly pre-suppose the existence of cash denominated in

[77]References for a sceptical view on these instruments are given by Selmayr, note 53 above, at margin n. 27.

[78]See footnote 69 above.

[79]Smits, note 47 above, p. 204.

[80]For more details on the (possible) violation of this principle, see Sect. 10.5 below.

[81]Article 1 paragraph 1 and 4 TEU and Protocol (no 2) on the Application of the Principles of Subsidiarity and Proportionality, Official Journal of 26 October 2012, C 326/206.

[82]Annette Theissen, "Die Wirksamkeit des Subsidiaritätsprinzips im Europäischen System der Zentralbanken", Diss. Jur. Augsburg 2005, p. 110; with reservations concurring, see Freimuth, note 7 above, Art. 128 at margin n. 30.

[83]Article 1a and Articles 10-12 of Council Regulation (EC) No 974/98 of 3 May 1998 on the introduction of the euro, Official Journal of 11.5.1998, L 139/1.

[84]Council Regulation (EC) No 975/98 of 3 May 1998 on denominations and technical specifications of euro coins intended for circulation, Official Journal of 11.5.1998, L 139/6.

euro. Their existence blocks the abolition of cash by the ECB and the Member States as well.

10.3.2.6 Interim Result

The abolition of cash would not be in conformity with the laws of the EU. Nor would the Member States have the legal power to enact any changes in the definition of legal tender. This power belongs to the "*ius monetae*" transferred in total to the EU as its exclusive competence.

10.4 The Conformity of Restriction with EU Law

Although a total abolition of cash would not be consistent with the law of the EU, it is still to be questioned whether it would be in conformity with EU law to impose restrictions for its use or to erect obstacles which would de facto prevent the use of legal tender.

Quite frequently, restrictions imposed by Member States are justified with reference to a recital used by Regulation 974/98.[85] In fact, recital 19 of Regulation (EC) 974/98[86] declares "limitations on payments in notes and coins, established by Member States for public reasons" not to be "incompatible with the status of legal tender of euro banknotes and coins, provided that other lawful means for the settlement of monetary debts are available". This line of argumentation is, however, not convincing, mainly for two reasons:

(1) First, it is questionable whether these considerations are compatible with the primary law of the EU. They would allow the (partial) removal of an essential trait of legal tender: the virtue that it has to be accepted for settlement of any kind of monetary obligation.[87] In contrast to all other monetary instruments, it has to be accepted by the creditor if it is offered to him or her. Complementing this characteristic, the creditor of a monetary obligation only has a claim for legal tender. This also holds for payments to a government entity, authority or agency. In 2010, the EU Commission explicitly accepted this trait:

[85] See, for example, Giuseppe Napoletano, "The Legal Protection of the Euro as a Means of Payment", in: European Central Bank (ed), note 30 above, p. 257, at 260; Papapaschalis note 45 above, p. 48, without seeing the problems discussed in the following.

[86] See note 29 above.

[87] Freimuth, note 7 above, Article 128 no 78; Benjamin Beck and Dominik König, "Bitcoin: Der Versuch einer vertragstypologischen Einordnung von kryptographischem Geld", (2015) *Juristen Zeitung*, p. 130, at 135; Beck, note 31 above, p. 581.

> The creditor of a payment obligation may not refuse euro banknotes and coins unless the parties have agreed on other means of payment.[88]

The expectation that legal tender has to be accepted, namely, by cashiers of government entities, has been considered as its inherent characteristic.[89] These traits are perfectly consistent with the "State Theory of Money" as outlined above.[90]

In its judgment on the admissibility of introducing the euro, the German Federal Constitutional Court considered, as an essential trait of "money", that it can be "freely" exchanged into other goods. In this context, it emphasised the special protection of this type of legitimate expectation (*Einlösungsvertrauen*), which it derived from the fundamental protection of property by Article 14 of the Basic Law (*Grundgesetz*), of the German Federal Constitution.[91]

(2) The second argument follows from the nature of a recital. A recital is legally not part of the norm. At most, it gives some insight into the motives of the lawmaker and may serve as argument in interpretation, but it is in no way binding. However, interpretation is only possible if a norm or a clause is open for interpretation and is in need of it; mainly because it is vague, opaque or inconsistent. Such a norm or clause is, however, not in sight. Moreover, the theme of recital 19 is nowhere to be found in the normative part of the regulation to be expounded. For these reasons, arguments from recital 19 have to be dismissed. They lack any normative significance for the legal question to be answered here.

From the property of legal tender it follows that it must be accepted (*Zwangsgeld*).[92] Only marginal modifications, such as the amount of coins that have to be accepted for a payment and the obligation to change notes in cases in which not the exact amount of the owed sum of money is offered, may be consistent with the quality of legal tender in the framework of a "fiat" currency. It is the task of the issuing authority to enforce these rules regardless of whether Articles 128, 133, and 282 paragraph 3 sentence 2 TFEU are mainly interpreted as (mere) empowerments. Empowerments may not only be used at will by the beneficiary. In principle, they also contain an obligation for the empowered to use them. The wording of Article 282 paragraph 4 TFEU confirms this view.

A factual pressure to to refrain from using legal tender is legally questionable and undermines substantially the credibility of a central bank and its task to perform monetary policy. In the end, it would lose control over the currency. The idea of a

[88]Commission Recommendation of 22 March 2010 on the scope and effects of legal tender of euro banknotes and coins (2010/191/EU), Official Journal of 30.3.2010, L 83/70.

[89]Clearly expressed for the Federal Reserve System of the U.S.; however, limited to public cashiers, 12 USC Chapter 3 Sub-chapter XII section 411; for further references, see note 31 above.

[90]See Sect. 10.2.

[91]BVerfGE 97, 350 at 371 *et seq.*

[92]For references, see note 31 above.

"single currency" would be abolished if a multitude of different rules of the Member States on the use of legal tender had to be obeyed. The infringement of the fundamental rights of the individual, specifically, the right to privacy is apparent.

The somewhat more lenient view of the ECB in the past when asked for an opinion in the process of consultation[93] has to be questioned and is under scrutiny; without prejudice to the right of private parties to agree on different rules about how to settle a claim, as long as it is, in fact, a truly free consent and no monopolistic power is employed.

The ECB requires, however, proportionality of the measure under scrutiny. This principle is discussed in the context of civil rights (Sect. 10.5.1 below).

10.5 The Requirements of the German Constitutional Law

10.5.1 Civil Rights

The abolition of cash or restrictions of its use are encroachments of fundamental freedoms. The freedom of profession protected by Article 12 paragraph 1 Basic Law is touched upon, as such measures are, at least in part, aimed at professional activities. For measures changing the monetary system, the German Federal Constitutional Court has also drawn on the protection of property by Article 14 paragraph 1 sentence 1 Basic Law.[94] In any case, the general freedom of action protected by Article 2 paragraph 1 Basic Law could be relevant, not least in its manifestation as commercial freedom. The constitutional right to privacy is touched upon as well.

The severity of the encroachment depends on the nature of the specific measure. The abolition of cash would, of course, be the most intrusive. The indispensable constitutional justification appears to be questionable. Eventually, a final legal assessment would boil down to a test of the proportionality of the specific measure to be judged.

Applying the principle of proportionality, it has to be examined whether the measure under scrutiny has a constitutionally legitimate objective, is suitable to fulfil this objective, is necessary for attaining it, and is proportional in a narrow sense. This means, whether its benefits outweigh its burdens.

[93]See CON/2012/83, CON/2014/4 and CON/2014/37. In France, the restrictions on using cash in Articles L. 112-5, L. 112-6 and L 112-7 of the French Monetary and Financial Code are treated as a "loi de police" even if it is still a criminal offence to refuse to accept legal tender as long as it is the exact amount due, see Caroline Kleiner (2010), *La Monnaie dans les Relations Privées Internationales*, LGDJ: Paris, p. 67, 146, discussing in depth the various meanings of "*lex monetae*" pp. 94–129; see, also, ibid (2009), "Money in Private International Law: What are the Problems? What are the Solutions?", *Yearbook of Private International Law*, Vol. XI, p. 565.

[94]BverfGE 97, 350 at 370.

Arguments in Favour of Restrictions

1. The main argument in favour of reducing the use of cash was cost-effectiveness. The handling of cash was declared expensive and risky; mainly by economists. Empirical evidence is, however, scarce, and in fact tends to show the opposite; at least for small amounts of money to be paid.[95]
2. Another important argument is fighting terrorism and crime in general. For money laundering, the use of cash or at least the availability of high denomination banknotes is allegedly essential. Sound evidence is, however, not visible, and the most dangerous criminals are sophisticated enough to use other means of payment, such as Bitcoins.[96]
3. A third argument is not disclosed so much in public but is probably most important: making the use of cash more costly or abolishing it completely may finally bestow upon the present "unconventional" monetary policy the effectiveness that it appears to be lacking to date.

Arguments in Favour of an Unrestricted Use of Cash

1. Cash does not discriminate.
2. Cash does not imply the risk of insolvency of the issuer.
3. Cash protects privacy. It does not leave traces. This is an interest acknowledged and protected by constitutional law.
4. Cash is, in many situations, efficient. The functionality of other means of payments abroad is dubious, to say the least.
5. Tinkering with a currency, which is solely based upon confidence, is highly imprudent.
6. This holds especially for a multinational currency like the euro.
7. Restrictions unnecessarily augment anti-EU sentiments.

In the words of the German Federal Constitutional Court, money is minted freedom ("*geprägte Freiheit*").[97] No sufficient grounds for such an intrusive measure as the elimination of cash are visible. The overall assessment by Kenneth Rogoff in favour of phasing out paper money is not convincing since it slanted towards the argument of fighting tax evasion and money laundering. To a lesser degree, but also similar, is the verdict on the restrictions of its use. The former president of the German Federal Constitutional Court, Hans-Jürgen Papier

[95] Malte Krüger and Franz Seitz, "Kosten und Nutzen des Bargelds und unbarer Zahlungsinstrumente", Studie im Auftrag der Deutschen Bundesbank, (2014), p. 108.

[96] In contrast to opinions expressed widely by politicians and the media, experts confirm the statement given here; see for example, Friedrich Schneider, "Der Umfang der Geldwäsche in Deutschland und weltweit", Friedrich Naumann Stiftung Freiheit, Potsdam-Babelsberg, 2016, pp. 16–21, criticising substantially the dissenting view of a study by Kai-D. Bussmann on the volume of money laundering, whose results are in part publicised as Kai-D. Bussmann and Marcel Vockrodt, "Geldwäsche-Compliance im Nicht-Finanzsektor: Ergebnisse einer Dunkelfeldstudie", *Compliance-Berater* (2016) 5, pp. 138–143.

[97] BVerfGE 97, 350 (372).

expressed serious doubts regarding the conformity of restrictions of the use of legal tender with German constitutional law. He judges them as non-justified intrusions into civil rights and doubts whether they are suitable and necessary.[98] The population has a right to be left alone by the government unless adequate and convincing grounds for onerous actions can be shown. The effectiveness of the restrictions for using cash in fighting (major) criminality has not been proven adequately and the argument that the use of cash serves as an incentive for vandalism and petty criminality is at best ambigous. It is more a confession of state failure.

What is most important, however, is that all substitutes for legal tender are issued by commercial institutions which potentially can become insolvent. This risk is an unnecessary burden for the economy and the population. It can be avoided by using legal tender. Using cash also allows the direct transfer of values from person to person without depending on a third party.

10.5.2 Social State

The same result may be derived from Article 20 paragraph 1 Basic Law ("social state", *Sozialstaat*). Restricting the use of issued banknotes and coins denominated in euro would mainly affect the least affluent parts of the population. In particular, the aspired "financial repression" has substantial and largely disregarded distributional effects. The distributional effects of greatly reduced interest payments of governmental budgets are unclear, but zero interest on savings destroys retirement plans for the lower middle class. In Germany, at least, the main assets of this section of the population are bank accounts, life insurance, and other monetary instruments. On average, they do not own assets that have profited from the policy such as real estate or common stock. Clearly, the judgment has to differentiate: the abolition or repression of high denominated banknotes may be onerous for business but not in view of the "not so well-to-do" population, mainly protected by the principle of the social state. The existence of easy to handle legal tender with the legitimate expectation that it will be accepted at every business and at every government entity at face value is part of the social-state principle.[99]

---

[98]See Rogoff, note 8 above, after assessing the various arguments in favour and against the elimination of paper money. Papier is cited in the assessment by the research service of the Federal Parliament, note 4 above, p. 7; also cited in: "Große Bedenken gegen Bargeldobergrenzen", *Frankfurter Allgemeine Zeitung*, 14 June 2016; "Verfassungswidrig?", *Frankfurter Neue Presse*, 14 June 2016, p. 4.

[99]A general reference to this principle is already expressed by Selmayr, note 25 above, p. 36.

10.6 The Legal Consequences of not Accepting Cash

Euro banknotes and coins are legal tender in the Member States whose currency is the euro. They have to be accepted by all creditors of monetary claims—public or private[100]—with some (minor) exceptions such as the amount of coins that can be accepted or the use of high denomination banknotes for paying small debts.[101] If creditors refuse to comply, sanctions from public law or even criminal law might be imposed,[102] which cannot be expounded in detail here. For practical purposes, the consequences in private law are more relevant: the creditor does not lose his or her claim, but has to bear the negative effects of being in the status of "default of acceptance". This may be an argument in favour of the decision of the Administrative Court in the case of the contributions for the public law broadcasting system in Germany.[103] For private persons, Section 293 of the German Civil Code would be relevant. In general, the issuer of legal tender, which does not have a material value close to the nominal value, must enforce the acceptance of this money, otherwise it is a deception of the public, who trust in the inherent promise that this token can be freely exchanged into goods and services.

10.7 Conclusion

From a legal point of view, the elimination of cash would be questionable. It would be an infraction of both the law of the European Union and of German constitutional law. In principle—albeit to a lesser degree and depending on the details—this also holds for mere restrictions of its use. They are, in principle, incompatible with the concept of legal tender whose issuance or authorisation is reserved to the ECB. Moreover they undermine the confidence in the currency and jeopardise the power of the central bank to execute its monetary policy.

[100]Article 10 sentence 2, article 11 sentence 2 Council Regulation (EC) No 974/98 above n. 29; Recital 1(a) of Commission Recommendation of 22 March 2010 on the scope and effects of the legal tender of euro banknotes and coins (2010/191/EU), Official Journal of 30.3.2010, L 83/70; for further references, see Sect. 10.4.

[101]In France, since the time of the revolution, the "code monétaire et financier" requires that a cash payment has to be accepted if it is the exact sum owed. A right for change does not exist; see Angel and Margerit, note 4 above, p. 589.

[102]Examples are given by Angel and Margerit, note 4 above, p. 588.

[103]See footnote 2 above. The court failed, however, to understand the monetary law dimension of the case and completely misinterpreted Section 14 of the Bundesbank Act stating the property of legal tender. Article 128 TFEU was totally ignored.

References

Angel B, Margerit A (2009) Quelle est la portée du cours légal de l'euro? Revue du Marché commun et de l'Union européenne, p. 587

Auerbach AJ, Kotlikoff LJ (1998) Macroeconomics, 2nd edn. The MIT Press, Cambridge

Beck B (2015) Bitcoins als Geld im Rechtssinne. Neue Juristische Wochenschrift, p. 580

Beck B, König D (2015) Bitcoin: Der Versuch einer vertragstypologischen Einordnung von kryptographischem Geld. Juristen Zeitung, p. 130

Becker F (2013) Article 133 AEUV [TFEU]. In: Siekmann H (ed) Kommentar zur Europäischen Währungsunion. Mohr Siebeck, Tübingen

Blanke H-J (1991) Föderalismus und Integrationsgewalt - Die Bundesrepublik Deutschland, Spanien, Italien und Belgien als dezentralisierte Staaten in der EG. Duncker & Humblot, Berlin

Borio C (2015) Comment. In: Bean C, Broda C, Ito T, Kroszner R (eds) Low for long? Causes and consequences of low interest rates. International Center for Monetary and Banking Studies/ ICMB, Geneva/London, Center for Economic Policy Research – CEPR-Press, 2015, Geneva Reports on the World Economy 17, p. 93

Bussmann K, Vockrodt M (2016) Geldwäsche-Compliance im Nicht-Finanzsektor: Ergebnisse einer Dunkelfeldstudie. Compliance-Berater 5:138

Calliess C (2016) Article 2 AEUV [TFEU]. In: Calliess and Ruffert (eds) EUV/AEUV, 5th edn. C. H. Beck, Munich

Dahlmann OR (1960) Das Recht des Geldes. Metzner, Berlin

de Lapasse P (2005) The legal status of the Euro. In: European Central Bank (ed) Legal aspects of the European system of central banks, Liber Amicorum Paolo Zamboni Garavelli. European Central Bank, Frankfurt am Main, p. 235

de Lhoneux E (2005) The eurosystem. In: European Central Bank (ed) Legal aspects of the European system of central banks, Liber Amicorum Paolo Zamboni Garavelli. European Central Bank, Frankfurt aM

Diekmann H, Bernauer C (2012) Mögliche Rechtsfolgen für vertragliche Verhältnisse bei einer Währungsumstellung eines Mitgliedstaates der Europäischen Währungsunion. Neue Zeitschrift für Gesellschaftsrecht, p. 1172

Eberhartinger M (1998) Ausgewählte Rechtsfragen zu den Euro-Verordnungen. Zeitschrift für Verwaltung, p. 771

Endler J (1998) Europäische Zentralbank und Preisstabilität. Boorberg, Stuttgart

Fögen H (1969) Geld- und Währungsrecht. Beck, Munich

Fox D, Velde FR, Ernst W (2016) Monetary history between law and economics. In: Fox D, Ernst W (eds) Money in the western legal tradition. Oxford University Press, Oxford, p. 3

Freimuth C (2013) Article 128 AEUV. In: Siekmann H (ed) Kommentar zur Europäischen Währungsunion. Tübingen, Mohr Siebeck

Goodhart C (1988) The evolution of Central Banks. The MIT Press, Boston, MA

Hahn HJ, Häde U (2010) Währungsrecht, 2nd edn. C.H. Beck, Munich

Häde U (2016) Article 133 AEUV [TFEU]. In: Calliess, Ruffert (eds) EUV/AEUV, 5th edn. C. H. Beck, Munich

Häring N (2015) Beitragsservice reagiert auf Handelsblatt-Experiment, Handelsblatt, 16 June 2015

Häring N (2016) Bargeld auf dem Rückzug. Handelsblatt, 26 January 2016, p. 29

Hartmann G (1868) Über den rechtlichen Begriff des Geldes und den Inhalt von Geldschulden. Leibrock, Braunschweig

Herrmann C (2010a) Griechische Tragödie – der währungsverfassungsrechtliche Rahmen für die Rettung, den Austritt oder den Ausschluss von überschuldeten Staaten aus der Eurozone, 2010, Europäische Zeitschrift für Wirtschaftsrecht, p. 413

Herrmann C (2010b) Währungshoheit, Währungsverfassung und subjektive Rechte. Mohr Siebeck, Tübingen

Hippin A (2016) 'Zivilisationsaufbau' durch digitales Bezahlen. Börsen-Zeitung, 27 Jan 2016, p. 2

Jarass HD, Beljin S (2004) Die Bedeutung von Vorrang und Durchführung des EG-Rechts für die nationale Rechtsetzung und Rechtsanwendung. Neue Z eitschrift für Verwaltungsrecht, p. 1
Jost S (2016) Die Welt. 13 Feb 2016
Kaetzler J (2016) Börsen-Zeitung, 3 March 2016, p. 7
Karlowa O (1869) Kritische Vierteljahresschrift für Gesetzgebung und Rechtswissenschaft. 11(4): 526
Kleiner C (2009) Money in private international law: what are the problems? What are the solutions. Yearb Priv Int Law XI:565
Kleiner C (2010) La Monnaie dans les Relations Privée Internationales. LGDJ, Paris
Knapp FG (1905) Staatliche Theorie des Geldes. Duncker & Humblot, Leipzig
Krauskopf B (2005) How euro banknotes acquire the properties of money. In: European Central Bank (ed) Legal aspects of the European System of Central Banks, Liber Amicorum Paolo Zamboni Garavelli. European Central Bank, ECB, Frankfurt am Main, p. 243
Krüger M, Seitz F (2014) Kosten und Nutzen des Bargelds und unbarer Zahlungsinstrumente. Studie im Auftrag der Deutschen Bundesbank
Lastra R (2015) International Financial and Monetary Law, 2nd edn. Oxford University Press, Oxford
Lenaerts K, van Nuffels P (2011) European Union Law, 3rd edn. Sweet & Maxwell, Thomson Reuters, London
Louis JV (2009) L'Union européenne et sa monnaie. In: Commentaire J. Maigret, 3ème edn. Editions de l'Université de Bruxelles
Mann FA (1992) The legal aspects of money, 5th edn. Clarendon Press, Oxford
Menger C (1883) Untersuchungen über die Methode der Sozialwissenschaften, und der politischen Oekonomie. Duncker & Humblot, Leipzig
Mishkin FS (2016) The economics of money, banking, and financial markets, 11th edn. Pearson, Harlow
Napolitano G (2005) The legal protection of the euro as a means of payment. In: European Central Bank (ed) European Central Bank, Legal aspects of the European System of Central Banks, Liber Amicorum Paolo Zamboni Garavelli. European Central Bank, ECB, Frankfurt am Main, p. 243
Odendahl C (2016) Es gibt kein Grundrecht auf Bargeld. Zeit online, 20 February 2016
Ohler C (2009) Die hoheitlichen Grundlagen der Geldordnung. Juristen Zeitung, 317
Papapaschalis P (2015) Article 128 AEUV [TFEU]. In: von der Groeben H, Schwarze J, Hatje A (eds) Europäisches Unionsrecht, 7th edn. Baden-Baden, Nomos
Papier H-J (2016) Cited in Große Bedenken gegen Bargeldobergrenzen. Frankfurter Allgemeine Zeitung, 14 June 2016; also cited in, "Verfassungswidrig?", Frankfurter Neue Presse, 14 June 2016, p. 4
Procter C (2012) Mann on the legal aspects of money, 7th edn. Oxford University Press, Oxford, p. 631
Ravit JC (1862) Beiträge zur Lehre vom Gelde. Aschenfeldt, Lübeck
Richter R (1990) Geldtheorie, 2nd edn. Springer, Berlin
Rogoff K (2014) Costs and benefits of phasing out paper currency, NBER macroeconomics annual conference, 11 Apr 2014
Rogoff K (2016) Handelsblatt Nr. 185, weekend edition, 23/24/25 September 2016, p. 28
Roosevelt FD (1938) The public papers and addresses of Franklin D. Roosevelt, The year of crisis, 1933: with a special introduction and explanatory notes by President Roosevelt, vol 2. Random House, New York, p. 111
Samm C-T (1997) 'Geld' und 'Währung' – begrifflich und mit Blick auf den Vertrag von Maastricht. In: Weber A (ed) Währung und Wirtschaft, Festschrift für Prof. Dr. Hugo J. Hahn zum 70. Geburtstag. Nomos, Baden-Baden
Sandrock O (1997) Der Euro und sein Einfluß auf nationale und internationale privatrechtliche Verträge. Betriebs Berater, p. 1

Schaefer C (2008) Die Ermächtigung von Mitgliedstaaten bei ausschließlicher Gemeinschaftszuständigkeit: Regelwidrigkeit in der Kompetenzordnung? EuR, p. 721
Schefold D (1996) Die Europäischen Verordnungen über die Einführung des Euro, WM Sonderbeilage 4/1996, p. 1
Schmidt K (1997a) Die 'Staatliche Theorie des Geldes': Jahrhundertwerk oder Makulatur? In: Weber A (ed) Währung und Wirtschaft, Festschrift für Prof. Dr. Hugo J. Hahn zum 70. Geburtstag. Nomos, Baden-Baden, p. 81
Schmidt K (1997b/1998) Vorbem. zu §§ 244 ff. In: von Staundingers, Kommentar zum Bürgerlichen Gesetzbuch mit Einführungsgesetz und Nebengesetzen, Zweites Buch, 13. Bearbeitung. Sellier and Walter de Gruyter, Berlin
Schneider F (2016) Der Umfang der Geldwäsche in Deutschland und weltweit. Friedrich Naumann Stiftung Freiheit, Potsdam-Babelsberg
Schöbener B (2011) Das Verhältnis des EU-Rechts zum nationalen Recht der Bundesrepublik Deutschland. Juristische Arbeitsblätter 43, p. 885
Schumpeter JA (1970) In: Mann FA (ed) Das Wesen des Geldes. Vandenhoeck & Ruprecht, Göttingen
Seidel M (2010) Der Euro – Schutzschild oder Falle? Zentrum für Europäische Integrationsforschung, ZEI, Working Paper B 01/2010
Selmayr M (2002) Das Recht der Wirtschafts- und Währungsunion. Nomos, Baden-Baden
Selmayr M (2015) Article 133 AEUV [TFEU]. In: von der Groeben H, Schwarze J, Hatje H (eds) Europäisches Unionsrecht, 7th edn. Nomos, Baden-Baden
Siekmann H (2013) Einführung. In: Siekmann H (ed) Kommentar zur Europäischen Währungsunion. Mohr Siebeck, Tübingen
Siekmann H (2014) Article 88. In: Sachs M (ed) Grundgesetz, 7th edn. Munich, C. H. Beck
Siekmann H (2015) The legal frameworks for the European system of Central Banks. In: Rövekamp F, Bälz M, Hilpert HG (eds) Central banking and financial stability in East Asia. Springer International Publishing, London, p. 43
Siekmann H (2016) Deposit banking and the use of monetary instruments. In: Fox D, Ernst W (eds) Money in the western legal tradition. Oxford University Press, Oxford, p. 489
Smits R (1997) The European Central Bank. Kluwer, The Hague
Stelter D (2016) Mit der Abschaffung der 500er Note ist ein Tabu gefallen. Börsen-Zeitung, 7 May 2016, p. 4
Stern K (1980) Das Staatsrecht der Bundesrepublik Deutschland, Band II. C.H. Beck, Munich
Summers L (2016) It's time to kill the $100 bill, Washington Post, 16 February 2016
Theile H (2014) Der Sündenbock. Frankfurter Allgemeine Zeitung, 16 November 2014
Theissen A (2005) Die Wirksamkeit des Subsidiaritätsprinzips im Europäischen System der Zentralbanken. Diss. Jur. Augsburg
Thiele C-L (2015) Diskussion um das Bargeld: Hätte eine Abschaffung von Banknoten und Münzen wirklich Vorteile? Ifo-Schnelldienst 13/2015 of 16 July 2015, p. 3
Vischer F Geld und Währungsrecht im nationalen und internationalen Kontext. Helbing Lichtenhahn, Basel
von Spindler J, Becker W, Starke O-E (1973) Die Deutsche Bundesbank, 4th edn. Kohlhammer, Stuttgart
Weidmann J (2016) Handelsblatt, 25 February 2016, p. 30
Wieland V (2016) Cited in: "Große Bedenken gegen Bargeldobergrenzen", Frankfurter Allgemeine Zeitung, 14 June 2016, also cited in, Frankfurter Neue Presse, 14 June 2016, p. 4
Wittkowski B 2016 Börsen-Zeitung, 6 May 2016, p. 1
Wray R (2016) From the state theory of money to modern money: an alternative to economic orthodoxy. In: Fox D, Ernst W (eds) Money in the western legal tradition. Oxford University Press, Oxford, p. 631
Zurbruegg F (2015) Comment. In: Bean C, Broda C, Ito T, Kroszner R (eds) Low for long? Causes and consequences of low interest rates. International Center for Monetary and Banking Studies – ICMB, Center for Economic Policy Research – CEPR-Press, Geneva/London, Geneva Reports on the World Economy 17, p. 94

Index

F. Rövekamp et al. (eds.), *Cash in East Asia*, Financial and Monetary Policy Studies 44, DOI 10.1007/978-3-319-59846-8

MIX
Papier aus verantwortungsvollen Quellen
Paper from responsible sources
FSC® C105338
FSC
www.fsc.org

If you have any concerns about our products,
you can contact us on
ProductSafety@springernature.com

In case Publisher is established outside the EU,
the EU authorized representative is:
Springer Nature Customer Service Center GmbH
Europaplatz 3, 69115 Heidelberg, Germany

Printed by Libri Plureos GmbH
in Hamburg, Germany